Second Edition

English for Today

Book Six: Literature in English

for "Reading in Bed about Foul Weather," "Giving Advice," "Departing Guests," "Dreams," "Transport in Films," "Making Stew," "Moments in the Morning," from *Delight* by J. B. Priestley, published by William Heinemann, Ltd., London. Reprinted by permission of A. D. Peters and Company.

Laurence Pollinger Limited for "A Most Forgiving Ape," from *No Room in the Ark* by Alan Moorehead, published by Hamish Hamilton Ltd..

William Saroyan, Fresno, California, for *My Heart's in the Highlands*, from *Three Plays* by William Saroyan.

Charles Scribner's Sons, New York, for "A Clean, Well-Lighted Place," from *Winner Take Nothing* by Ernest Hemingway. Copyright 1933 by Charles Scribner's Sons, renewal copyright © 1961 by Ernest Hemingway. Also for *The Will* from *Half Hours* by J. M. Barrie, copyright 1914 by Charles Scribner's Sons, renewal copyright 1942 by Cynthia Asquith and Peter Llewelyn Davies. Reprinted by permission of Charles Scribner's Sons.

The Society of Authors, London, for the poems of A. E. Housman (as the Literary Representative of the Estate of the late A. E. Housman).

The Viking Press, Inc., New York, for "The Open Window" from *The Short Stories of Saki* (H. H. Munro), all rights reserved. Also for "The Great Mountains" from *The Long Valley* by John Steinbeck, copyright 1933, © 1961 by John Steinbeck. Reprinted by permission of the Viking Press, Inc.

A. P. Watt & Son, London, for the poems by William Butler Yeats. Reprinted by permission of Mr. M. B. Yeats, the Macmillan Co. of London and Basingstoke, and the Macmillan Co. of Canada, Ltd.

HEMINGWAY

Section One
Fiction

Joseph Conrad, a famous English novelist, said that his goal as a writer was "to make you hear, to make you feel—it is, before all, to make you *see*. That—and no more, and it is everything." A good short story tries to give the reader a sense of the actual experience. Often it leaves a single sharp impression to be turned over and over in the mind. After finishing the story, the reader should have something to think about: the pathos or humor of life, its ironies, or the unpredictability of human behavior.

In order to read a short story with full understanding, the reader must approach the content on two levels. The first and most obvious level is conveyed through the plot. *Plot* refers to the sequence of events, to the actions of the characters and the situations in which they are involved. To explain the plot, then, is to tell what happened in the story and to whom. In some short stories, plot is the dominating element. "The Open Window," the first of the selections that follow, is a good example of a short story in which plot dominates. The impact on the reader comes from the sudden and unexpected revelation of Vera's speciality of providing "romance at short notice." In other short stories, plot plays a very minor role. In "A Clean, Well-Lighted Place," for example, all that "happens" is that an old man sits drinking in a café while the two waiters talk about him and about themselves. When the old man leaves, we follow the older of the two waiters to an all-night bar where he thinks about the restless night he will spend in a lonely room and an empty bed.

In Hemingway's story, then, we must approach the content on another level. The impact of the story comes from the insight it gives us into the needs and desires of youth and old age. To understand and appreciate the story, the reader must be able to identify its general topic or *theme* (youth versus old age). The next step is to identify the device by which the author comments on this theme—in this case, through the dialogue of the younger and older waiters. Finally, the reader should be able to articulate the insights which the author has given into the theme—that is, to explain the meaning of the story. In complex stories such as this one, careful readers may not always agree in their interpretations. One possible interpretation might be stated in this way: "Hemingway suggests that both youth and old age can be sad and lonely. But there is a difference. Old age has fewer expectations; it can be contented with less, sometimes with little more than a quiet drink in a clean, well-lighted place."

Readers cannot appreciate a short story fully—they cannot hear and see and feel it—unless they react not only to *what* has been said but also to *how* it has been said. They must look for style and structure, as well as for content. *Style* grows out of the writer's own personality and can be seen in the choice of words and phrases, the arrangement of sentences, the rhythm and tone. *Structure* refers to the architecture of the story—the ways in which the details are selected and arranged to produce the desired effect.

As you read the stories that are presented here, you should be prepared to encounter several kinds of English. The characters in the stories are from many different backgrounds and social levels, and they will often use words and phrases that do not appear in the standard writing of newspapers and magazines and books. They may use specialized terms and slang. The stories also have wide geographical range—from Willa Cather's small town, Sand City, in the Middle West to Frank O'Connor's Ireland. Irish English and Sand City English are very different. In addition, because literature uses language in a special way to achieve part of its artistic effect, some of these stories will contain words and phrases used figuratively—that is, they may have a symbolic meaning as well as the literal meaning found in the dictionary. The footnotes will attempt to give you some help in these matters: non-standard English, dialectal forms, and figurative language.

When you began to study English, the vocabulary and structure were carefully controlled to allow you to learn the basic words and sentence patterns efficiently. Now you are going to encounter a language used with all its variety and complexity, a language used by many people in many different countries to express complex truths about human life that cannot be simply expressed. The stories you are about to read are often difficult even for people who have spoken English all their lives. They must be read and reread and talked about and thought about. So you need not despair if the going is difficult. The rewards will be great. The rewards of literature always are.

The Open Window

by Saki (H. H. Munro)

In this story a very imaginative young lady of fifteen plays an amusing trick on a chance visitor to her aunt's house. As you read, watch closely how smoothly she conducts herself. The story is told with a charm and grace that is characteristic of this English author (1870–1916), who commonly wrote under the pen name of Saki.

"My aunt will be down presently, Mr. Nuttel," said a very self-possessed young lady of fifteen; "in the meantime you must try and put up with me."[1]

[1] *put up with me:* tolerate me.

Framton Nuttel endeavoured to say the correct something which should duly flatter the niece of the moment without unduly discounting[2] the aunt that was to come. Privately he doubted more than ever whether these formal visits on a succession of total strangers would do much towards helping the nerve cure which he was supposed to be undergoing.

"I know how it will be," his sister had said when he was preparing to migrate to this rural retreat; "you will bury yourself down there and not speak to a living soul, and your nerves will be worse than ever from moping. I shall just give you letters of introduction to all the people I know there. Some of them, as far as I can remember, were quite nice."

Framton wondered whether Mrs. Sappleton, the lady to whom he was presenting one of the letters of introduction, came into the nice division.

"Do you know many of the people round here?" asked the niece, when she judged that they had had sufficient silent communion.

"Hardly a soul," said Framton. "My sister was staying here, at the rectory[3] you know, some four years ago, and she gave me letters of introduction to some of the people here."

He made the last statement in a tone of distinct regret.

"Then you know practically nothing about my aunt?" pursued the self-possessed young lady.[4]

"Only her name and address," admitted the caller. He was wondering whether Mrs. Sappleton was in the married or widowed state. An undefinable something about the room seemed to suggest masculine habitation.[5]

"Her great tragedy happened just three years ago," said the child; "that would be since your sister's time."

"Her tragedy?" asked Framton; somehow in this restful country spot tragedies seemed out of place.

"You may wonder why we keep that window wide open on an October afternoon," said the niece, indicating a large French window that opened on to a lawn.

"It is quite warm for the time of the year," said Framton; "but has that window got anything to do with the tragedy?"

"Out through that window, three years ago to a day, her husband and her two young brothers went off for their day's shooting. They never came back. In crossing the moor to their favourite snipe-shooting ground they were all three engulfed in a treacherous piece of bog.[6] It had been that dreadful wet summer, you know, and places that were safe in other years gave way suddenly without warning. Their bodies were

[2] *unduly discounting:* showing too little respect for.
[3] *rectory:* a house in which a minister lives.
[4] Note this question well, for it looks forward to the whole point of the story.
[5] *seemed to suggest masculine habitation:* gave Framton the idea that there were men living in the house.
[6] *engulfed in a treacherous piece of bog:* swallowed up by a swamp.

never recovered. That was the dreadful part of it." Here the child's voice lost its self-possessed note and became falteringly human. "Poor aunt always thinks that they will come back some day, they and the little brown spaniel that was lost with them, and walk in at that window just as they used to do. That is why the window is kept open every evening till it is quite dusk. Poor dear aunt, she has often told me how they went out, her husband with his white waterproof coat over his arm, and Ronnie, her youngest brother, singing, 'Bertie, why do you bound?' as he always did to tease her, because she said it got on her nerves. Do you know, sometimes on still, quiet evenings like this, I almost get a creepy feeling that they will all walk in through that window—"

She broke off with a little shudder. It was a relief to Framton when the aunt bustled into the room with a whirl of apologies for being late in making her appearance.

"I hope Vera has been amusing you?" she said.

"She has been very interesting," said Framton.

"I hope you don't mind the open window," said Mrs. Sappleton briskly; "my husband and brothers will be home directly from shooting, and they always come in this way. They've been out for snipe in the marshes today, so they'll make a fine mess over my poor carpets. So like you menfolk, isn't it?"

She rattled on cheerfully about the shooting and the scarcity of birds, and the prospects for duck in the winter. To Framton it was all purely horrible. He made a desperate but only partially successful effort to turn the talk on to a less ghastly topic; he was conscious that his hostess was giving him only a fragment of her attention, and her eyes were constantly straying past him to the open window and the lawn beyond. It was certainly an unfortunate coincidence that he should have paid his visit on this tragic anniversary.

"The doctors agree in ordering me complete rest, an absence of mental excitement, and avoidance of anything in the nature of violent physical exercise," announced Framton, who laboured under the tolerably wide-spread delusion[7] that total strangers and chance acquaintances are hungry for the least detail of one's ailments and infirmities, their cause and cure. "On the matter of diet they are not so much in agreement," he continued.

"No?" said Mrs. Sappleton, in a voice which only replaced a yawn at the last moment. Then she suddenly brightened into alert attention—but not to what Framton was saying.

"Here they are at last!" she cried. "Just in time for tea, and don't they look as if they were muddy up to the eyes!"

Framton shivered slightly and turned towards the niece with a look intended to convey sympathetic comprehension. The child was

[7] *laboured under the tolerably wide-spread delusion:* believed in a common, but false, idea.

staring out through the open window with dazed horror in her eyes. In a chill shock of nameless fear Framton swung round in his seat and looked in the same direction.

In the deepening twilight three figures were walking across the lawn towards the window; they all carried guns under their arms, and one of them was additionally burdened with a white coat hung over his shoulders. A tired brown spaniel kept close at their heels. Noiselessly they neared the house, and then a hoarse young voice chanted out of the dusk: "I said, Bertie, why do you bound?"

Framton grabbed wildly at his stick and hat; the hall-door, the gravel-drive, and the front gate were dimly noted stages in his headlong retreat. A cyclist coming along the road had to run into the hedge to avoid imminent collision.

"Here we are, my dear," said the bearer of the white mackintosh, coming in through the window; "fairly muddy, but most of it's dry. Who was that who bolted out as we came up?"

"A most extraordinary man, a Mr. Nuttel," said Mrs. Sappleton; "could only talk about his illnesses, and dashed off without a word of good-bye or apology when you arrived. One would think he had seen a ghost."

"I expect it was the spaniel," said the niece calmly; "he told me he had a horror of dogs. He was once hunted into a cemetery somewhere on the banks of the Ganges[8] by a pack of pariah dogs,[9] and had to spend the night in a newly dug grave with the creatures snarling and grinning and foaming just above him. Enough to make any one lose their nerve."

Romance at short notice was her specialty.

Comprehension

1. How old is Mrs. Sappleton's niece?
2. How well does Mr. Nuttel know Mrs. Sappleton?
3. What kind of "cure" was Mr. Nuttel undergoing?
4. Who gave Mr. Nuttel his letters of introduction? Why did she give him the letters?
5. Was Mr. Nuttel anxious to meet new people? Find two sentences in the reading that give you the answer.
6. When, according to the niece, did Mrs. Sappleton's "great tragedy" occur?
7. Why, according to the niece, does Mrs. Sappleton keep the window open?
8. Why did Mr. Nuttel try to change the subject of the conversation—"to turn the talk on to a less ghastly topic"?

[8] *the Ganges:* a river in India.

[9] *pariah dogs:* A pariah was a person who belonged to one of the lower social castes. A pariah dog would be an outcast, a stray.

9. What subject did Mr. Nuttel begin to talk about?
10. What did Mr. Nuttel do when he saw the three figures walking across the lawn?
11. What did Mrs. Sappleton say about Mr. Nuttel's sudden departure?
12. How did Vera explain Mr. Nuttel's departure?

Toward Interpretation

1. How did it happen that Mr. Nuttel came to call on the Sappletons? How did this fact give Vera an advantage over him?
2. When Vera saw the returning hunters, was her "dazed horror" real or pretended?
3. In what other way, besides deceiving Mr. Nuttel, does Vera prove that "romance . . . was her specialty"?

Why Tortoise's Shell Is Not Smooth

by Chinua Achebe

The use of English as a literary medium in Nigeria has increased at an impressive pace since the late 1950s. Today the works of Nigerian novelists, playwrights, and poets are attracting more and more attention in the English-speaking world and beyond. Among the best-known novelists is Chinua Achebe, an Ibo writer whose first novel, Things Fall Apart *(1958), has been translated into German, Italian, and Spanish.*

Achebe is deeply interested in the traditional life of the Ibo people. In Things Fall Apart, *he tells the story of a "strong man," a village leader named Okonkwo. At the beginning of the novel, Okonkwo is a successful and highly respected member of his community. But as influences from the outside world begin to affect the traditional values that he has upheld, he gradually comes to realize that the way of life he knew will never be the same: "Okonkwo was deeply grieved. And it was not just a personal grief. He mourned for the clan, which he saw breaking up and falling apart, and he mourned for the warlike men of [his village], who had so unaccountably become soft like women."*

Achebe has appropriately chosen a phrase from Yeats's poem "The Second Coming" for his title:

> *Things fall apart; the centre cannot hold;*
> *Mere anarchy is loosed upon the world,*
> *The blood-dimmed tide is loosed, and everywhere*
> *The ceremony of innocence is drowned. . . .*

The excerpt that follows is from Chapter 11 of the novel. It opens with a typical evening scene in Okonkwo's compound. The day's work is done, and his three wives, each of whom occupies a separate hut in the compound, are sharing songs and stories with their children. As we read the delightful legend of the tortoise and the birds, we can only hope that all such folk stories will be preserved in the writings of regional authors like Achebe and will not be forgotten as the Ibo villages gradually become part of a new and different world.

The night was impenetrably dark. The moon had been rising later and later every night until now it was seen only at dawn. And whenever the moon forsook evening and rose at cock-crow the nights were as black as charcoal.

Ezinma and her mother sat on a mat on the floor after their supper of yam foo-foo[1] and bitter-leaf soup. A palm-oil lamp gave out yellowish light. Without it, it would have been impossible to eat; one could not have known where one's mouth was in the darkness of that night. There was an oil lamp in all the four huts on Okonkwo's compound, and each hut seen from the others looked like a soft eye of yellow half-light set in the solid massiveness of night.

The world was silent except for the shrill cry of insects, which was part of the night, and the sound of wooden mortar and pestle as Nwayieke pounded her foo-foo. Nwayieke lived four compounds away, and she was notorious for her late cooking. Every woman in the neighborhood knew the sound of Nwayieke's mortar and pestle. It was also part of the night.

Okonkwo had eaten from his wives' dishes and was now reclining with his back against the wall. He searched his bag and brought out his snuff-bottle. He turned it on to his left palm, but nothing came out. He hit the bottle against his knee to shake up the tobacco. That was always the trouble with Okeke's snuff. It very quickly went damp, and there was too much saltpeter in it. Okonkwo had not bought snuff from him for a long time. Idigo was the man who knew how to grind good snuff. But he had recently fallen ill.

[1] *yam foo-foo:* a dish made from a variety of the yam plant that is boiled and pounded into a paste.

Low voices, broken now and again by singing, reached Okonkwo from his wives' huts as each woman and her children told folk stories. Ekwefi and her daughter, Ezinma, sat on a mat on the floor. It was Ekwefi's turn to tell a story.

"Once upon a time," she began, "all the birds were invited to a feast in the sky. They were very happy and began to prepare themselves for the great day. They painted their bodies with red cam wood and drew beautiful patterns on them with *uli*.[2]

"Tortoise saw all these preparations and soon discovered what it all meant. Nothing that happened in the world of the animals ever escaped his notice; he was full of cunning. As soon as he heard of the great feast in the sky his throat began to itch at the very thought. There was a famine in those days and Tortoise had not eaten a good meal for two moons.[3] His body rattled like a piece of dry stick in his empty shell. So he began to plan how he would go to the sky."

"But he had no wings," said Ezinma.

"Be patient," replied her mother. "That is the story. Tortoise had no wings, but he went to the birds and asked to be allowed to go with them.

'We know you too well,' said the birds when they had heard him. 'You are full of cunning and you are ungrateful. If we allow you to come with us you will soon begin your mischief.'

'You do not know me,' said Tortoise. 'I am a changed man. I have learned that a man who makes trouble for others is also making it for himself.'

"Tortoise had a sweet tongue, and within a short time all the birds agreed that he was a changed man, and they each gave him a feather, with which he made two wings.

"At last the great day came and Tortoise was the first to arrive at the meeting place. When all the birds had gathered together, they set off in a body. Tortoise was very happy and voluble as he flew among the birds, and he was soon chosen as the man to speak for the party because he was a great orator.

'There is one important thing which we must not forget,' he said as they flew on their way. 'When people are invited to a great feast like this, they take new names for the occasion. Our hosts in the sky will expect us to honor this age-old custom.'

"None of the birds had heard of this custom but they knew that Tortoise, in spite of his failings in other directions, was a widely-traveled man who knew the customs of different peoples. And so they each took a new name. When they had all taken, Tortoise also took one. He was to be called *All of you*.

[2] *uli*: a liquid dye obtained from a tree and used for cosmetic purposes (or body decoration).
[3] *two moons*: two months.

"At last the party arrived in the sky and their hosts were very happy to see them. Tortoise stood up in his many-colored plumage and thanked them for their invitation. His speech was so eloquent that all the birds were glad they had brought him, and nodded their heads in approval of all he said. Their hosts took him as the king of the birds, especially as he looked somewhat different from the others.

"After kola nuts had been presented and eaten, the people of the sky set before their guests the most delectable dishes Tortoise had ever seen or dreamed of. The soup was brought out hot from the fire and in the very pot in which it had been cooked. It was full of meat and fish. Tortoise began to sniff aloud. There was pounded yam and also yam pottage cooked with palm-oil and fresh fish. There were also pots of palm-wine. When everything had been set before the guests, one of the people of the sky came forward and tasted a little from each pot. He then invited the birds to eat. But Tortoise jumped to his feet and asked: 'For whom have you prepared this feast?'

'For all of you,' replied the man.

"Tortoise turned to the birds and said: 'You remember that my name is *All of you*. The custom here is to serve the spokesman first and the others later. They will serve you when I have eaten.'

"He began to eat and the birds grumbled angrily. The people of the sky thought it must be their custom to leave all the food for their king. And so Tortoise ate the best part of the food and then drank two pots of palm-wine, so that he was full of food and drink and his body filled out in his shell.

"The birds gathered round to eat what was left and to peck at the bones he had thrown all about the floor. Some of them were too angry to eat. They chose to fly home on an empty stomach. But before they left each took back the feather he had lent to Tortoise. And there he stood in his hard shell full of food and wine but without any wings to fly home. He asked the birds to take a message for his wife, but they all refused. In the end Parrot, who had felt more angry than the others, suddenly changed his mind and agreed to take the message.

"'Tell my wife,' said Tortoise, 'to bring out all the soft things in my house and cover the compound with them so that I can jump down from the sky without very great danger.'

"Parrot promised to deliver the message, and then flew away. But when he reached Tortoise's house he told his wife to bring out all the hard things in the house. And so she brought out her husband's hoes, machetes, spears, guns, and even his cannon. Tortoise looked down from the sky and saw his wife bringing things out, but it was too far to see what they were. When all seemed ready he let himself go. He fell and fell and fell until he began to fear that he would never stop falling. And then like the sound of his cannon he crashed on the compound."

"Did he die?" asked Ezinma.

"No," replied Ekwefi. "His shell broke into pieces. But there was a great medicine man in the neighborhood. Tortoise's wife sent for him and he gathered all the bits of shell and stuck them together. That is why Tortoise's shell is not smooth.

"There is no song in the story," Ezinma pointed out.

"No," said Ekwefi. "I shall think of another one with a song. But it is your turn now."

Comprehension

1. When was the moon seen? How dark were the nights?
2. What did Ezinma and her mother have for supper?
3. Where did the light in the huts come from?
4. How many huts were there in Okonkwo's compound?
5. What did Okonkwo do after supper?
6. Where did the low voices and the singing come from? What were the women and children doing?
7. Whose turn was it to tell a story?
8. What were the birds invited to?
9. How long had it been since Tortoise had eaten a good meal?
10. Did the birds want Tortoise to go with them at first? What did he say that changed their minds?
11. Where did Tortoise get his wings?
12. Why was Tortoise chosen to speak for the group?
13. What new name did Tortoise take for the occasion?
14. What did the man reply when Tortoise asked who the feast was prepared for?
15. Who did Tortoise tell the birds was the first to be served?
16. How much did Tortoise eat?
17. Did all the birds eat?
18. What did Tortoise ask the birds to do?
19. Which bird was angrier than the others but suddenly agreed to take the message?
20. What message did Tortoise give Parrot?
21. Did Parrot report the message accurately? How did he change it?
22. What did Tortoise's wife cover the compound with?
23. What happened to Tortoise when he hit the ground?
24. Why isn't Tortoise's shell smooth?

Toward Interpretation

1. Does the story have a moral? Is there anything to be learned about human nature by observing the behavior of the birds and Tortoise?

A Clean, Well-Lighted Place
by Ernest Hemingway

Not much happens in this story—only a brief conversation between two waiters in a Spanish café. They talk about a client who is sitting by himself and drinking brandy, just before closing time. Yet the impact of the story, for all its brevity and simplicity, is tremendous. Here is a glimpse into *rather than* at *life which jars the reader into somber thoughts about the stark tragedy of loneliness.*

Ernest Hemingway (1899–1961), an American Nobel Prize winner in literature, spent part of his life in Spain and frequently used it as a setting for his novels and short stories.

It was late and everyone had left the café except an old man who sat in the shadow the leaves of the tree made against the electric light. In the daytime the street was dusty, but at night the dew settled the dust and the old man liked to sit late because he was deaf and now at night it was quiet and he felt the difference. The two waiters inside the café knew that the old man was a little drunk, and while he was a good client they knew that if he became too drunk he would leave without paying, so they kept watch on him.

"Last week he tried to commit suicide," one waiter said.

"Why?"

"He was in despair."

"What about?"

"Nothing."

"How do you know it was nothing?"

"He has plenty of money."

They sat together at a table that was close against the wall near the door of the café and looked at the terrace where the tables were all empty except where the old man sat in the shadow of the leaves of the tree that moved slightly in the wind. A girl and a soldier went by in the street. The street-light shone on the brass number on his collar. The girl wore no head covering and hurried beside him.

"The guard will pick him up," one waiter said.

"What does it matter if he gets what he's after?"

"He had better get off the street now. The guard will get him. They went by five minutes ago."

The old man sitting in the shadow rapped on his saucer with his glass. The younger waiter went over to him.

"What do you want?"

The old man looked at him. "Another brandy," he said.

"You'll be drunk," the waiter said. The old man looked at him. The waiter went away.

"He'll stay all night," he said to his colleague. "I'm sleepy now. I never get into bed before three o'clock. He should have killed himself last week."

The waiter took the brandy bottle and another saucer from the counter inside the café and marched out to the old man's table. He put down the saucer and poured the glass full of brandy.

"You should have killed yourself last week," he said to the deaf man. The old man motioned with his finger. "A little more," he said. The waiter poured on into the glass so that the brandy slopped over and ran down the stem into the top saucer of the pile. "Thank you," the old man said. The waiter took the bottle back inside the café. He sat down at the table with his colleague again.

"He's drunk now," he said.

"He's drunk every night."

"What did he want to kill himself for?"

"How should I know?"

"How did he do it?"

"He hung himself with a rope."

"Who cut him down?"

"His niece."

"Why did they do it?"

"Fear for his soul."

"How much money has he got?"

"He's got plenty."

"He must be eighty years old."

"Anyway I should say he was eighty."

"I wish he would go home. I never get to bed before three o'clock. What kind of hour is that to go to bed?"

"He stays up because he likes it."

"He's lonely. I'm not lonely. I have a wife waiting in bed for me."

"He had a wife once too."

"A wife would be no good to him now."

"You can't tell. He might be better with a wife."

"His niece looks after him."

"I know. You said she cut him down."

"I wouldn't want to be that old. An old man is a nasty thing."

"Not always. This old man is clean. He drinks without spilling. Even now, drunk. Look at him."

"I don't want to look at him. I wish he would go home. He has no regard for those who must work."

The old man looked from his glass across the square,[1] then over at the waiters.

"Another brandy," he said, pointing to his glass. The waiter who was in a hurry came over.

"Finished," he said, speaking with that omission of syntax[2] stupid people employ when talking to drunken people or foreigners. "No more tonight. Close now."

"Another," said the old man.

"No. Finished." The waiter wiped the edge of the table with a towel and shook his head.

The old man stood up, slowly counted the saucers,[3] took a leather coin purse from his pocket and paid for the drinks, leaving half a peseta tip.

The waiter watched him go down the street, a very old man walking unsteadily but with dignity.

"Why didn't you let him stay and drink?" the unhurried waiter asked. They were putting up the shutters.[4] "It is not half past two."

[1] *across the square:* Here "square" refers to the plaza. The café is on the sidewalk.

[2] You can note for yourself how the waiter "omits syntax": "Close now" should be "We are closing now."

[3] The saucers record the number of drinks he must pay for.

[4] They were closing the café for the night.

"I want to go home to bed."

"What is an hour?"

"More to me than to him."

"An hour is the same."

"You talk like an old man yourself. He can buy a bottle and drink at home."

"It's not the same."

"No, it is not," agreed the waiter with a wife. He did not wish to be unjust. He was only in a hurry.

"And you? You have no fear of going home before your usual hour?"

"Are you trying to insult me?"[5]

"No, hombre,[6] only to make a joke."

"No," the waiter who was in a hurry said, rising from pulling down the metal shutters. "I have confidence. I am all confidence."

"You have youth, confidence, and a job," the older waiter said. "You have everything."

"And what do you lack?"

"Everything but work."

"You have everything I have."

"No. I have never had confidence and I am not young."

"Come on. Stop talking nonsense and lock up."

"I am of those who like to stay late at the café," the older waiter said. "With all those who do not want to go to bed. With all those who need a light for the night."

"I want to go home and into bed."

"We are of two different kinds," the older waiter said. He was now dressed to go home. "It is not only a question of youth and confidence although those things are very beautiful. Each night I am reluctant to close up because there may be someone who needs the café."

"Hombre, there are bodegas[7] open all night long."

"You do not understand. This is a clean and pleasant café. It is well lighted. The light is very good and also, now, there are shadows of the leaves."

"Good night," said the younger waiter.

"Good night," the other said. Turning off the electric light he continued the conversation with himself.[8] It is the light of course, but it is necessary that the place be clean and pleasant. You do not want music. Certainly you do not want music. Nor can you stand before a bar with dignity although that is all that is provided for these hours. What did

[5] The implication is that the younger waiter, if he arrived home unexpectedly, might discover he had a rival.

[6] *hombre*: Spanish for "man." This is a friendly form of address.

[7] *bodegas*: Spanish for "wine cellars."

[8] Note this sentence well as you read on, for it is an important clue to understanding what follows.

he fear? It was not fear or dread. It was a nothing that he knew too well. It was all a nothing and a man was nothing too. It was only that the light was all it needed and a certain cleanness and order. Some lived in it and never felt it but he knew it all was nada y pues nada y nada y pues nada.[9] Our nada who art in nada, nada be thy name thy kingdom nada thy will be nada in nada as it is in nada. Give us this nada our daily nada and nada us our nada as we nada our nadas and nada us not into nada but deliver us from nada; pues nada.[10] Hail nothing full of nothing, nothing is with thee.[11] He smiled and stood before a bar with a shining steam pressure coffee machine.

"What yours?" asked the barman.

"Nada."

"Otro loco mas,"[12] said the barman and turned away.

"A little cup," said the waiter.

The barman poured it for him.

"The light is very bright and pleasant but the bar is unpolished," the waiter said.

The barman looked at him but did not answer. It was too late at night for conversation.

"You want another copita?"[13] the barman asked.

"No, thank you," said the waiter and went out. He disliked bars and bodegas. A clean, well-lighted café was a very different thing. Now, without thinking further, he would go home to his room. He would lie in the bed and finally, with daylight, he would go to sleep. After all, he said to himself, it was probably only insomnia. Many must have it.

Comprehension

1. Did the old man come often to the café?
2. Why did the two waiters keep watching the old man?
3. Why, according to one of the waiters, did the old man try to commit suicide?
4. How did the old man try to kill himself? Why didn't he succeed?
5. What reason does the older waiter give for the old man's staying up late? What reason does the younger waiter give?

[9] *nada y pues nada*: Spanish for "nothing and then nothing."

[10] This is a paraphrase of the Lord's Prayer. The Spanish word *nada* ("nothing") takes the place of some of the English words. Note the effect: "Our Father, who art in heaven, hallowed be thy name. Thy kingdom come, thy will be done on earth as it is in heaven. Give us this day our daily bread and forgive us our debts as we forgive our debtors. And lead us not into temptation, but deliver us from evil; amen."

[11] This is a paraphrase of a prayer to the Virgin Mary: "Hail Mary, full of grace, the Lord is with thee." After this sentence there is a break: we move from the inner reverie of the waiter to an actual scene in a bar.

[12] *Otro loco mas*: Spanish for "another crazy one."

[13] *copita*: Spanish for "little cup."

6. Were both waiters in a hurry to leave?
7. Why is the older waiter reluctant to close up for the night?
8. What doesn't the older waiter like about bars?
9. What did the older waiter do on the way home?
10. Would the older waiter go to sleep as soon as he went to bed? What does he think might keep him awake?

Toward Interpretation

1. Neither of the two waiters in the story is named, and their dialogue is written without the usual identification of the speaker. They are distinguished chiefly by the difference in their attitude toward the old man drinking his brandy. What is that difference? What other differences are there between them? What phrases can you find in the story that distinguished them?
2. The two waiters lead different kinds of lives, which are responsible for the different attitude each has toward the old man. What kind of life does each waiter lead? What kind of home docs each waiter have?
3. What is the difference in the attitude of the two men toward the café? By what signs can you tell?
4. What is the significance of the garbled Lord's Prayer?
5. What do you think is the significance of the title of the story? Find the lines in the story that reveal it. How do these lines reveal the significance of the title?

The Snob
by Morley Callaghan

Morley Callaghan (born in 1903) began to write short stories while he was still a student. Later, encouraged by Ernest Hemingway—whom he had met in Paris during the late twenties—he published his stories in a wide range of American magazines. For twelve successive years he was represented in Edward O'Brien's Best Short Stories, *an annual anthology of distinguished writing. These short stories, along with his later novels, made him one of Canada's best-known writers.*

In "The Snob," Callaghan shows some of Hemingway's keen awareness of the hidden conflicts that determine people's behavior. What is the nature of snobbery? How can it affect our lives? John Harcourt, the young man in the story, is suddenly confronted with a situation in which "something very precious that he wanted to hold seemed close to destruction."

It was at the book counter in the department store that John Harcourt, the student, caught a glimpse of his father. At first he could not be sure in the crowd that pushed along the aisle, but there was something about the color of the back of the elderly man's neck, something about the faded felt hat, that he knew very well. Harcourt was standing with the girl he loved, buying a book for her. All afternoon he had been talking to her, eagerly, but with an anxious diffidence, as if there still remained in him an innocent wonder that she should be delighted to be with him. From underneath her wide-brimmed straw hat, her face, so fair and beautifully strong with its expression of cool independence, kept turning up to him and sometimes smiled at what he said. That was the way they always talked, never daring to show much full, strong feeling. Harcourt had just bought the book, and had reached into his pocket for the money with a free, ready gesture to make it appear that he was accustomed to buying books for young ladies, when the white-haired man in the faded felt hat, at the other end of the counter, turned half-toward him, and Harcourt knew he was standing only a few feet away from his father.

The young man's easy words trailed away and his voice became little more than a whisper, as if he were afraid that everyone in the store might recognize it. There was rising in him a dreadful uneasiness; something very precious that he wanted to hold seemed close to destruction. His father, standing at the end of the bargain counter, was planted squarely on his two feet, turning a book over thoughtfully in his hands. Then he took out his glasses from an old, worn leather case and adjusted them on the end of his nose, looking down over them at the book. His coat was thrown open, two buttons on his vest were undone, his hair was too long, and in his rather shabby clothes he looked very much like a workingman, a carpenter perhaps. Such a resentment rose in young Harcourt that he wanted to cry out bitterly, "Why does he dress as if he never owned a decent suit in his life? He doesn't care what the whole world thinks of him. He never did. I've told him a hundred times he ought to wear his good clothes when he goes out. Mother's told him the same thing. He just laughs. And now Grace may see him. Grace will meet him."

So young Harcourt stood still, with his head down, feeling that something very painful was impeding. Once he looked anxiously at Grace, who had turned to the bargain counter. Among those people drifting aimlessly by with hot red faces, getting in each other's way, using their elbows but keeping their faces detached and wooden, she looked tall and splendidly alone. She was so sure of herself,[1] her relation to the people in the aisles, the clerks behind the counters, the books on the shelves, and everything around her. Still keeping his head down and moving close, he whispered uneasily, "Let's go and have tea somewhere, Grace."

[1] *sure of herself*: In other words, her manner expressed poise and self-confidence.

"In a minute, dear," she said.

"Let's go now."

"In just a minute, dear," she repeated absently.

"There's not a breath of air in here. Let's go now."

"What makes you so impatient?"

"There's nothing but old books on that counter."

"There may be something here I've wanted all my life," she said, smiling at him brightly and not noticing the uneasiness in his face.

So Harcourt had to move slowly behind her, getting closer to his father all the time. He could feel the space that separated them narrowing. Once he looked up with a vague, sidelong glance. But his father, red-faced and happy, was still reading the book, only now there was a meditative expression on his face, as if something in the book had stirred him and he intended to stay there reading for some time.

Old Harcourt had lots of time to amuse himself, because he was on a pension after working hard all his life. He had sent John to the university and he was eager to have him distinguish himself. Every night when John came home, whether it was early or late, he used to go into his father and mother's bedroom and turn on the light and talk to them about the interesting things that had happened to him during the day. They listened and shared this new world with him. They both sat up in their night clothes, and, while his mother asked all the questions, his father listened attentively with his head cocked on one side and a smile or a frown on his face. The memory of all this was in John now, and there was also a desperate longing and a pain within him growing harder to bear as he glanced fearfully at his father, but he thought stubbornly, "I can't introduce him. It'll be easier for everybody if he doesn't see us. I'm not ashamed. But it will be easier. It'll be more sensible. It'll only embarrass him to see Grace." By this time he knew he was ashamed, but he felt that his shame was justified, for Grace's father had the smooth, confident manner of a man who had lived all his life among people who were rich and sure of themselves. Often when he had been in Grace's home talking politely to her mother, John had kept on thinking of the plainness of his own home and of his parent's laughing, good-natured untidiness, and he resolved desperately that he must make Grace's people admire him.

He looked up cautiously, for they were about eight feet away from his father, but at that moment his father, too, looked up and John's glance shifted swiftly far over the aisle, over the counters, seeing nothing. As his father's blue, calm eyes stared steadily over the glasses, there was an instant when their glances might have met. Neither one could have been certain, yet John, as he turned away and began to talk hurriedly to Grace, knew surely that his father had seen him. He knew it by the steady calmness in his father's blue eyes. John's shame grew, and then humiliation sickened him as he waited and did nothing.

His father turned away, going down the aisle, walking erectly in his shabby clothes, his shoulders very straight, never once looking back. His father would walk slowly down the street, he knew, with that meditative expression deepening and becoming grave.

Young Harcourt stood beside Grace, brushing against her soft shoulder, and was made faintly aware again of the delicate scent she used. There, so close beside him, she was holding within her everything he wanted to reach out for, only now he felt a sharp hostility that made him sullen and silent.

"You were right, John," she was drawling in her soft voice. "It does get unbearable in here on a hot day. Do let's go now. Have you ever noticed that department stores after a time can make you really hate people?" But she smiled when she spoke, so he might see that she really hated no one.

"You don't like people, do you?" he said sharply.

"People? What people? What do you mean?"

"I mean," he went on irritably, "you don't like the kind of people you bump into here, for example."

"Not especially. Who does? What are you talking about?"

"Anybody could see you don't," he said recklessly, full of a savage eagerness to hurt her. "I say you don't like simple, honest people, the kind of people you meet all over the city." He blurted the words out as if he wanted to shake her, but he was longing to say, "You wouldn't like my family. Why couldn't I take you home to have dinner with them? You'd turn your nose at them, because they've no pretensions. As soon as my father saw you, he knew you wouldn't want to meet him. I could tell by the way he turned."

His father was on his way home now, he knew, and that evening at dinner they would meet. His mother and sister would talk rapidly, but his father would say nothing to him, or to anyone. There would only be Harcourt's memory of the level look in the blue eyes, and the knowledge of his father's pain as he walked away.

Grace watched John's gloomy face as they walked through the store, and she knew he was nursing some private rage, and so her own resentment and exasperation kept growing, and she said crisply, "You're entitled to your moods on a hot afternoon, I suppose, but if I feel I don't like it here, then I don't like it. You wanted to go yourself. Who likes to spend very much time in a department store on a hot afternoon? I begin to hate every stupid person that bangs into me, everybody near me. What does that make me?"

"It makes you a snob."

"So I'm a snob now?" she asked angrily.

"Certainly you're a snob," he said. They were at the door going out to the street. As they walked in the sunlight, in the crowd moving slowly down the street, he was groping for words to describe the secret he had always had about her. "I've always known how you'd feel about people I like who didn't fit into your private world," he said.

"You're a very stupid person," she said. Her face was flushed now, and it was hard for her to express her indignation, so she stared straight ahead as she walked along.

They had never talked in this way, and now they were both quickly eager to hurt each other. With a flow of words, she started to argue with him, then she checked herself and said calmly, "Listen, John, I imagine you're tired of my company. There's no sense in having tea together. I think I'd better leave you right here."

"That's fine," he said. "Good afternoon."

"Good-by."

"Good-by."

She started to go, she had gone two paces, but he reached out desperately and held her arm, and he was frightened, and pleading, "Please don't go, Grace."

All the anger and irritation had left him; there was just a desperate anxiety in his voice as he pleaded, "Please forgive me. I've no right to talk to you like that. I don't know why I'm so rude or what's the matter. I'm ridiculous. I'm very, very ridiculous. Please, you must forgive me. Don't leave me."

He had never talked to her so brokenly, and his sincerity, the depth of his feeling, began to stir her. While she listened, feeling all the yearning in him, they seemed to have been brought closer together, by opposing each other, than ever before, and she began to feel almost shy. "I don't know what's the matter. I suppose we're both irritable. It must be the weather," she said. "But I'm not angry, John."

He nodded his head miserably. He longed to tell her that he was sure she would have been charming to his father, but he had never felt so wretched in his life. He held her arm tight, as if he must hold it or what he wanted most in the world would slip away from him, yet he kept thinking, as he would ever think, of his father walking away quietly with his head never turning.

Comprehension

1. Was John Harcourt sure at first that he had seen his father in the department store?
2. Who was John Harcourt standing with?
3. What was he doing at the department store?
4. How was John's father dressed?
5. How did John react to his father's appearance? Why did he want to leave right away?
6. Did John's parents have a university education? Were they happy that John was going to the university?

7. Did John's father see him in the store?
8. How did John feel after he had failed to speak to his father? How did he feel toward Grace?
9. What fault did John accuse Grace of?
10. Did he apologize to Grace?
11. Was John happy after he and Grace had made up? What single word describes how he felt?

Toward Interpretation

1. What was the cause of John Harcourt's "dreadful uneasiness" as he and the girl he loved stood at the book counter in the department store?
2. What reasons did John Harcourt give himself for deliberately not recognizing his father in the bookstore?
3. When did John's uneasiness turn suddenly to deep humiliation?
4. What was the real cause of John's sudden hostility toward Grace? What did he accuse her of?
5. What sudden change in John's attitude occurred? What did Grace suddenly realize about him?
6. What secret guilt would oppress John for the rest of his life?

My Oedipus Complex
by Frank O'Connor

Small children often resent sharing their mother's attention with anyone else. In the story that follows, a little boy resents sharing his mother's attention with his father. This tendency of a boy to become attached to his mother and to resent his father is referred to as the "Oedipus complex." *Oedipus is a character in an old Greek legend. Oedipus, so the legend says, killed a man—without knowing that the man was his father—and married the man's wife—without knowing that she was his mother. In this way he fulfilled a strange prophecy that he had heard and had been unable to believe.*

Just how this "natural" hostility toward a father can arise and complicate normal family life is humorously told in the story that follows. O'Connor, a popular Irish author (1903–1966), shows us a grown-up man remembering how it felt to be a small boy. The result is an amusing commentary on the strange business of growing up and leaving the self-centered world of childhood.

Father was in the army all through the war—the first war, I mean—so, up to the age of five, I never saw much of him, and what I saw did not worry me. Sometimes I woke and there was a big figure in khaki[1] peering down at me in the candlelight. Sometimes in the early morning I heard the slamming of the front door and the clatter of nailed boots down the cobbles of the lane. These were Father's entrances and exits. Like Santa Claus[2] he came and went mysteriously.

In fact, I rather liked his visits, though it was an uncomfortable squeeze between Mother and him when I got into the big bed in the early morning. He smoked, which gave him a pleasant musty smell, and shaved, an operation of astounding interest. Each time he left a trail of souvenirs—model tanks and Gurkha knives[3] with handles made of bullet cases, and German helmets and cap badges and button-sticks,[4] and all sorts of military equipment—carefully stowed away in a long box on top of the wardrobe, in case they ever came in handy. There was a bit of the magpie about Father; he expected everything to come in handy. When his back was turned, Mother let me get a chair and rummage through his treasures. She didn't seem to think so highly of them as he did.

The war was the most peaceful period of my life. The window of my attic faced southeast. My mother had curtained it, but that had small effect. I always woke with the first light and, with all the responsibilities of the previous day melted, feeling myself rather like the sun, ready to illumine and rejoice. Life never seemed so simple and clear and full of possibilities as then. I put my feet out from under the clothes—I called them Mrs. Left and Mrs. Right—and invented dramatic situations for them in which they discussed the problems of the day. At least Mrs. Right did; she was very demonstrative, but I hadn't the same control of Mrs. Left, so she mostly contented herself with nodding agreement.

They discussed what Mother and I should do during the day, what Santa Claus should give a fellow for Christmas, and what steps should be taken to brighten the home. There was that little matter of the baby, for instance. Mother and I could never agree about that. Ours was the only house in the terrace without a new baby, and Mother said we couldn't afford one till Father came back from the war because they cost seventeen and six. That showed how simple she was. The Geneys up the road had a baby, and everyone knew they couldn't afford seventeen and six. It was probably a cheap baby, and Mother wanted something

[1] *khaki:* a material often used in military uniforms. This helps set the scene. The father was in the army and thus away from home.

[2] *Santa Claus:* Santa Claus is supposed to make toys all during the year and distribute them at Christmas. He visits the house when the child is asleep.

[3] *Gurkha knives:* short swords with broad blades first used by a tribe (the Gurkha) in India.

[4] *button-sticks:* strips of brass, slotted for buttons, on a military uniform—so devised that buttons may be polished without soiling the cloth.

really good, but I felt she was too exclusive. The Geney's baby would have done us fine.

Having settled my plans for the day, I got up, put a chair under the attic window, and lifted the frame high enough to stick out my head. The window overlooked the front gardens of the terrace behind ours, and beyond these it looked over a deep valley to the tall, red-brick houses terraced up the opposite hillside, which were all still in shadow, while those at our side of the valley were all lit up, though with long strange shadows that made them seem unfamiliar; rigid and painted.

After that I went into Mother's room and climbed into the big bed. She woke and I began to tell her of my schemes. By this time, though I never seem to have noticed it, I was petrified in my nightshirt, and I thawed as I talked until, the last frost melted, I fell asleep beside her and woke again only when I heard her below in the kitchen, making the breakfast.

After breakfast we went into town; heard Mass[5] at St. Augustine's and said a prayer for Father, and did the shopping. If the afternoon was fine we either went for a walk in the country or a visit to Mother's great friend in the convent, Mother St. Dominic. Mother had them all praying for Father, and every night, going to bed, I asked God to send him back safe from the war to us. Little, indeed, did I know what I was praying for!

One morning, I got into the big bed, and there, sure enough, was Father in his usual Santa Claus manner, but later, instead of a uniform, he put on his best blue suit, and Mother was as pleased as anything. I saw nothing to be pleased about, because, out of uniform, Father was altogether less interesting, but she only beamed, and explained that our prayers had been answered, and off we went to Mass to thank God for having brought Father safely home.

The irony of it! That very day when he came in to dinner he took off his boots and put on his slippers, donned the dirty old cap he wore about the house to save him from colds, crossed his legs, and began to talk gravely to Mother, who looked anxious. Naturally, I disliked her looking anxious, because it destroyed her good looks, so I interrupted him.

"Just a moment, Larry!" she said gently.

This was only what she said when we had boring visitors, so I attached no importance to it and went on talking.

"Do be quiet, Larry!" she said impatiently. "Don't you hear me talking to Daddy?"

This was the first time I had heard those ominous words, "talking to Daddy," and I couldn't help feeling that if this was how God answered prayers, he couldn't listen to them very attentively.

[5] *heard Mass:* That is, they went to church and heard the priest say Mass. They are Roman Catholics.

"Why are you talking to Daddy?" I asked with as great a show of indifference as I could muster.

"Because Daddy and I have business to discuss. Now, don't interrupt again!"

In the afternoon, at Mother's request, Father took me for a walk. This time we went into town instead of out to the country, and I thought at first, in my usual optimistic way, that it might be an improvement. It was nothing of the sort. Father and I had quite different notions of a walk in town. He had no proper interest in trams, ships, and horses, and the only thing that seemed to divert him was talking to fellows as old as himself. When I wanted to stop he simply went on, dragging me behind him by the hand; when he wanted to stop I had no alternative but to do the same. I noticed that it seemed to be a sign that he wanted to stop for a long time whenever he leaned against a wall. The second time I saw him do it I got wild. He seemed to be settling himself forever. I pulled him by the coat and trousers, but, unlike Mother who, if you were too persistent, got into a wax[6] and said: "Larry, if you don't behave yourself, I'll give you a good slap," Father had an extraordinary capacity for amiable inattention.[7] I sized him up and wondered would I cry, but he seemed to be too remote to be annoyed even by that. Really, it was like going for a walk with a mountain! He either ignored the wrenching and pummeling entirely, or else glanced down with a grin of amusement from his peak. I had never met anyone so absorbed in himself as he seemed.

At teatime, "talking to Daddy" began again, complicated this time by the fact that he had an evening paper, and every few minutes he put it down and told Mother something new out of it. I felt this was foul play. Man for man, I was prepared to compete with him any time for Mother's attention, but when he had it all made up for him by other people it left me no chance. Several times I tried to change the subject without success.

"You must be quiet while Daddy is reading, Larry," Mother said impatiently.

It was clear that she either genuinely liked talking to Father better than talking to me, or else that he had some terrible hold on her which made her afraid to admit the truth.

"Mummy," I said that night when she was tucking me up, "do you think if I prayed hard God would send Daddy back to the war?"

She seemed to think about that for a moment.

"No, dear," she said with a smile. "I don't think he would."

"Why wouldn't he, Mummy?"

[6] *got into a wax*: slang for "became very angry."

[7] *extraordinary capacity for amiable inattention*: Larry's father paid little or no attention to anything Larry said.

"Because there isn't a war any longer, dear."

"But, Mummy, couldn't God make another war, if he liked?"

"He wouldn't like to, dear. It's not God who makes wars, but bad people."

"Oh!" I said.

I was disappointed about that. I began to think that God wasn't quite what he was cracked up to be.[8]

Next morning I woke at my usual hour, feeling like a bottle of champagne. I put out my feet and invented a long conversation in which Mrs. Right talked of the trouble she had with her own father till she put him in the Home. I didn't quite know what the Home was but it sounded the right place for Father. Then I got my chair and stuck my head out of the attic window. Dawn was just breaking, with a guilty air that made me feel I had caught it in the act. My head bursting with stories and schemes, I stumbled in next door, and in the half-darkness scrambled into the big bed. There was no room at Mother's side so I had to get between her and Father. For the time being I had forgotten about him, and for several minutes I sat bolt upright, racking my brains to know[9] what I could do with him. He was taking up more than his fair share of the bed, and I couldn't get comfortable, so I gave him several kicks that made him grunt and stretch. He made room all right, though. Mother waked and felt for me. I settled back comfortably in the warmth of the bed with my thumb in my mouth.

"Mummy!" I hummed, loudly and contentedly.

"Sssh! dear," she whispered. "Don't wake Daddy!"

This was a new development, which threatened to be even more serious than "talking to Daddy." Life without my early-morning conferences was unthinkable.

"Why?" I asked severely.

"Because poor Daddy is tired."

This seemed to me a quite inadequate reason, and I was sickened by the sentimentality of her "poor Daddy." I never liked that sort of gush; it always struck me as insincere.

"Oh!" I said lightly. Then in my most winning tone: "Do you know where I want to go with you today, Mummy?"

"No, dear," she sighed.

"I want to go down the Glen and fish for thornybacks with my new net, and then I want to go out to the Fox and Hounds,[10] and—"

"Don't-wake-Daddy!" she hissed angrily, clapping her hand across my mouth.

[8] *wasn't quite what he was cracked up to be:* slang for "did not measure up to what people said about him."

[9] *racking my brains to know:* trying hard to think.

[10] *Fox and Hounds:* perhaps the name of an inn.

But it was too late. He was awake, or nearly so. He grunted and reached for the matches. Then he stared incredulously at his watch.

"Like a cup of tea, dear?" asked Mother in a meek, hushed voice I had never heard her use before. It sounded almost as though she were afraid.

"Tea?" he exclaimed indignantly. "Do you know what the time is?"

"And after that I want to go up the Rathcooney Road," I said loudly, afraid I'd forget something in all those interruptions.

"Go to sleep at once, Larry!" she said sharply.

I began to snivel. I couldn't concentrate, the way that pair went on, and smothering my early-morning schemes was like burying a family from the cradle.[11]

Father said nothing, but lit his pipe and sucked it, looking out into the shadows without minding Mother or me. I knew he was mad. Every time I made a remark Mother hushed me irritably. I was mortified. I felt it wasn't fair; there was even something sinister in it. Every time I had pointed out to her the waste of making two beds when we could both sleep in one, she had told me it was healthier like that, and now here was this man, this stranger, sleeping with her without the least regard for her health!

He got up early and made tea, but though he brought Mother a cup he brought none for me.

"Mummy," I shouted, "I want a cup of tea, too."

"Yes, dear," she said patiently. "You can drink from Mummy's saucer."

That settled it. Either Father or I would have to leave the house. I didn't want to drink from Mother's saucer; I wanted to be treated as an equal in my own home, so, just to spite her, I drank it all and left none for her. She took that quietly, too.

But that night when she was putting me to bed she said gently:

"Larry, I want you to promise me something."

"What is it?" I asked.

"Not to come in and disturb poor Daddy in the morning. Promise?"

"Poor Daddy" again! I was becoming suspicious of everything involving that quite impossible man.

"Why?" I asked.

"Because poor Daddy is worried and tired and he doesn't sleep well."

"Why doesn't he, Mummy?"

"Well, you know, don't you, that while he was at war Mummy got the pennies from the Post Office?"

[11] *like burying a family from the cradle:* not letting them have any life.

"From Miss MacCarthy?"[12]

"That's right. But now, you see, Miss MacCarthy hasn't any more pennies, so Daddy must go out and find us some. You know what would happen if he couldn't?"

"No," I said, "tell us."

"Well, I think we might have to go out and beg for them like the poor old woman on Fridays. We wouldn't like that, would we?"

"No," I agreed. "We wouldn't."

"So you'll promise not to come in and wake him?"

"Promise."

Mind you, I meant that. I knew pennies were a serious matter, and I was all against having to go out and beg like the old woman on Fridays. Mother laid out all my toys in a complete ring round the bed so that, whatever way I got out, I was bound to fall over one of them.

When I woke I remembered my promise all right. I got up and sat on the floor and played—for hours, it seemed to me. Then I got my chair and looked out the attic window for more hours. I wished it was time for Father to wake; I wished someone would make me a cup of tea. I didn't feel in the least like the sun; instead, I was bored and so very, very cold! I simply longed for the warmth and depth of the big featherbed.

At last I could stand it no longer. I went into the next room. As there was still no room at Mother's side I climbed over her and she woke with a start.

"Larry," she whispered, gripping my arm very tightly, "what did you promise?"

"But I did, Mummy," I wailed, caught in the very act. "I was quiet for ever so long."

"Oh, dear, and you're perished!" she said sadly, feeling me all over. "Now, if I let you stay will you promise not to talk?"

"But I want to talk, Mummy," I wailed.

"That has nothing to do with it," she said with a firmness that was new to me. "Daddy wants to sleep. Now, do you understand that?"

I understood it only too well. I wanted to talk, he wanted to sleep —whose house was it, anyway?

"Mummy," I said with equal firmness, "I think it would be healthier for Daddy to sleep in his own bed."

That seemed to stagger her, because she said nothing for a while.

"Now, once for all," she went on, "you're to be perfectly quiet or go back to your own bed. Which is it to be?"

The injustice of it got me down.[13] I had convicted her out of her

[12] *from the Post Office:* In other words, Father's pay from the government came through the mail. We may assume that Miss MacCarthy is the postmistress.

[13] *got me down:* really annoyed me.

own mouth of inconsistency and unreasonableness,[14] and she hadn't even attempted to reply. Full of spite, I gave Father a kick, which she didn't notice but which made him grunt and open his eyes in alarm.

"What time is it?" he asked in a panic-stricken voice, not looking at Mother but the door, as if he saw someone there.

"It's early yet," she replied soothingly. "It's only the child. Go to sleep again. . . . Now, Larry," she added, getting out of bed, "you've wakened Daddy and you must go back."

This time, for all her quiet air, I knew she meant it, and knew that my principal rights and privileges were as good as lost unless I asserted them at once. As she lifted me, I gave a screech, enough to wake the dead, not to mind[15] Father. He groaned.

"That damned child! Doesn't he ever sleep?"

"It's only a habit, dear," she said quietly, though I could see she was vexed.

"Well, it's time he got out of it," shouted Father, beginning to heave in the bed. He suddenly gathered all the bedclothes about him, turned to the wall, and then looked back over his shoulder with nothing showing only two small, spiteful dark eyes. The man looked very wicked.

To open the bedroom door, Mother had to let me down, and I broke free and dashed for the farthest corner, screeching. Father sat bolt upright in bed.

"Shut up, you little puppy!" he said in a choking voice.

I was so astonished that I stopped screeching. Never, never had anyone spoken to me in that tone before. I looked at him incredulously and saw his face convulsed with rage. It was only then that I fully realized how God had codded me,[16] listening to my prayers for the safe return of this monster.

"Shut up, you!" I bawled, beside myself.

"What's that you said?" shouted Father, making a wild leap out of bed.

"Mick, Mick!" cried Mother. "Don't you see the child isn't used to you?"

"I see he's better fed than taught,"[17] snarled Father, waving his arms wildly. "He wants his bottom smacked."

All his previous shouting was as nothing to these obscene words referring to my person. They really made my blood boil.[18]

"Smack your own!" I screamed hysterically. "Smack your own! Shut up! Shut up!"

[14] *convicted her out of her own mouth of inconsistency and unreasonableness:* had proved from his mother's remarks that she was undependable (inconsistent) and unfair.

[15] *not to mind:* not to mention.

[16] *codded me:* hoaxed, or played a trick on me.

[17] *better fed than taught:* an Irish saying. Larry was well fed but not well disciplined.

[18] *made my blood boil:* made me furiously angry.

At this he lost his patience and let fly at me.[19] He did it with the lack of conviction you'd expect of a man under Mother's horrified eyes, and it ended up as a mere tap, but the sheer indignity of being struck at all by a stranger, a total stranger who had cajoled his way back from the war into our big bed as a result of my innocent intercession, made me completely dotty. I shrieked and shrieked, and danced in my bare feet, and Father, looking awkward and hairy in nothing but a short grey army shirt, glared down at me like a mountain out for murder. I think it must have been then that I realized he was jealous too. And there stood Mother in her nightdress, looking as if her heart was broken between us. I hoped she felt as she looked. It seemed to me that she deserved it all.

From that morning out my life was a hell. Father and I were enemies, open and avowed. We conducted a series of skirmishes[20] against one another, he trying to steal my time with Mother and I his. When she was sitting on my bed, telling me a story, he took to looking for some pair of old boots which he alleged he had left behind him at the beginning of the war. While he talked to Mother I played loudly with my toys to show my total lack of concern. He created a terrible scene one evening when he came in from work and found me at his box, playing with his regimental badges, Gurkha knives and button-sticks. Mother got up and took the box from me.

"You mustn't play with Daddy's toys unless he lets you, Larry," she said severely. "Daddy doesn't play with yours."

For some reason Father looked at her as if she had struck him and then turned away with a scowl.

"Those are not toys," he growled, taking down the box again to see had I lifted anything. "Some of those curios are very rare and valuable."

But as time went on I saw more and more how he managed to alienate Mother and me. What made it worse was that I couldn't grasp his method or see what attraction he had for Mother. In every possible way he was less winning than I. He had a common[21] accent and made noises at his tea. I thought for a while that it might be the newspapers she was interested in, so I made up bits of news of my own to read to her. Then I thought it might be the smoking, which I personally thought attractive, and took his pipes and went round the house dribbling into them till he caught me. I even made noises at my tea, but Mother only told me I was disgusting. It all seemed to hinge round that unhealthy habit of sleeping together, so I made a point of dropping into their bedroom and nosing around, talking to myself, so that they wouldn't know

[19] *let fly at me:* hit me.

[20] *conducted a series of skirmishes:* had a number of small fights or arguments.

[21] *common:* unrefined; lower-class.

I was watching them, but they were never up to anything that I could see. In the end it beat me.[22] It seemed to depend on being grown-up and giving people rings, and I realized I'd have to wait.

But at the same time I wanted him to see that I was only waiting, not giving up the fight. One evening when he was being particularly obnoxious, chatting away well above my head, I let him have it.

"Mummy," I said, "do you know what I'm going to do when I grow up?"

"No, dear," she replied. "What?"

"I'm going to marry you," I said quietly.

Father gave a great guffaw out of him, but he didn't take me in.[23] I knew it must only be pretense. And Mother, in spite of everything, was pleased. I felt she was probably relieved to know that one day Father's hold on her would be broken.

"Won't that be nice?" she said with a smile.

"It'll be very nice," I said confidently. "Because we're going to have lots and lots of babies."

"That's right, dear," she said placidly. "I think we'll have one soon, and then you'll have plenty of company."

I was no end pleased about that because it showed that in spite of the way she gave in to Father she still considered my wishes. Besides, it would put the Geneys in their place.

It didn't turn out like that, though. To begin with, she was very preoccupied—I supposed about where she would get the seventeen and six[24]—and though Father took to staying out late in the evenings it did me no particular good. She stopped taking me for walks, became as touchy as blazes, and smacked me for nothing at all. Sometimes I wished I'd never mentioned the confounded baby—I seemed to have a genius for bringing calamity on myself.

And calamity it was! Sonny arrived in the most appalling hullabaloo—even that much he couldn't do without a fuss—and from the first moment I disliked him. He was a difficult child—so far as I was concerned he was always difficult—and demanded far too much attention. Mother was simply silly about him, and couldn't see when he was only showing off. As company he was worse than useless. He slept all day, and I had to go round the house on tiptoe to avoid waking him. It wasn't any longer a question of not waking Father. The slogan now was "Don't-wake-Sonny!" I couldn't understand why the child wouldn't sleep at the proper time, so whenever Mother's back was turned I woke him. Sometimes to

[22] *beat me:* It defeated me. That is, Larry could not solve the puzzle.

[23] *take me in:* fool me.

[24] *the seventeen and six:* the price of a baby. Earlier, his mother had told him that this is what babies cost.

keep him awake I pinched him as well. Mother caught me at it one day and gave me a most unmerciful flaking.[25]

One evening, when Father was coming in from work, I was playing trains in the front garden. I let on[26] not to notice him; instead, I pretended to be talking to myself, and said in a loud voice: "If another bloody baby comes into this house, I'm going out."

Father stopped dead and looked at me over his shoulder.

"What's that you said?" he asked sternly.

"I was only talking to myself," I replied, trying to conceal my panic. "It's private."

He turned and went in without a word. Mind you, I intended it as a solemn warning, but its effect was quite different. Father started being quite nice to me. I could understand that, of course. Mother was quite sickening about Sonny. Even at mealtimes she'd get up and gawk at him in the cradle with an idiotic smile, and tell Father to do the same. He was always polite about it, but he looked so puzzled you could see he didn't know what she was talking about. He complained of the way Sonny cried at night, but she only got cross and said that Sonny never cried except when there was something up with him[27]—which was a flaming lie, because Sonny never had anything up with him, and only cried for attention. It was really painful to see how simple-minded she was. Father wasn't attractive, but he had a fine intelligence. He saw through Sonny, and now he knew that I saw through him as well.

One night I woke with a start. There was someone beside me in the bed. For one wild moment I felt sure it must be Mother, having come to her senses and left Father for good, but then I heard Sonny in convulsions in the next room, and Mother saying: "There! There! There!" and I knew it wasn't she. It was Father. He was lying beside me, wide awake, breathing hard and apparently as mad as hell.

After a while it came to me what he was mad about. It was his turn now. After turning me out of the big bed, he had been turned out himself. Mother had no consideration now for anyone but that poisonous pup, Sonny. I couldn't help feeling sorry for Father. I had been through it all myself, and even at that age I was magnanimous. I began to stroke him down and say: "There! There!" He wasn't exactly responsive.

"Aren't you asleep either?" he snarled.

"Ah, come on and put your arm around us, can't you?" I said, and he did, in a sort of way. Gingerly, I suppose, is how you'd describe it. He was very bony but better than nothing.

At Christmas he went out of his way to buy me a really nice model railway.

[25] *flaking:* slang for "spanking."
[26] *let on:* pretended.
[27] *something up with him:* something the matter with him.

Comprehension

1. Who tells the story—that is, who is the narrator?
2. Why was the boy's father away from home?
3. Why did the boy enjoy his father's occasional visits?
4. What "little matter" couldn't the boy and his mother agree about?
5. What did the boy do every morning after he had made his plans for the day and looked out the attic window?
6. What did the boy pray for every night when he was going to bed?
7. What "ominous" words did Larry hear for the first time shortly after his father had come home to stay?
8. Did Larry enjoy his first walk with his father? What didn't his father have "any proper interest in"? What was the "only thing that seemed to divert him"?
9. What did Larry tell his mother when she was tucking him in bed? What did he want to pray to God for?
10. What incident "settled it"—that is, what finally made Larry decide that either he would have to leave or his father would?
11. Did Larry keep his promise not to wake up his father?
12. What did Larry and his father try to steal from each other?
13. What did Larry's mother say to him when his father found him playing with his regimental badges?
14. Why did Larry's mother give him "a most unmerciful flaking"?
15. What did Larry say that seemed to change his father's attitude toward him—that made his father start to be "quite nice"?

Toward Interpretation

1. How can you describe the theme of the story in general terms—that is, in terms of the relationships that various members of a family establish with each other?

The Great Mountains
by John Steinbeck

The American novelist John Steinbeck (1902–1968) received the Nobel Prize for literature in 1962. He was the sixth American author to be so honored. Steinbeck's books have been praised both for their insight into character and for their insight into social problems. Many of Steinbeck's stories have been made into motion pictures.

A favorite setting for his stories is his native California, whose mountains and valleys he knew and loved. It is here that the scene of the following story is laid, an episode taken from one of his shorter novels entitled The Red Pony. *Here the farm boy Jody looks at the faraway mountains and wonders if they have anything to tell him. An old Mexican farm hand helps him to find an answer.*

The hills were dry at this season and the wild grass was golden, but where the spring-pipe filled the round tub and the tub spilled over, there lay a stretch of fine green grass, deep and sweet and moist. Jody drank from the mossy tub, then lay on his back in the grass and looked up at the dumpling summer clouds.[1] By closing one eye and destroying perspective he brought them down within reach so that he could put up his fingers and stroke them. He helped the gentle wind push them down the sky; it seemed to him that they went faster for his help. One fat white cloud he helped clear to the mountain rims and pressed it firmly over, out of sight. Jody wondered what it was seeing, then. He sat up the better to look at the great mountains where they went piling back, growing darker and more savage until they finished with one jagged ridge, high up against the west. Curious secret mountains; he thought of the little he knew about them.

"What's on the other side?" he asked his father once.

"More mountains, I guess. Why?"

"And on the other side of them?"

"More mountains. Why?"

"More mountains on and on?"

"Well, no. At last you come to the ocean."

"But what's in the mountains?"

"Just cliffs and brush and rocks and dryness."

"Were you ever there?"

"No."

"Has anybody ever been there?"

"A few people, I guess. It's dangerous, with cliffs and things. Why, I've read there's more unexplored country in the mountains of Monterey County[2] than any place in the United States." His father seemed proud that this should be so.

"And at last the ocean?"

"At last the ocean."

"But," the boy insisted, "but in between? No one knows?"

"Oh, a few people do, I guess. But there's nothing there to get. And not much water. Just rocks and cliffs and greasewood.[3] Why?"

"It would be good to go."

"What for? There's nothing there."

Jody knew something was there, something very wonderful because it wasn't known, something secret and mysterious. He could feel within himself that this was so. He said to his mother, "Do you know what's in the big mountains?"

She looked at him and then back at the ferocious range,[4] and she said, "Only the bear, I guess."

"What bear?"

[1] *dumpling summer clouds*: clouds that suggested dumplings—a light, fluffy mass of dough—to the boy's imagination.

[2] *Monterey County:* in southwestern California.

[3] *greasewood:* a low-growing prickly shrub found in dry areas of the western United States.

[4] *ferocious range:* the mountains. Steinbeck has also called them "savage."

"Why the one that went over the mountain to see what he could see."[5]

Jody questioned Billy Buck, the ranch hand, about the possibility of ancient cities lost in the mountains, but Billy agreed with Jody's father.

"It ain't likely," Billy said. "There'd be nothing to eat unless a kind of people that can eat rocks live there."

That was all the information Jody ever got, and it made the mountains dear to him, and terrible. He thought often of the miles of ridge after ridge until at last there was the sea. When the peaks were pink in the morning they invited him among them: and when the sun had gone over the edge in the evening and the mountains were a purple-like despair,[6] then Jody was afraid of them; then they were so impersonal and aloof that their very imperturbability was a threat.

Now he turned his head toward the mountains of the east, the Gabilans, and they were jolly mountains, with hill ranches in their creases, and with pine trees growing on the crests. People lived there, and battles had been fought against the Mexicans[7] on the slopes. He looked back for an instant at the Great Ones and shivered a little at the contrast. The foothill cup of the home ranch[8] below him was sunny and safe. The house gleamed with white light and the barn was brown and warm. The red cows on the farther hill ate their way slowly toward the north. Even the dark cypress tree by the bunkhouse was usual and safe. The chickens scratched about in the dust of the farmyard with quick waltzing steps.

Then a moving figure caught Jody's eye. A man walked slowly over the brow of the hill, on the road from Salinas, and he was headed toward the house. Jody stood up and moved down toward the house too, for if someone was coming, he wanted to be there to see. By the time the boy had got to the house the walking man was only halfway down the road, a lean man, very straight in the shoulders. Jody could tell he was old only because his heels struck the ground with hard jerks. As he approached nearer, Jody saw that he was dressed in blue jeans and in a coat of the same material. He wore clodhopper shoes and an old flat-

[5] Jody's mother is teasing him. She refers to this song that is commonly learned by American children:

The bear went over the mountain	The other side of the mountain
The bear went over the mountain	The other side of the mountain
The bear went over the mountain	The other side of the mountain
To see what he could see.	Was all that he could see.

In other words, Jody's mother is saying that there is nothing on the other side of the mountain.

[6] *purple-like despair:* Mountains often have a purple color just as the sun goes down behind them in the evening. To Jody, this purple was unfriendly and impersonal—the mountains offered no hope. They did not invite him, as the morning mountains did.

[7] Much of the present state of California once belonged to Mexico.

[8] The ranch where Jody lived was located in a valley (shaped like a cup) among the foothills of the mountain range.

brimmed Stetson hat.[9] Over his shoulder he carried a gunny sack, lumpy and full. In a few moments he had trudged close enough so that his face could be seen. And his face was as dark as dried beef. A moustache, blue-white against the dark skin, hovered over his mouth, and his hair was white, too, where it showed at his neck. The skin of his face had shrunk back against the skull until it defined bone, not flesh, and made the nose and chin seem sharp and fragile. The eyes were large and deep and dark, with eyelids stretched tightly over them. Irises and pupils were one, and very black, but the eyeballs were brown. There were no wrinkles in the face at all. This old man wore a blue denim coat buttoned to the throat with brass buttons, as all men do who wear no shirts. Out of the sleeves came strong bony wrists and hands gnarled and knotted and hard as peach branches. The nails were flat and blunt and shiny.

The old man drew close to the gate and swung down his sack when he confronted Jody. His lips fluttered a little and a soft impersonal voice came from between them.

"Do you live here?"

Jody was embarrassed. He turned and looked at the house, and he turned back and looked toward the barn where his father and Billy Buck were. "Yes," he said, when no help came from either direction.

"I have come back," the old man said. "I am Gitano, and I have come back."

Jody could not take all this responsibility. He turned abruptly, and ran into the house for help, and the screen door banged after him. His mother was in the kitchen poking out the clogged holes of a colander with a hairpin, and biting her lower lip with concentration.

"It's an old man," Jody cried excitedly. "It's an old paisano[10] man, and he says he's come back."

His mother put down the colander and stuck the hairpin behind the sink board. "What's the matter now?" she asked patiently.

"It's an old man outside. Come on out."

"Well, what does he want?" She untied the strings of her apron and smoothed her hair with her fingers.

"I don't know. He came walking."

His mother smoothed down her dress and went out, and Jody followed her. Gitano had not moved.

"Yes?" Mrs. Tiflin asked.

Gitano took off his old black hat and held it with both hands in front of him. He repeated, "I am Gitano, and I have come back."

"Come back? Back where?"

[9] *clodhopper shoes . . . Stetson hat:* Clodhoppers are large, heavy work shoes. Stetson, originally a trade name, refers to men's hats that have wide brims and high crowns. Cowboys are often pictured wearing this kind of hat.

[10] *paisano:* farm worker.

Gitano's whole straight body leaned forward a little. His right hand described the circle of the hills, the sloping fields and the mountains, and ended at his hat again. "Back to the rancho.[11] I was born here, and my father, too."

"No, there," he said, pointing to the western ridge. "On the other side there, in a house that is gone."

At last she understood. "The old 'dobe[12] that's washed almost away, you mean?"

"Yes, señora. When the rancho broke up they put no more lime on the 'dobe, and the rains washed it down."

Jody's mother was silent for a little, and curious homesick thoughts ran through her mind, but quickly she cleared them out. "And what do you want here now, Gitano?"

"I will stay here," he said quietly, "until I die."

"But we don't need an extra man here."

"I can not work hard any more, señora. I can milk a cow, feed chickens, cut a little wood; no more. I will stay here." He indicated the sack on the ground beside him. "Here are my things."

She turned to Jody. "Run down to the barn and call your father."

Jody dashed away, and he returned with Carl Tiflin and Billy Buck behind him. The old man was standing as he had been, but he was resting now. His whole body had sagged into a timeless repose.

"What is it?" Carl Tiflin asked. "What's Jody so excited about?"

Mrs. Tiflin motioned to the old man. "He wants to stay here. He wants to do a little work and stay here."

"Well, we can't have him. We don't need any more men. He's too old. Billy does everything we need."

They had been talking over him as though he did not exist, and now, suddenly, they both hesitated and looked at Gitano and were embarrassed.

He cleared his throat. "I am too old to work. I come back where I was born."

"You weren't born here," Carl said sharply.

"No. In the 'dobe house over the hill. It was all one rancho before you came."

"In the mud house that's all melted down?"

"Yes. I and my father. I will stay here now on the rancho."

"I tell you you won't stay," Carl said angrily. "I don't need an old man. This isn't a big ranch. I can't afford food and doctor bills for an

[11] *rancho:* Gitano is using the Spanish form. The English word "ranch" is a borrowing from Mexican Spanish.

[12] *The old 'dobe*: the old adobe house. Adobe is made of sun-dried earth and washes away easily in heavy rain.

old man. You must have relatives and friends. Go to them. It is like begging to come to strangers."

"I was born here," Gitano said patiently and inflexibly.

Carl Tiflin didn't like to be cruel, but he felt he must. "You can eat here tonight," he said. "You can sleep in the little room of the old bunkhouse. We'll give you your breakfast in the morning, and then you'll have to go along. Go to your friends. Don't come to die with strangers."

Gitano put on his black hat and stooped for the sack. "Here are my things," he said.

Carl turned away. "Come on, Billy, we'll finish down at the barn. Jody, show him the little room in the bunkhouse."

He and Billy turned back toward the barn. Mrs. Tiflin went into the house, saying over her shoulder, "I'll send some blankets down."

Gitano looked questioningly at Jody. "I'll show you where it is," Jody said.

There was a cot with a shuck mattress, an apple box[13] holding a tin lantern, and a backless rocking-chair in the little room of the bunkhouse. Gitano laid his sack carefully on the floor and sat down on the bed. Jody stood shyly in the room, hesitating to go. At last he said,

"Did you come out of the big mountains?"

Gitano shook his head slowly. "No, I worked down the Salinas Valley."

The afternoon thought[14] would not let Jody go. "Did you ever go into the big mountains back there?"

The old dark eyes grew fixed, and their light turned inward on the years that were living in Gitano's head. "Once—when I was a little boy. I went with my father."

"Way back, clear into the mountains?"

"Yes."

"What was there?" Jody cried. "Did you see any people or any houses?"

"No."

"Well, what was there?"

Gitano's eyes remained inward. A little wrinkled strain came between his brows.

"What did you see in there?" Jody repeated.

"I don't know," Gitano said. "I don't remember."

"Was it terrible and dry?"

"I don't remember."

In his excitement, Jody had lost his shyness. "Don't you remember anything about it?"

Gitano's mouth opened for a word, and remained open while

[13] *apple box:* a box that had originally been used to pack apples in.

[14] Jody, you remember, had been thinking all afternoon about the mountains.

his brain sought the word. "I think it was quiet—I think it was nice."

Gitano's eyes seemed to have found something back in the years, for they grew soft and a little smile seemed to come and go in them.

"Didn't you ever go back in the mountains again?" Jody insisted.

"No."

"Didn't you ever want to?"

But now Gitano's face became impatient. "No," he said in a tone that told Jody he didn't want to talk about it any more. The boy was held by a curious fascination. He didn't want to go away from Gitano. His shyness returned.

"Would you like to come down to the barn and see the stock?" he asked.

Gitano stood up and put on his hat and prepared to follow.

It was almost evening now. They stood near the watering trough while the horses sauntered in from the hillsides for an evening drink. Gitano rested his big twisted hands on the top rail of the fence. Five horses came down and drank, and then stood about, nibbling at the dirt or rubbing their sides against the polished wood of the fence. Long after they had finished drinking, an old horse appeared over the brow of the hill and came painfully down. It had long yellow teeth; its hooves were flat and sharp as spades, and its ribs and hipbones jutted out under its skin. It hobbled up to the trough and drank water with a loud sucking noise.

"That's old Easter," Jody explained. "That's the first horse my father ever had. He's thirty years old." He looked up into Gitano's old eyes for some response.

"No good any more," Gitano said.

Jody's father and Billy Buck came out of the barn and walked over. "Too old to work," Gitano repeated. "Just eats and pretty soon dies."

Carl Tiflin caught the last words. He hated his brutality toward old Gitano, and so he became brutal again.

"It's a shame not to shoot Easter," he said. "It'd save him a lot of pains and rheumatism." He looked secretly at Gitano, to see whether he noticed the parallel, but the big bony hands did not move, nor did the dark eyes turn from the horse. "Old things ought to be put out of their misery," Jody's father went on. "One shot, a big noise, one big pain in the head maybe, and that's all. That's better than stiffness and sore teeth."

Billy Buck broke in. "They got a right to rest after they worked all of their life. Maybe they like to just walk around."

Carl had been looking steadily at the skinny horse. "You can't imagine now what Easter used to look like," he said softly. "'High neck, deep chest, fine barrel.[15] He could jump a five-bar gate in stride.[16] I won

[15] *fine barrel:* Here, "barrel" refers to the body of the horse.
[16] *in stride:* without change in his normal pace.

a flatrace[17] on him when I was fifteen years old. I could of got two hundred dollars for him any time. You wouldn't think how pretty he was." He checked himself, for he hated softness. "But he ought to be shot now," he said.

"He's got a right to rest," Billy Buck insisted.

Jody's father had a humorous thought. He turned to Gitano. "If ham and eggs grew on a side-hill I'd turn you out to pasture too," he said. "But I can't afford to pasture you in my kitchen."

He laughed to Billy Buck about it as they went on toward the house. "Be a good thing for all of us if ham and eggs grew on the side-hills."

Jody knew how his father was probing for a place to hurt in Gitano. He had been probed often. His father knew every place in the boy where a word would fester.

"He's only talking," Jody said. "He didn't mean it about shooting Easter. He likes Easter. That was the first horse he ever owned."

The sun sank behind the high mountains as they stood there, and the ranch was hushed. Gitano seemed to be more at home in the evening. He made a curious sharp sound with his lips and stretched one of his hands over the fence. Old Easter moved stiffly to him, and Gitano rubbed the the lean neck under the mane.

"You like him?" Jody asked softly.

"Yes—but he's no damn good."

The triangle[18] sounded at the ranch house. "That's supper," Jody cried. "Come on up to supper."

As they walked up toward the house Jody noticed again that Gitano's body was as straight as that of a young man. Only by a jerkiness in his movements and by the scuffling of his heels could it be seen that he was old.

The turkeys were flying heavily into the lower branches of the cypress tree by the bunkhouse. A fat sleek ranch cat walked across the road carrying a rat so large that its tail dragged on the ground. The quail on the side-hills were still sounding the clear water call.

Jody and Gitano came to the back steps and Mrs. Tiflin looked out through the screen door at them.

"Come running, Jody. Come in to supper, Gitano."

Carl and Billy Buck had started to eat at the long oilcloth-covered table. Jody slipped into his chair without moving it, but Gitano stood holding his hat until Carl looked up and said, "Sit down, sit down. You might as well get your belly full before you go on." Carl was afraid he

[17] *flatrace:* a short straight race on level ground.

[18] *triangle:* as used here, a metal triangle. The noise made by hitting the triangle with a metal rod summons people to meals.

might relent and let the old man stay, and so he continued to remind himself that this couldn't be.

Gitano laid his hat on the floor and diffidently sat down. He wouldn't reach for food. Carl had to pass it to him. "Here, fill yourself up." Gitano ate very slowly, cutting tiny pieces of meat and arranging little pats of mashed potatoes on his plate.

The situation would not stop worrying Carl Tiflin. "Haven't you got any relatives in this part of the country?" he asked.

Gitano answered with some pride, "My brother-in-law is in Monterey. I have cousins there, too."

"Well, you can go and live there, then."

"I was born here," Gitano said in gentle rebuke.

Jody's mother came in from the kitchen, carrying a large bowl of tapioca pudding.

Carl chuckled to her, "Did I tell you what I said to him? I said if ham and eggs grew on the side-hills I'd put him out to pasture, like old Easter."

Gitano stared unmoved at his plate.

"It's too bad he can't stay," said Mrs. Tiflin.

"Now don't you start anything," Carl said crossly.

When they had finished eating, Carl and Billy Buck and Jody went into the living-room to sit for a while, but Gitano, without a word of farewell or thanks, walked through the kitchen and out the back door. Jody sat and secretly watched his father. He knew how mean his father felt.

"This country's full of these old paisanos," Carl said to Billy Buck.

"They're damn good men," Billy defended them. "They can work older than white men. I saw one of them a hundred and five years old, and he could still ride a horse. You don't see any white men as old as Gitano walking twenty or thirty miles."

"Oh, they're tough, all right," Carl agreed. "Say, are you standing up for him too? Listen, Billy," he explained, "I'm having a hard enough time keeping this ranch out of the Bank of Italy[19] without taking on anybody else to feed. You know that, Billy."

"Sure, I know," said Billy. "If you was rich, it'd be different."

"That's right, and it isn't like he didn't have relatives to go to. A brother-in-law and cousins right in Monterey. Why should I worry about him?"

Jody sat quietly listening, and he seemed to hear Gitano's gentle voice and its unanswerable, "But I was born here." Gitano was mysterious like the mountains. There were ranges back as far as you could see, but behind the last range piled up against the sky there was a great unknown country. And Gitano was an old man, until you got to the dull dark eyes.

[19] In other words, Carl was having a hard enough time keeping up the payments on the mortgage—presumably held by a bank called the Bank of Italy.

And in behind them was some unknown thing. He didn't ever say enough to let you guess what was inside, under the eyes. Jody felt himself irresistibly drawn toward the bunkhouse. He slipped from his chair while his father was talking and he went out the door without making a sound.

The night was very dark and far-off noises carried in clearly. The hamebells of a wood team sounded from way over the hill on the country road. Jody picked his way across the dark yard. He could see a light through the window of the little room of the bunkhouse. Because the night was secret he walked quietly up to the window and peered in. Gitano sat in the rocking-chair and his back was toward the window. His right arm moved slowly back and forth in front of him. Jody pushed the door open and walked in. Gitano jerked upright and, seizing a piece of deerskin, he tried to throw it over the thing in his lap, but the skin slipped away. Jody stood overwhelmed by the thing in Gitano's hand, a lean and lovely rapier with a golden basket hilt. The blade was like a thin ray of dark light. The hilt was pierced and intricately carved.

"What is it?" Jody demanded.

Gitano only looked at him with resentful eyes, and he picked up the fallen deerskin and firmly wrapped the beautiful blade in it.

Jody put out his hand. "Can't I see it?"

Gitano's eyes smoldered angrily and he shook his head.

"Where'd you get it? Where'd it come from?"

Now Gitano regarded him profoundly, as though he pondered. "I got it from my father."

"Well, where'd he get it?"

Gitano looked down at the long deerskin parcel in his hand. "I don't know."

"Didn't he ever tell you?"

"No."

"What do you do with it?"

Gitano looked slightly surprised. "Nothing. I just keep it."

"Can't I see it again?"

The old man slowly unwrapped the shining blade and let the lamplight slip along it for a moment. Then he wrapped it up again. "You go now. I want to go to bed." He blew out the lamp almost before Jody had closed the door.

As he went back toward the house, Jody knew one thing more sharply than he had ever known anything. He must never tell anyone about the rapier. It would be a dreadful thing to tell anyone about it, for it would destroy some fragile structure of truth. It was a truth that might be shattered by division.[20]

[20] Jody knew what the old man was going to do with the rapier and dimly sensed its rightness. Still he would never tell anyone about it. Talking about it might shatter the "truth" he dimly perceived.

On the way across the dark yard Jody passed Billy Buck. "They're wondering where you are," Billy said.

Jody slipped into the living-room, and his father turned to him. "Where have you been?"

"I just went out to see if I caught any rats in my new trap."

"It's time you went to bed," his father said.

Jody was first at the breakfast table in the morning. Then his father came in, and last, Billy Buck. Mrs. Tiflin looked in from the kitchen.

"Where's the old man, Billy?" she asked.

"I guess he's out walking," Billy said. "I looked in his room and he wasn't there."

"Maybe he started early to Monterey," said Carl. "It's a long walk."

"No," Billy explained. "His sack is in the little room."

After breakfast Jody walked down to the bunkhouse. Flies were flashing about in the sunshine. The ranch seemed especially quiet this morning. When he was sure no one was watching him, Jody went into the little room, and looked into Gitano's sack. An extra pair of long cotton underwear was there, an extra pair of jeans and three pairs of worn socks. Nothing else was in the sack. A sharp loneliness fell on Jody. He walked slowly back toward the house. His father stood on the porch talking to Mrs. Tiflin.

"I guess old Easter's dead at last," he said. "I didn't see him come down to water with the other horses."

In the middle of the morning Jess Taylor from the ridge ranch rode down.

"You didn't sell that old grey crowbait[21] of yours, did you, Carl?"

"No, of course not. Why?"

"Well," Jess said. "I was out this morning early, and I saw a funny thing. I saw an old man on an old horse, no saddle, only a piece of rope for a bridle. He wasn't on the road at all. He was cutting right up straight through the brush. I think he had a gun. At least I saw something shine in his hand."

"That's old Gitano," Carl Tiflin said. "I'll see if any of my guns are missing." He stepped into the house for a second. "Nope, all here. Which way was he heading, Jess?"

"Well, that's the funny thing. He was heading straight back into the mountains."

Carl laughed. "They never get too old to steal," he said. "I guess he just stole old Easter."

"Want to go after him, Carl?"

[21] *grey crowbait:* In other words, the old horse about to die would serve as bait to attract crows, which feed on dead flesh.

"Hell no, just save me burying that horse. I wonder where he got the gun. I wonder what he wants back there."

Jody walked up through the vegetable patch, toward the brush line. He looked searchingly at the towering mountains—ridge after ridge after ridge until at last there was the ocean. For a moment he thought he could see a black speck crawling up the farthest ridge. Jody thought of the rapier and of Gitano. And he thought of the great mountains. A longing caressed him, and it was so sharp that he wanted to cry to get it out of his breast. He lay down in the green grass near the round tub at the brush line. He covered his eyes with his crossed arms and lay there a long time, and he was full of a nameless sorrow.

Comprehension

1. What did Jody's father say was on the other side of the mountains?
2. Was some of the country near Jody's ranch still unexplored?
3. Did Jody want to explore the mountains? Did his father?
4. What did Jody's mother say was in the big mountains?
5. What did Billy Buck think about the possibility of Jody's finding ancient cities lost in the mountains?
6. What did Gitano carry over his shoulder?
7. What did Gitano tell Jody when they first met? What did he tell Jody's mother?
8. How long did Gitano intend to stay?
9. Did Jody's father tell Gitano that he could stay at the ranch?
10. Had Gitano ever gone into the big mountains?
11. What did Gitano say about the old horse named Easter?
12. Did Jody tell Gitano that his father was serious about shooting Easter?
13. What did Gitano say when Carl asked him why he didn't go to his relatives?
14. What did Jody see in Gitano's hand when he went to the bunkhouse after dinner?
15. Where did the old man get the rapier?
16. Did Jody tell anyone about the rapier?
17. What did Jess Taylor report that he saw?
18. Where was Gitano heading?
19. What did Jody do when he heard about Gitano?

Toward Interpretation

1. What fascination did the great mountains hold for Jody? On a more abstract level, what important element do you think they could symbolize in the character of this young boy?

2. What function does the old horse Easter serve in the story? What parallels are drawn between Easter and Gitano?
3. Describe the character of Carl Tiflin as revealed in the following quotes:

> He hated his brutality toward old Gitano, and so he became brutal again.

> Jody knew how his father was probing for a place to hurt in Gitano. He had been probed often. His father knew every place in the boy where a word would fester.

4. Contrast Carl Tiflin's reaction to the news of Gitano and Easter with Jody's reaction.

The Sculptor's Funeral

by Willa Cather

There is wonder in this story—the wonder of a man's triumph over his environment. The sculptor whose funeral you are to read about achieved a very special victory—a victory over the "jaw-biting ugliness" in which he grew up, an ugliness which could so easily have defeated him as it did others. Look for sharp contrasts as you read—contrasts between the way people think and feel and act and live. The ability to depict such contrasts is one of the special talents for which this American author (1873–1947) is noted.

A group of the townspeople stood on the station siding of a little Kansas town, awaiting the coming of the night train, which was already twenty minutes overdue. The snow had fallen thick over everything; in the pale starlight the line of bluffs across the wide, white meadows south of the town made soft, smoke-coloured curves against the clear sky. The men on the siding stood first on one foot and then on the other, their hands thrust deep into their trousers pockets, their overcoats open, their shoulders screwed up with the cold; and they glanced from time to time toward the southeast, where the railroad track wound along the river shore. They conversed in low tones and moved about restlessly, seeming uncertain as to what was expected of them. There was but one of the company who looked as if he knew exactly why he was there, and he kept conspicuously apart; walking to the far end of the platform, returning to the station door, then pacing up the track again, his chin sunk in the high collar of his overcoat, his burly shoulders drooping forward, his gait heavy and dogged. Presently he was approached by a tall, spare, grizzled man clad in a faded Grand Army suit,[1] who shuffled out from the group and advanced with a certain deference, craning his neck forward until his back made the angle of a jack-knife three-quarters open.

"I reckon she's a-goin' to be pretty late agin tonight, Jim," he remarked in a squeaky falsetto. "S'pose it's the snow?"[2]

"I don't know," responded the other man with a shade of annoyance, speaking from out an astonishing cataract of red beard that grew fiercely and thickly in all directions.

The spare man shifted the quill toothpick he was chewing to the other side of his mouth. "It ain't likely that anybody from the East will come with the corpse, I s'pose," he went on reflectively.

"I don't know," responded the other, more curtly than before.

"It's too bad he didn't belong to some lodge or other. I like an order funeral[3] myself. They seem more appropriate for people of some repytation,"[4] the spare man continued, with an ingratiating concession in his shrill voice, as he carefully placed his toothpick in his vest pocket. He always carried the flag at the G.A.R.[5] funerals in the town.

The heavy man turned on his heel, without replying, and walked up the siding. The spare man rejoined the uneasy group. "Jim's ez full ez a tick, ez ushel,"[6] he commented commiseratingly.

Just then a distant whistle sounded, and there was a shuffling of feet on the platform. A number of lanky boys, of all ages, appeared as suddenly and slimily as eels wakened by the crack of thunder; some came from the waiting-room, where they had been warming themselves by

[1] *Grand Army suit:* the uniform of Northern soldiers in the American Civil War. The Grand Army of the Republic was an association of Northern veterans.

[2] Throughout the story, Willa Cather attempts to represent the folk dialect of Sand City, the little town in Kansas. Most of it is easy to understand with some respelling: "I reckon (think) she's (referring to the train) a-going to be pretty late again tonight, Jim. . . . Suppose it's the snow?"

[3] *order funeral:* a funeral sponsored and directed by a military order or organization.

[4] *repytation:* an attempt to represent the dialectal pronunciation of "reputation."

[5] *G.A.R.:* stands for Grand Army of the Republic, mentioned in footnote 1.

[6] Dialect. "Jim is as full as a tick, as usual." "As full as a tick" is slang for very drunk. A tick is an insect that drinks so much blood its body swells up.

the red stove, or half asleep on the slat benches; others uncoiled themselves from baggage trucks or slid out of express wagons. Two clambered down from the driver's seat of a hearse that stood backed up against the siding. They straightened their stooping shoulders and lifted their heads, and a flash of momentary animation kindled their dull eyes at that cold, vibrant scream, the world-wide call for men. It stirred them like the note of a trumpet; just as it had often stirred the man who was coming tonight, in his boyhood.

The night express shot, red as a rocket, from out the eastward marsh lands and wound along the river shore under the long lines of shivering poplars that sentinelled the meadows, the escaping steam hanging in grey masses against the pale sky and blotting out the Milky Way.[7] In a moment the red glare from the headlight streamed up the snow-covered track before the siding and glittered on the wet, black rails. The burly man with the dishevelled red beard walked swiftly up the platform toward the approaching train, uncovering his head as he went. The group of men behind him hesitated, glanced questioningly at one another, and awkwardly followed his example. The train stopped, and the crowd shuffled up to the express car just as the door was thrown open, the man in the G.A.R. suit thrusting his head forward with curiosity. The express messenger appeared in the doorway, accompanied by a young man in in a long ulster and travelling cap.

"Are Mr. Merrick's friends here?" inquired the young man.

The group on the platform swayed uneasily. Philip Phelps, the banker, responded with dignity: "We have come to take charge of the body. Mr. Merrick's father is very feeble and can't be about."

"Send the agent out here," growled the express messenger, "and tell the operator to lend a hand."

The coffin was got out of its rough-box and down on the snowy platform. The townspeople drew back enough to make room for it and then formed a close semicircle about it, looking curiously at the palm leaf[8] which lay across the black cover. No one said anything. The baggage man stood by his truck, waiting to get at the trunks. The engine panted heavily, and the fireman dodged in and out among the wheels with his yellow torch and long oil-can, snapping the spindle boxes.[9] The young Bostonian, one of the dead sculptor's pupils who had come with the body, looked about him helplessly. He turned to the banker, the only one of that black, uneasy, stoop-shouldered group who seemed enough of an individual to be addressed.

[7] *Milky Way:* a certain broad band of stars so far away that they cannot be seen separately—thus "milky." The steam hides the band of stars from view.

[8] *palm leaf:* a symbol of the sculptor's achievement as an artist. The palm leaf is a traditional sign of victory or excellence.

[9] *spindle boxes:* In oiling the wheels, the fireman snaps the covers of the spindles.

"None of Mr. Merrick's brothers are here?" he asked uncertainly.

The man with the red beard for the first time stepped up and joined the others. "No, they have not come yet; the family is scattered. The body will be taken directly to the house." He stooped and took hold of one of the handles of the coffin.

"Take the long hill road up, Thompson, it will be easier on the horses," called the liveryman as the undertaker snapped the door of the hearse and prepared to mount to the driver's seat.

Laird, the red-bearded lawyer, turned again to the stranger: "We didn't know whether there would be any one with him or not," he explained. "It's a long walk, so you'd better go up in the hack." He pointed to a single battered conveyance, but the young man replied stiffly: "Thank you, but I think I will go up with the hearse. If you don't object," turning to the undertaker, "I'll ride with you."

They clambered up over the wheels and drove off in the starlight up the long, white hill toward the town. The lamps in the still village were shining from under the low, snow-burdened roofs; and beyond, on every side, the plains reached out into emptiness, peaceful and wide as the soft sky itself, and wrapped in a tangible, white silence.

When the hearse backed up to a wooden sidewalk before a naked, weather-beaten frame house, the same composite, ill-defined group that had stood upon the station siding was huddled about the gate. The front yard was an icy swamp, and a couple of warped planks, extending from the sidewalk to the door, made a sort of rickety foot-bridge. The gate hung on one hinge, and was opened wide with difficulty. Steavens, the young stranger, noticed that something black [10] was tied to the knob of the front door.

The grating sound made by the casket, as it was drawn from the hearse, was answered by a scream from the house; the front door was wrenched open, and a tall, corpulent woman rushed out bareheaded into the snow and flung herself upon the coffin, shrieking: "My boy, my boy! And this is how you've come home to me!"

As Steavens turned away and closed his eyes with a shudder of unutterable repulsion, another woman, also tall, but flat and angular, dressed entirely in black, darted out of the house and caught Mrs. Merrick by the shoulders, crying sharply: "Come, come, mother; you mustn't go on like this!" Her tone changed to one of obsequious solemnity as she turned to the banker: "The parlour is ready, Mr. Phelps."

The bearers carried the coffin along the narrow boards, while the undertaker ran ahead with the coffin-rests. They bore it into a large, unheated room that smelled of dampness and disuse and furniture polish, and set it down under a hanging lamp ornamented with jingling glass

[10] *something black:* perhaps a black ribbon. Black is symbolic of mourning.

prisms and before a "Rogers group" of John Alden and Priscilla, wreathed with smilax.[11] Henry Steavens stared about him with the sickening conviction that there had been a mistake, and that he had somehow arrived at the wrong destination. He looked at the clover-green Brussels,[12] the fat plush upholstery, among the hand-painted china placques and panels and vases, for some mark of identification,—for something that might once conceivably have belonged to Harvey Merrick. It was not until he recognized his friend in the crayon portrait of a little boy in kilts and curls, hanging above the piano, that he felt willing to let any of these people approach the coffin.

"Take the lid off, Mr. Thompson; let me see my boy's face," wailed the elder woman between her sobs. This time Steavens looked fearfully, almost beseechingly into her face, red and swollen under its masses of strong, black, shiny hair. He flushed, dropped his eyes, and then, almost incredulously, looked again. There was a kind of power about her face—a kind of brutal handsomeness, even; but it was scarred and furrowed by violence, and so coloured and coarsened by fiercer passions that grief seemed never to have laid gentle finger there. The long nose was distended and knobbed at the end, and there were deep lines on either side of it; her heavy, black brows almost met across her forehead, her teeth were large and square, and set far apart—teeth that could tear. She filled the room; the men were obliterated, seemed tossed about like twigs in an angry water, and even Steavens felt himself being drawn into the whirlpool.

The daughter—the tall, raw-boned woman in crêpe, with a mourning comb[13] in her hair which curiously lengthened her long face—sat stiffly upon the sofa, her hands, conspicuous for their large knuckles, folded in her lap, her mouth and eyes drawn down, solemnly awaiting the opening of the coffin. Near the door stood a mulatto woman, evidently a servant in the house, with a timid bearing and an emaciated face pitifully sad and gentle. She was weeping silently, the corner of her calico apron lifted to her eyes, occasionally suppressing a long, quivering sob. Steavens walked over and stood beside her.

Feeble steps were heard on the stairs, and an old man, tall and frail, odorous of pipe smoke, with shaggy, unkempt grey hair and a dingy beard, tobacco stained about the mouth, entered uncertainly. He went slowly up to the coffin and stood rolling a blue cotton handkerchief

[11] *"Rogers group" . . . smilax:* John Rogers was a popular American sculptor whose pieces—this one of Priscilla and John Alden—became known as "Rogers groups" and were reproduced in quantity by machine. The romantic attachment between John Alden and Priscilla is known to every American schoolchild who has studied the colonial period in American history. This group was wreathed with an artificial vine (smilax is a kind of vine). The group typifies the bad taste of the entire house, in Steavens's eyes. Steavens is contrasting the drab room with the world of culture and art that the dead sculptor lived in.

[12] *Brussels:* in this case, a Brussels carpet.

[13] *mourning comb:* a special ornamental comb worn at funerals.

between his hands, seeming so pained and embarrassed by his wife's orgy of grief that he had no consciousness of anything else.

"There, there, Annie, dear, don't take on so," he quavered timidly, putting out a shaking hand and awkwardly patting her elbow. She turned and sank upon his shoulder with such violence that he tottered a little. He did not even glance toward the coffin, but continued to look at her with a dull, frightened, appealing expression, as a spaniel looks at the whip. His sunken cheeks slowly reddened and burned with miserable shame. When his wife rushed from the room, her daughter strode after her with set lips. The servant stole up to the coffin, bent over it for a moment, and then slipped away to the kitchen, leaving Steavens, the lawyer, and the father to themselves. The old man stood looking down at his dead son's face. The sculptor's splendid head seemed even more noble in its rigid stillness than in life. The dark hair had crept down upon the wide forehead; the face seemed strangely long, but in it there was not that repose we expect to find in the faces of the dead. The brows were so drawn that there were two deep lines above the beaked nose, and the chin was thrust forward defiantly. It was as though the strain of life had been so sharp and bitter that death could not at once relax the tension and smooth the countenance into perfect peace—as though he were still guarding something precious, which might even yet be wrested from him.

The old man's lips were working under his stained beard. He turned to the lawyer with timid deference: "Phelps and the rest are comin' back to set up with Harve, ain't they?" he asked. "Thank 'ee, Jim, thank 'ee." He brushed the hair back gently from his son's forehead. "He was a good boy, Jim; always a good boy. He was ez gentle ez a child and the kindest of 'em all—only we didn't none of us ever onderstand him."[14] The tears trickled slowly down his beard and dropped upon the sculptor's coat.

"Martin, Martin! Oh, Martin! come here," his wife wailed from the top of the stairs. The old man started timorously: "Yes, Annie, I'm coming." He turned away, hesitated, stood for a moment in miserable indecision; then reached back and patted the dead man's hair softly, and stumbled from the room.

"Poor old man, I didn't think he had any tears left. Seems as if his eyes would have gone dry long ago. At his age nothing cuts very deep," remarked the lawyer.

Something in his tone made Steavens glance up. While the mother had been in the room, the young man had scarcely seen any one else; but now, from the moment he first glanced into Jim Laird's florid face and blood-shot eyes, he knew that he had found what he had been heartsick

[14] Dialect. "Thank you. . . . He was as gentle as a child (when he was a child) and the kindest of them all—only we didn't none of us ever understand him."

at not finding before—the feeling, the understanding, that must exist in some one, even here.[15]

The man was red as his beard, with features swollen and blurred by dissipation, and a hot, blazing blue eye. His face was strained—that of a man who is controlling himself with difficulty—and he kept plucking at his beard with a sort of fierce resentment. Steavens, sitting by the window, watched him turn down the glaring lamp, still its jangling pendants with an angry gesture, and then stand with his hands locked behind him, staring down into the master's face. He could not help wondering what link there had been between the porcelain vessel and so sooty a lump of potter's clay.[16]

From the kitchen an uproar was sounding; when the dining-room door opened, the import of it was clear. The mother was abusing the maid for having forgotten to make the dressing for the chicken salad which had been prepared for the watchers.[17] Steavens had never heard anything in the least like it; it was injured, emotional, dramatic abuse, unique and masterly in its excruciating cruelty, as violent and unrestrained as had been her grief of twenty minutes before. With a shudder of disgust the lawyer went into the dining-room and closed the door into the kitchen.

"Poor Roxy's getting it now," he remarked when he came back. "The Merricks took her out of the poor-house years ago; and if her loyalty would let her, I guess the poor old thing could tell tales that would curdle your blood. She's the mulatto woman who was standing in here a while ago, with her apron to her eyes. The old woman is a fury; there never was anybody like her. She made Harvey's life a hell for him when he lived at home; he was so sick ashamed of it. I never could see how he kept himself sweet."

"He was wonderful," said Steavens slowly, "wonderful; but until tonight I have never known how wonderful."[18]

"That is the eternal wonder of it, anyway; that it can come even from such a dung heap as this," the lawyer cried, with a sweeping gesture which seemed to indicate much more than the four walls within which they stood.

"I think I'll see whether I can get a little air. The room is so close I am beginning to feel rather faint," murmured Steavens, struggling with

[15] This is an important paragraph. Here Steavens recognizes the feeling and understanding which Jim Laird is capable of. Jim Laird can see the town and the sculptor's home in the same light as Steavens.

[16] In other words, Steavens is wondering what the bond had been between Jim Laird and the dead sculptor. To Steavens, the sculptor was a fine finished product of a man (a porcelain vessel) and Jim Laird was but raw material (a lump of potter's clay).

[17] *watchers:* those who sat up all night with the dead.

[18] Previously Steavens had judged the sculptor on his own merits. Tonight he saw him against the background of the environment from which he sprang and recognized him as a man who had triumphed over that environment.

one of the windows. The sash was stuck, however, and would not yield, so he sat down dejectedly and began pulling at his collar. The lawyer came over, loosened the sash with one blow of his red fist and sent the window up a few inches. Steavens thanked him, but the nausea which had been gradually climbing into his throat for the last half hour left him with but one desire—a desperate feeling that he must get away from this place with what was left of Harvey Merrick. Oh, he comprehended well enough now the quiet bitterness of the smile that he had seen so often on his master's lips!

Once when Merrick returned from a visit home, he brought with him a singularly feeling and suggestive bas-relief[19] of a thin, faded old woman, sitting and sewing something pinned to her knee; while a full-lipped, full-blooded little urchin, his trousers held up by a single gallows, stood beside her, impatiently twitching her gown to call her attention to a butterfly he had caught. Steavens, impressed by the tender and delicate modelling of the thin, tired face, had asked him if it were his mother. He remembered the dull flush that had burned up in the sculptor's face.

The lawyer was sitting in a rocking-chair beside the coffin, his head thrown back and his eyes closed. Steavens looked at him earnestly, puzzled at the line of the chin, and wondering why a man should conceal a feature of such distinction under that disfiguring shock of beard. Suddenly, as though he felt the young sculptor's keen glance, Jim Laird opened his eyes.

"Was he always a good deal of an oyster?"[20] he asked abruptly. "He was terribly shy as a boy."

"Yes, he was an oyster, since you put it so," rejoined Steavens. "Although he could be very fond of people, he always gave one the impression of being detached. He disliked violent emotion; he was reflective, and rather distrustful of himself—except, of course, as regarded his work. He was sure enough there. He distrusted men pretty thoroughly and women even more, yet somehow without believing ill of them. He was determined, indeed, to believe the best; but he seemed afraid to investigate."

"A burnt dog dreads the fire,"[21] said the lawyer grimly, and closed his eyes.

Steavens went on and on, reconstructing that whole miserable boyhood. All this raw, biting ugliness had been the portion of the man whose mind was to become an exhaustless gallery of beautiful impressions

[19] *singularly feeling and suggestive bas-relief:* In a bas-relief (sculpture in which the figures are partly raised on a flat surface), Merrick had pictured a boy and his mother in a very appealing way.

[20] An oyster closes up and lives within its shell. A person who is quiet and lives much alone is sometimes called an oyster.

[21] *A burnt dog dreads the fire:* This old expression means that Merrick avoided people because he had been hurt (burnt) and did not trust them.

—so sensitive that the mere shadow of a poplar leaf flickering against a sunny wall would be etched and held there for ever. Surely, if ever a man had the magic word in his finger tips, it was Merrick. Whatever he touched, he revealed its holiest secret; liberated it from enchantment and restored it to its pristine loveliness. Upon whatever he had come in contact with, he had left a beautiful record of the experience—a sort of ethereal signature;[22] a scent, a sound, a colour that was his own.

Steavens understood now the real tragedy of his master's life; neither love nor wine, as many had conjectured; but a blow which had fallen earlier and cut deeper than anything else could have done—a shame not his, and yet so unescapably his, to hide in his heart from his very boyhood. And without—the frontier warfare; the yearning of a boy, cast ashore upon a desert of newness and ugliness and sordidness, for all that is chastened and old, and noble with traditions.

At eleven o'clock the tall, flat woman in black announced that the watchers were arriving, and asked them to "step into the dining-room." As Steavens rose, the lawyer said dryly: "You go on—it'll be a good experience for you. I'm not equal to that crowd tonight; I've had twenty years of them."

As Steavens closed the door after him he glanced back at the lawyer, sitting by the coffin in the dim light, with his chin resting on his hand.

The same misty group that had stood before the door of the express car shuffled into the dining-room. In the light of the kerosene lamp they separated and became individuals. The minister, a pale, feeble-looking man with white hair and blond chin-whiskers, took his seat beside a small side table and placed his Bible upon it. The Grand Army man sat down behind the stove and tilted his chair back comfortably against the wall, fishing his quill toothpick from his waistcoat pocket. The two bankers, Phelps and Elder, sat off in a corner behind the dinner-table, where they could finish their discussion of the new usury law and its effect on chattel security loans.[23] The real estate agent, an old man with a smiling, hypocritical face, soon joined them. The coal and lumber dealer and the cattle shipper sat on opposite sides of the hard coal-burner, their feet on the nickel-work. Steavens took a book from his pocket and began to read. The talk around him ranged through various topics of local interest while the house was quieting down. When it was clear that the members of the family were in bed, the Grand Army man hitched his shoulders and, untangling his long legs, caught his heels on the rounds of his chair.

"S'pose there'll be a will, Phelps?" he queried in his weak falsetto.

The banker laughed disagreeably, and began trimming his nails with a pearl-handled pocket-knife.

"There'll scarcely be any need for one, will there?" he queried in his turn.

[22] *a sort of ethereal signature:* Merrick's work had a spiritual quality which he alone possessed.
[23] *usury law . . . chattel security loans:* These are terms related to borrowing money.

The restless Grand Army man shifted his position again, getting his knees still nearer his chin. "Why the ole man says Harve's done right well lately," he chirped.

The other banker spoke up. "I reckon he means by that Harve ain't asked him to mortgage any more farms lately, so as he could go on with his education."

'Seems like my mind don't reach back to a time when Harve wasn't bein' edycated," tittered the Grand Army man.

There was a general chuckle. The minister took out his handkerchief and blew his nose sonorously. Banker Phelps closed his knife with a snap. "It's too bad the old man's sons didn't turn out better," he remarked with reflective authority. "They never hung together. He spent money enough on Harve to stock a dozen cattle-farms, and he might as well have poured it into Sand Creek. If Harve had stayed at home and helped nurse what little they had, and gone into stock on the old man's bottom farm, they might all have been well fixed. But the old man had to trust everything to tenants and was cheated right and left."

"Harve never could have handled stock none," interposed the cattleman. "He hadn't it in him to be sharp. Do you remember when he bought Sander's mules for eight-year olds, when everybody in town knew that Sander's father-in-law give 'em to his wife for a wedding present eighteen years before, an' they was full-grown mules then?"

The company laughed discreetly, and the Grand Army man rubbed his knees with a spasm of childish delight.

"Harve never was much account for anything practical, and he shore was never fond of work," began the coal and lumber dealer. "I mind the last time he was home; the day he left, when the old man was out to the barn helpin' his hand hitch up to take Harve to the train, and Cal Moots was patchin' up the fence; Harve, he come out on the step and sings out, in his ladylike voice: 'Cal Moots, Cal Moots! please come cord my trunk.'"

"That's Harve for you," approved the Grand Army man. "I kin hear him howlin' yet, when he was a big feller in long pants and his mother used to whale him with a rawhide in the barn for lettin' the cows git foundered in the cornfield when he was drivin' 'em home from pasture. He killed a cow of mine that-a-way onct—a pure Jersey and the best milker I had, an' the ole man had to put up for her. Harve, he was watchin' the sun set acrost the marshes when the anamile got away."[24]

[24] Dialect. "I can hear him howling (crying) yet, when he was a big fellow in long pants and his mother used to whale (whip) him with a rawhide (whip made of untanned hide) in the barn for letting the cows get foundered (become sick from eating too much) in the cornfield when he was driving them home from pasture. He killed a cow of mine that way once—a pure Jersey (breed of cow) and the best milker I had, and the old man had to put up (pay) for her. Harve, he was watching the sun set across the marshes when the animal got away."

"Where the old man made his mistake was in sending the boy East to school," said Phelps, stroking his goatee and speaking in a deliberate, judicial tone. "There was where he got his head full of nonsense. What Harve needed, of all people, was a course in some first-class Kansas City business college."

The letters were swimming before Steaven's eyes.[25] Was it possible that these men did not understand, that the palm on the coffin meant nothing to them? The very name of their town would have remained for ever buried in the postal guide had it not been now and again mentioned in the world in connection with Harvey Merrick's. He remembered what his master had said to him on the day of his death, after the congestion of both lungs had shut off any probability of recovery, and the sculptor had asked his pupil to send his body home. "It's not a pleasant place to be lying while the world is moving and doing and bettering," he had said with a feeble smile, "but it rather seems as though we ought to go back to the place we came from, in the end. The townspeople will come in for a look at me; and after they have had their say, I shan't have much to fear from the judgment of God!"

The cattleman took up the comment. "Forty's young for a Merrick to cash in;[26] they usually hang on pretty well. Probably he helped it along with whisky."

"His mother's people were not long lived, and Harvey never had a robust constitution," said the minister mildly. He would have liked to say more. He had been the boy's Sunday-school teacher, and had been fond of him; but he felt that he was not in a position to speak. His own sons had turned out badly, and it was a year since one of them had made his last trip home in the express car, shot in a gambling-house in the Black Hills.

"Nevertheless, there is no disputin' that Harve frequently looked upon the wine when it was red, also variegated, and it shore made an oncommon fool of him," moralized the cattleman.

Just then the door leading into the parlour rattled loudly and every one stared involuntarily, looking relieved when only Jim Laird came out. The Grand Army man ducked his head when he saw the spark in his blue, blood-shot eye. They were all afraid of Jim; he was a drunkard, but he could twist the law to suit his client's needs as no other man in all western Kansas could do, and there were many who tried. The lawyer closed the door behind him, leaned back against it and folded his arms, cocking his head a little to one side. When he assumed this attitude in

[25] Steavens, you should remember, "took a book from his pocket" just as the talk began. Now, as he listens, he is so shocked by the conversation that he cannot read.

[26] *to cash in:* The full expression is "to cash in your chips." The phrase is used in gambling. Here, it means "to die." The cattleman is accusing Harve of drinking to excess.

the court-room, ears were always pricked up, as it usually foretold a flood of withering sarcasm.

"I've been with you gentlemen before," he began in a dry, even tone, "when you've sat by the coffins of boys born and raised in this town; and, if I remember rightly, you were never any too well satisfied when you checked them up. What's the matter, anyhow? Why is it that reputable young men are as scarce as millionaires in Sand City? It might almost seem to a stranger that there was some way something the matter with your progressive town. Why did Ruben Sayer, the brightest young lawyer you ever turned out, after he had come home from the university as straight as a die,[27] take to drinking and forge a check and shoot himself? Why did Bill Merrit's son die of the shakes[28] in a saloon in Omaha? Why was Mr. Thomas's son, here, shot in a gambling-house? Why did young Adams burn his mill to beat the insurance companies and go to the pen?"

The lawyer paused and unfolded his arms, laying one clenched fist quietly on the table. "I'll tell you why. Because you drummed nothing but money and knavery into their ears from the time they wore knickerbockers; because you carped away at them as you've been carping here tonight, holding your friends Phelps and Elder up to them for their models, as our grandfathers held up George Washington and John Adams. But the boys were young, and raw at the business you put them to, and how could they match coppers with such artists as Phelps and Elder? You wanted them to be successful rascals; they were only unsuccessful ones—that's all the difference. There was only one boy ever raised in this borderland between ruffianism and civilization who didn't come to grief, and you hated Harvey Merrick more for winning out than you hated all the other boys who got under the wheels. Lord, Lord, how you did hate him! Phelps, here, is fond of saying that he could buy and sell us all out any time he's a mind to; but he knew Harve wouldn't have given a tinker's damn for his bank and all his cattlefarms put together; and a lack of appreciation, that way, goes hard with Phelps.

"Old Nimrod[29] thinks Harve drank too much; and this from such as Nimrod and me!

"Brother Elder says Harve was too free with the old man's money —fell short in filial consideration,[30] maybe. Well, we can all remember the very tone in which brother Elder swore his own father was a liar, in the county court; and we all know that the old man came out of that partnership with his son as bare as a sheared lamb.[31] But maybe I'm getting personal, and I'd better be driving ahead at what I want to say."

[27] *straight as a die:* This figure of speech means extremely honest and dependable.
[28] *the shakes:* shaking and trembling as a result of addiction to alcohol.
[29] *Old Nimrod:* In the Bible, Nimrod is described as a mighty hunter and ruler. As used here, the term seems to refer ironically to Phelps, the banker.
[30] *fell short in filial consideration:* did not act as a son should act toward his father.
[31] *bare as a sheared lamb:* In other words, Brother Elder's father lost his money and his reputation.

The lawyer paused a moment, squared his heavy shoulders, and went on: "Harvey Merrick and I went to school together, back East. We were dead in earnest,[32] and we wanted you all to be proud of us some day. We meant to be great men. Even I, and I haven't lost my sense of humour, gentlemen, I meant to be a great man. I came back here to practise, and I found you didn't in the least want me to be a great man. You wanted me to be a shrewd lawyer—oh, yes! Our veteran[33] here wanted me to get him an increase of pension, because he had dyspepsia; Phelps wanted a new county survey that would put the widow Wilson's little bottom farm inside his south line; Elder wanted to lend money at 5 per cent a month, and get it collected; and Stark here wanted to wheedle old women up in Vermont into investing their annuities in real-estate mortgages that are not worth the paper they are written on. Oh, you needed me hard enough and you'll go on needing me!

"Well, I came back here and became the damned shyster[34] you wanted me to be. You pretend to have some sort of respect for me; and yet you'll stand up and throw mud at Harvey Merrick, whose soul you couldn't dirty and whose hands you couldn't tie. Oh, you're a discriminating lot of Christians! There have been times when the sight of Harvey's name in some Eastern paper has made me hang my head like a whipped dog; and, again, times when I liked to think of him off there in the world, away from all this hog-wallow, climbing the big, clean upgrade he'd set for himself.

"And we? Now that we've fought and lied and sweated and stolen, and hated as only the disappointed strugglers in a bitter, dead little Western town know how to do, what have we got to show for it? Harvey Merrick wouldn't have given one sunset over your marshes for all you've got put together, and you know it. It's not for me to say why, in the inscrutable wisdom of God, a genius should ever have been called from this place of hatred and bitter waters; but I want this Boston man to know that the drivel he's been hearing here tonight is the only tribute any truly great man could have from such a lot of sick, side-tracked, burnt-dog, land-poor sharks as the here-present financiers of Sand City—upon which town may God have mercy!"

The lawyer thrust out his hand to Steavens as he passed him, caught up his overcoat in the hall, and had left the house before the Grand Army man had had time to lift his ducked head and crane his long neck about at his fellows.

Next day Jim Laird was drunk and unable to attend the funeral services. Steavens called twice at his office, but was compelled to start East without seeing him. He had a presentiment that he would hear from

[32] *dead in earnest:* very serious.
[33] *Our veteran:* Jim is referring to the Grand Army man.
[34] *shyster:* a tricky lawyer.

him again, and left his address on the lawyer's table; but if Laird found it, he never acknowledged it. The thing in him that Harvey Merrick had loved must have gone under ground with Harvey Merrick's coffin; for it never spoke again, and Jim got the cold he died of driving across the Colorado mountains to defend one of Phelps's sons who had got into trouble out there by cutting government timber.

Comprehension

1. What was the crowd at the railway station waiting for?
2. Who had come with the sculptor's body?
3. Where was the coffin taken?
4. How did Henry Steavens react to the parlor where the coffin was placed?
5. What did Mrs. Merrick, the sculptor's mother, look like?
6. What did the sculptor's father say about him?
7. Did the family understand Harvey?
8. What did Jim Laird look like?
9. How did Mrs. Merrick treat the maid?
10. What, according to Jim Laird, was the "eternal wonder of it"?
11. How did Steavens describe Harvey Merrick? Was he a friendly, outgoing person?
12. What did Steavens do while the others were eating and talking?
13. Did banker Phelps appreciate Merrick's achievements as a sculptor? Did he think his life was well spent?
14. Did the company gathered in the dining room approve of Harvey Merrick's behavior as a boy?
15. What was Steaven's reaction to the conversation in the dining room? Did he continue to read?
16. Why had the capable and promising young men of Sand City gone wrong? Who was to blame?
17. Why, according to Laird, did the group hate Harvey Merrick?
18. Did Jim Laird return from the law school with high ideals? Was he able to put them into practice?
19. What, according to Jim Laird, would the sculptor have valued more—money or a beautiful sunset?
20. What happened to Jim Laird?

Toward Interpretation

1. Steavens was repelled by the behavior of Mrs. Merrick as the coffin was carried into the house. Why? What did she do? What incidents seemed to reveal her character? Why did this distress Steavens so much?

2. Somehow Harvey Merrick did not seem to fit into the room where his casket was brought. What kind of expression did he wear in death? How might that expression be interpreted by those who knew him?
3. Under what circumstances was Steavens's attention first drawn to Jim Laird, the lawyer? What had he missed in the Merrick home and then found in Jim Laird that reassured him? What was Jim Laird like? What did he tell Steavens about Merrick's boyhood?
4. What impression of Harvey Merrick do you get from Steavens? How did he rate as a sculptor? What was the tragedy in his life?
5. What did Steavens learn from the "watchers" about Merrick's reputation at home? What was the common mistake all the watchers made?
6. Jim Laird made an impassioned speech before the watchers. What was the substance of the speech? What did it tell you about Merrick? About the town's leading citizens? What made him do it? What was the effect of his speech on the watchers? On Steavens?
7. The theme of the story is a familiar, perhaps universal, one. How would you describe it?

SANDBURG

Section Two
Nonfiction

Through nonfiction prose—through letters, speeches, essays, biographies, and articles—much of the world's work is done, as men seek to persuade or convert, to inform or entertain, or simply to share the meaning of an experience.

Whatever its object or purpose, all good prose should be clear and interesting; and it should be structured so that the progression of the ideas is logically and dramatically effective. It should also have a distinctive style, a style that faithfully expresses the personality of the author. While stylistic effects are achieved by subtle and complex processes, there is one element of style that all students of literature would agree must be present—the element of choice. Given a variety of ways in which the same idea could be expressed, the author somehow selects the one that is most striking—the word or phrase, the word order, the image or comparison that is exactly right. This means that the ability to appreciate style requires a long and intimate acquaintance with a language, an acquaintance so thorough that readers can match their expectations of how something might be said with the actual phrasing the author has chosen; it is only by their ability to compare what *could be* with what *is* that they can sense the "differentness," the uniqueness that is basic to an appreciation of the writer's style. And all this explains as well why appreciation of style is so difficult for those who lack the experience of a native speaker and why the ability to appreciate style in another language is perhaps the learner's ultimate and most impressive achievement.

Sometimes the style is so simple that it conveys the impression of artlessness. Lincoln delivered his "Gettysburg Address" at a critical moment in a civil war; Gandhi spoke to the American people at a similarly critical moment in a spiritual way. Both men knew that much was at stake. Both believed that they were speaking for human freedom. Both knew that vast energies and forces had been released, that their listeners' emotions were heightened. Both chose, therefore, to speak in simple words and phrases, in a quiet understatement that is brilliantly effective.

While Gandhi and Lincoln both wished to convey an impression of artlessness, Moorehead has openly created a clever design. He causes us to fear, for many reasons, that he will fail to see the magnificent ape. If he fails, so will we. Therefore, when the animal is finally seen, there is deep satisfaction and a release of tension in the reader.

Santha Rama Rau skillfully employs many concrete details to make familiar and sympathetic what might otherwise be an exotic and puzzling scene. At the same time she quietly manages to convey her own belief in the young teacher's idealism. Narayan, on the other hand, focuses on one detail, a seemingly trivial one, to wittily show significant differences between two cultures.

Nancy Hanks was a pioneer woman living a simple, uneventful life. But Carl Sandburg heightens and ennobles her life by the use of poetic devices, often an image supported by rhythm and sound, as in this memorable sentence: "She was sad with sorrow like dark stars in a blue mist."

J. B. Priestley, through the sprightliness of his style and the subtlety and penetration of his intellectual exploration, invests a series of common experiences with delight.

The selections that follow all illustrate the ability of a skillful writer to enter the reader's life, to induce a sharing of ideas and emotions, a common participation in a significant and heightened moment.

Rashid's School at Okhla

by Santha Rama Rau

Before India gained her independence, the Congress party was carrying on a vast educational program quietly and patiently, anticipating the time when the people of India would have to assume the responsibilities of citizenship in a democracy. The episode that follows tells of one very small but significant effort toward that goal, for it was out of countless such efforts that the new India was created.

The chapter is taken from the first of the author's many books about India and the Far East, a book entitled Home to India. *The book tells the absorbing story of the author's return to her native land as a sixteen-year-old girl, after ten years of attending school in London and spending her vacations traveling on the continents of Europe and Africa with her sister, Premila, and her parents. Her father was a member of the diplomatic service and her mother an ardent social and political worker for a free India. From this background came her own intense interest in the changes that were taking place in her native land: the breakup of the caste system, the changes in marriage customs, and the education of women. Her grandmother, in whose house she lived for a while on her return to India, belonged to the old India. But her parents and her mother's brother—whose wife, Kitty, is the first person mentioned in this chapter—all worked for social reform.*

After returning home from school in London at the outbreak of the Second World War in 1939, the author visited her aunt Kitty in Delhi, the capital of India. It was Kitty who suggested the trip to Rashid's School in Okhla. Kitty, a Viennese married to an Indian, had fallen in love with her husband's land. He was a newspaperman, she an educator with a training in psychology. Together they worked for the liberation of India.

In the years following the incident described here, the author completed her education in America. She graduated from Wellesley College in 1944; in 1947 she went to Japan with her father, who had become the first Ambassador of free India to that country. There she met her American husband. Santha Rama Rau (who was born in 1923) has written many travel books about India and the Far East and has become a well-known interpreter of the East to the West.

Kitty and I drove away from Delhi along the straight, flat Agra[1] road. It was hot, with all the stale accumulated heat of summer concentrated in that autumn day. Behind us the dust rolled upward in thick red clouds. Kitty kept her hand casually and frequently on the horn while we wound our way through the morning traffic. We passed the long lines of bullock carts, with their unoiled axles screaming—a device which is deliberately intended to keep the bullocks awake, but which seems to have no effect on the drivers who sleep calmly on top of their loads. The camel-trains were more orderly. Their drivers had threaded ropes through the noses of the animals to facilitate their control, yet it still took the train about a quarter of an hour to swing away from the center of the road and allow us to pass. The camel owners were more prosperous than the bullock owners; the household utensils on the last animal were made of silver instead of brass.

"Merchants," Kitty guessed, "on their way back to Agra."

Okhla, when we reached it, proved to be a scatter of huts with earthen walls plastered with cow-dung which kept the interiors cool during the day and was used as fuel when it had dried. There was an absurdly tiny shop whose proprietor was a member of the village *panchayat* —the five men who are traditionally elected as governors of the village.

[1] *Agra:* the city of the world-famous Taj Mahal, the beautiful tomb built by a Mogul emperor for his favorite wife. The Agra road is much traveled by those who go to see this architectural wonder.

He acted as the village bank as well as the village letter-writer. Like all Indian villages Okhla was deserted at that time in the morning. Most of the people were working in the fields, and the women had gathered at the well which was their meeting place and center of gossip. As we turned up the dry earth track towards the school, the women stood with their terracotta urns on their heads watching us.

Kitty stopped the car. "Is Rashidji[2] up at the school?" she called. After they had answered us we had to stay and talk to them, for there were countless things they wanted to know about me, a stranger. Where did I live? Who were my parents? Was I married? No? They told me comfortingly not to worry. I still looked young even if I was nearly seventeen; but it certainly wasn't too early to start looking if I didn't want to bring shame on my unfortunate mother. Why was I here? How long would I stay?

Rashid came out to meet us in front of the school. He was a small man, deceptively frail-looking for one of his immense energy. He made himself understood as much by the gestures of his hands as by his fluid English.

"I am so glad you could come," he said, enunciating each syllable clearly. "We, of course, have been at work since half past five. We like to begin early in the cool of the day so that we can let the children rest through the hot hours. . . ." He led us across the yard, on three sides of which were the earthen school buildings. Turning to me, he explained, "You must think this is all very primitive, but to us"—in a suddenly florid tone—"it is the realization of a dream. Sometimes I go into Delhi to have dinner with Kittyji, or see some other friends, and everywhere I hear people talking about this 'political consciousness' we must bring to the inarticulate millions of India. And I say to them this is not a present we can give the villagers; we cannot say 'Come, it is Christmas, here is a gift,' we can only help them. Perhaps we can even give an impetus—but the achievement? That lies with them." He looked at me, trying to gauge my reaction. "But I'm afraid I am only a voice crying in—er—an Indian village."[3]

As we reached the main school building I saw that all the doorways were decorated with enormous yellow sunflowers painted, I was told, by the children.

"They make the colors themselves," Rashid said, "because of course, we can't afford to buy them. Nevertheless, even in a matter as small as this, the earth looks after her own." This started him off on a

[2] *Rashidji:* The name of the schoolmaster whom Kitty and her niece have come to visit is Rashid. The addition of the syllable *-ji* denotes respect.

[3] *a voice crying in . . . village:* The Biblical phrase is "the voice of one crying in the wilderness" (Mark 1, 3). Rashid has adapted it to fit his own situation. In both cases the meaning is the same: The "voice" is solitary and isolated and may not be heard. Rashid is not sure that he can achieve his goals; success will depend upon the villagers.

new speech. He told me something of the history of the school, which in a small way was the history of the whole educational movement which the Congress Party had inaugurated through the medium of the village schools.

To begin with, the villagers were suspicious. It was hard, Rashid said, to persuade them that they were really getting something for nothing. And even when that was accomplished, they were not at all sure that they wanted their children to leave their homes. The adult villagers had found in their own lives no use for education, or indeed for literacy. A few of them spoke of a previous adult literacy campaign into which they had been drawn. They remembered that it had taken the quicker ones a short enough time to learn to read and write—and an equally short time to forget all they had learned. They were frankly skeptical.

As soon as the children of the village were old enough to work in the fields they became economically important to their families. Against that argument education carried very little weight.[4] Rashid assured them that the children would learn really useful things in school—how to enrich the soil, how to make the land more productive. Still the parents were not convinced.

"Finally," he said, "I told them that if they would send their children to my school I would provide the means for them to reel cotton for an hour every day. At last the villagers saw some concrete good in education. The spools of cotton can be sold for a few pice each—less than a penny, but enough to make a substantial difference to the family finances. I won my point; they helped build the schoolhouse, and the children come here every day until they are old enough to help their parents in the fields."

We reached a group of children in a corner of the yard who were building a relief map. Some were soaking mehendi leaves to make a red dye to color the countries.

"It is astonishing," said Kitty, "how they can accept the idea of world geography when they have never been further than twenty miles from their villages."

Rashid looked round the class with affection and triumph. "It was much easier to get the villagers to consent to co-education than it would have been to get the consent of townspeople. I hope industrialism doesn't draw our people into the cities too soon. They lose that independence of spirit that only ownership and the land can give."

Late that afternoon when we were leaving Okhla, Kitty asked Rashid to come into Delhi and have dinner at her house. "Or do you have your mothers' class tonight?" she remembered suddenly.

"No," he answered, "that isn't until tomorrow. I would like very much to dine with you."

[4] *carried little weight:* had little effect.

"Do tell my niece about your success with the ladies, Rashidji," Kitty suggested.

Rashid looked at me pinkly. "I'm afraid your aunt rather misrepresents the incident. Some of my pupils, you see, after they had been coming to school for some months must have carried home favorable reports to their parents. Indeed their mothers were so impressed that one day several of the men of the village came to me to ask whether their wives could learn as well. Of course I was delighted with the success of the school." He looked at Kitty. "But there was a serious drawback. Most of these women were Moslems and consequently could meet no men except their husbands. Imagine what a dilemma! I could not let the opportunity pass, yet I could not teach the women. Eventually I reached a solution that pleased all parties. Now, two evenings a week the women gather in the largest room of the school while I lecture to them from behind a screen with my eyes covered."

After some further discussion between Kitty and Rashid about extending the village school system to other communities around Delhi, Kitty and I left. But that evening at dinner talk of the school was resumed. Rashid had come in on the rickety bus that passes through Okhla twice a day, true to his promise, and Mother was much interested in what I had to tell of the visit to Okhla.

"It must have needed a great deal of courage to carry through a scheme like that," she said, turning to Rashid.

"Not courage so much as hard work and money," he replied. "The officials don't really interfere in matters like this. You see, theoretically they are on the side of education for all people."

"I believe," Kitty put in, "that there are even some laws to that effect—for all the good they do."

"But actually they might as well forbid people to go to school. The damage would be about the same, because naturally we cannot afford public schools on any national scale unless they are subsidized by the government. As long as we don't ask for financial aid we are left undisturbed." Rashid smiled timidly as though he were expecting to be contradicted.

"I didn't mean that kind of courage," Mother said. "I mean the courage it would need to build a world. I know if I had the job on my hands I wouldn't have the least idea what to put into it." She hesitated. "These children are never going to forget what you tell them now. It must be an almost frightening responsibility. Can you say to the Moslems, 'It is wrong to marry twice'? Or to the Hindus, 'It isn't sinful to eat beef'?" She looked across the table at Premila[5] and me, and added "In the West they get out of it easily. They teach their children rigidly, and then say,

[5] *Premila:* the sister of the author.

'Rely on your conscience, it will tell you good from bad.' My daughters hate generalizations like this, but I have always thought that Indians are rather rational people, and for us, I find, reason and conscience are mutual correctives." She smiled disarmingly. "Am I wrong, Rashidji?"

Comprehension

1. Who is telling the story? Who is the "I" in the first sentence? (Refer to the introduction that precedes the story.)
2. How old is the author? What did the villagers tell her not to worry about?
3. What language did Rashid speak in? What was his style of speaking?
4. What time did school begin? Why did it begin so early?
5. Had an earlier literacy campaign for adults in the village been successful?
6. In what way were the children "economically important" to their families?
7. How did Rashid manage to persuade the villagers that there was "some concrete good in education" and get them to help build the schoolhouse?
8. Was the school coeducational?
9. What, according to Rashid, gives the villagers an "independence of spirit"?
10. How did it come about that Rashid was asked to teach a group of mothers?
11. Why did Rashid have to lecture to the mothers from behind a screen with his eyes covered?
12. How did Rashid get from his village to Delhi in order to attend the dinner at Kitty's house?
13. Rashid denied that it took courage to open the school. What did he say it took?
14. The author's mother told Rashid that he had a "frightening responsibility." What was this responsibility?
15. How, according to the author's mother, are children in the West taught to distinguish between good and bad?
16. What does the author's mother say will serve as "mutual correctives" for the Indian people?

Toward Interpretation

1. What difficulties did Rashid have in persuading the villagers to send their children to his school?
2. What signs of educational activity among the children did the two visitors notice?
3. Why didn't the officials interfere with Rashid's school?

4. The author's mother described Rashid's responsibility as "almost frightening." What did she mean by "frightening"?
5. What do you think Rashid had in mind when he said that education is only an impetus to the achievement of "political consciousness"?

Over a Cup of Coffee

by R. K. Narayan

The Indian writer R. K. Narayan (born in 1906) spent nine months in the United States in 1956, seeing the whole of it, from New York to San Francisco. He kept a journal, published in 1960 as My Dateless Diary, *from which the following selection is taken. "It is not a book of information on America," he tells us, "nor is it a study of American culture. It is mainly autobiographical, full of 'I' in relation to some moments, scenes and personalities."*

In the episode below, his humorous observations "over a cup of coffee" give us such a moment—friendly, personal, and gently satiric—as he brings memories of coffee making in a South Indian household into affectionate relationship with his self-help experience in a New York cafeteria. Narayan makes the most of little things. He invests every experience, however small, with its own true wonder, mixed with equal parts of innocence and irony. His stories and novels about Malgudi, an imaginary town in South India, are full of worldly-wise insights. He writes in English, in which he is as much at home as in his native tongue, Kannada, the language of Mysore.

Yesterday, at the self-service cafeteria, I made the mistake of waiting for someone to ask what I wanted. Today I know better. You enter the cafeteria, pull out a "check" (on which prices are punched) from a machine, pick up a tray and spoons, and study the various dishes displayed on the long counter under a glass cover, trying to judge what's what and how far a vegetarian could venture—whether that attractive yellow stuff might not be some prohibited food such as lobster or chicken; the men here evidently do not like anyone to stare so long at their display; one of them asks in a surly manner, "What do you want?" (instead of the ever-polite "Can I help you?"). They are black-haired, hatchet-faced men, possessing a Latin temper perhaps; not the blond soft-spoken Mayflower descendants.[1] How differently you got through a restaurant-session in Mysore.[2] You took your seat, asked for the morning paper and a glass of water—just to mark time before deciding whether you should have *Masal Dosai* again or *Idli*,[3] or as you generally felt inclined (but resisted) both; but indecision could never be an end in itself, and you devised a further postponement of issues, by asking, when the reading of the paper was over, "What have you?" A routine question. The waiter would begin again a quick recital of the day's menu—nothing new or startling in it; but you liked to hear it all over again. It gave you time to make up your mind. Coming from a civilization used to this pace of life, I felt unequal to the speed of a Broadway Cafeteria. If you hesitated with the tray in hand, you held up the traffic behind you. I fumbled and obstructed only for a day. Today I was as good as my neighbour. I picked up my breakfast and assembled it with deftness, and had on the whole acquired so much smartness that when I approached coffee and was asked, "Black or white?" "Neither," I said haughtily. The server looked up rather puzzled. "What do you mean?" he asked. "I want it neither black nor white, but brown which ought to be the colour of honest coffee—that's how we make it in South India where devotees of perfection in coffee assemble from all over the world." He must have thought me crazy, but such leisurely talk is deliberate, like the extra-clutches on the track of a train rolling downhill. I wanted to apply a deliberate counter-action to Broadway's innate rush,

[1] *possessing a Latin temper perhaps; not the blond soft-spoken Mayflower descendants:* People in Latin countries (southern Europe, South America) are considered quick-tempered, while the Mayflower descendants, being of English origin, are supposedly calm and slow to get angry. *Mayflower* is the name of the ship that brought the first permanent English settlers to America.

[2] *Mysore:* capital city of the state of Tamilnadu in Southern India. Mysore is Narayan's hometown.

[3] *Masal Dosai* is a filled pancake. *Idli* are steamed rice patties. They are common foods of South India.

just to study the effect. It could prove disastrous as I learnt later about an Indian anthropologist who went to an Automat[4] and nearly brought the business there to a standstill as he beamed on every one with, "Well, my man, how are you?" or "Where do you come from?" or "How many children have you?" and so forth. He attempted to make genial conversation with all and sundry,[5] got in everybody's way, fumbled with his purse, asking elaborately: "Can you give me change please?" at the wrong place, while all the time five-cent coins were rolling out, as from the mint, at the right place.[6] He felt so discouraged at the end of it that he slipped away losing all hope of mastering the art of ordering food in New York; he was said to have subsisted for a week on hot chestnuts bought of a vendor at the street corner.

Today I wanted to discourse on the implications of brown coffee, but there were other breakfasters, with their trays, standing behind me inexorably, to secure their coffee and race for a table space. They were too well-mannered to push, but I knew they were fretting inside; each must have had a dozen things to do after breakfast, and how dare I block their business? Still I was in a communicative mood; I smiled at those behind me and said, "Sorry." I told the coffee server, "When you have more time, come to me, I'll tell you all about brown coffee." I bore away my tray and sat at a secluded table and began to work my way through cornflakes and milk, marmalade and toast, which were to be my main diet for the next ten months. A man in a sports-jacket came over and asked, "Do you mind?" "Not at all," I said. He set his tray on the table, and said, "I overheard your remark about coffee. You know of a special trick in making it?" God-given opportunity for me to start off on a lecture on coffee, its place in South India (in the North they favour tea), its place in our social life, how the darkest condemnation of a family would be the warning uttered at their back, "Their coffee is awful," how at wedding parties it was the responsibility of the bride's father to produce the best coffee and keep it flowing all day for five hundred at a time; how the decoction drawn at the right density, on the addition of fresh warm milk turned from black to sepia, from which ultimately emerged a brown akin to the foaming edge of a river in flood, how the whole thing depended upon one's feeling for quality and eye for colour; and then the adding of sugar, just enough to mitigate the bitterness but without producing sweetness. Coffee making is a task of precision at every stage. I could not help mentioning my mother who has maintained our house-reputation for coffee undimmed for half a century. She selects the right quality of seeds almost subjecting

[4] *Automat:* a self-service restaurant, where one obtains food from wall compartments by inserting coins which automatically open the compartment.

[5] *all and sundry:* everyone.

[6] *at the right place:* that is, at an automatic coin changer.

every bean to a severe scrutiny,[7] roasts them slowly over charcoal fire, and knows by the texture and fragrance of the golden smoke emanating from the chinks in the roaster whether the seeds within have turned the right shade and then grinds them into perfect grains; everything has to be right in this business. A daughter-in-law who comes into the family will have to go through several weeks of initiation before she may dare to make the family coffee. "Three spoons for six persons. Place the powder at the bottom of a stainless steel vessel and pour boiling water over it and then strain it slowly through a piece of cloth." She is a fanatic and insists on straining coffee only through thin cloth; no power on earth can ever make her change over to a percolater or the more common brass coffee-filter. She considers all such contraptions inimical to her coffee ideals. She gleefully boasted once, "I have made over a hundred persons throw away their coffee-filters and use the cloth for straining. I shall persuade many more before long. Ultimately coffee-filters should cease to have a market. . . ." Such a fanatic, I wondered what her reaction would be to the preposterous question "White or black?" She would be infuriated at the very terminology. "White" coffee actually means, according to her, milk with a dash of coffee which is administered only to sick persons, black coffee should never be drunk! "Cream" itself she would object to as it could never help good coffee. Only pure milk, untampered and taken straight from the cow could be a true coffee component.

After breakfast I emerged into Broadway. My life in New York had not yet fallen into a routine. I felt free to do what I liked.

Comprehension

1. What mistake did Narayan make when he first went to a self-service cafeteria in New York?
2. Why was Narayan afraid to select certain foods?
3. What was the first thing a customer did when he went to a restaurant in Mysore?
4. How did a customer find out what was on the menu?
5. Why did the customer ask "What have you?" when the menu was always the same?
6. Did Narayan ask for black or white coffee?
7. Why did Narayan tell the server about brown coffee? Why did he hold up the line?
8. What did the Indian anthropologist do to bring the business at the Automat nearly to a standstill?
9. What did the anthropologist lose all hope of?

[7] *subjecting every bean to a severe scrutiny:* looking carefully at each coffee bean.

10. What was Narayan's main diet for ten months?
11. How did Narayan finally get an opportunity to give a lecture on coffee?
12. What drink is favored in South India? In North India?
13. What is "the darkest condemnation of a family" in South India?
14. Is warm or cold milk added to the coffee?
15. How much sugar is added?
16. What "initiation" does a new daughter-in-law in Narayan's family have to go through?
17. What boast did Narayan's mother make?
18. What would have been her reaction to the question, "White or black?"
19. Did she use milk or cream in her coffee?
20. Had Narayan's life in New York fallen into a routine?

Toward Interpretation

1. How did ordering in a cafeteria in New York differ from ordering in a restaurant at home in Mysore? What does this incident reveal about the pace of life in New York and Mysore?
2. What happened to the Indian anthropologist who went to an automat?
3. What was the consequence of Narayan's final remark to the coffee server that he would tell him all about brown coffee?
4. How does Narayan's mother feel about other people's methods of making coffee?
5. Why would the phrase "black or white," applied to coffee, have been infuriating to Narayan's mother?

Nancy Hanks
by Carl Sandburg

Many biographies of Abraham Lincoln have been written, but Carl Sandburg's stands out for the devotion of the writer to his subject. The selection that follows is about Lincoln's mother, who died when he was a boy of eight. Through her story you will gain some insight into the harshness of frontier life in the America of Lincoln's youth.

Carl Sandburg, a poet as well as a biographer, sees Lincoln as America's most heroic figure. Sandburg (1878–1967) grew up in Illinois, Lincoln's home state, and he was introduced early to the stories about the small-town lawyer who was born in a log cabin and who eventually became President of the United States. In the biography and in his published poems, Sandburg conveys a deep faith in the American democracy from which such great men as Lincoln can and do emerge.

Tom Lincoln[1] was looking for a woman to travel through life with, for better or worse. One young woman Tom's eyes fell on was a brunette sometimes called Nancy Hanks because she was a daughter of Lucy Hanks, and sometimes called Nancy Sparrow because she was an adopted daughter of Thomas and Elizabeth Sparrow and lived with the Sparrow family.

Lucy Hanks had welcomed her child Nancy into life in Virginia in 1784 and had traveled the Wilderness Road[2] carrying what was to her a precious bundle through the Cumberland Gap and on into Kentucky.

The mother of Nancy was nineteen years old when she made this trip, leaving Nancy's father back in Virginia. She could croon in the moist evening twilight to the shining face in the sweet bundle, "Hush thee, hush thee,[3] thy father's a gentleman." She could toss the bundle into the air against a far, hazy line of blue mountains, catch it in her two hands as it came down, let it snuggle to her breast and feed, while she asked, "Here we come—where from?"

And while Nancy was still learning to walk and talk, her mother Lucy was talked about in and around Harrodsburg, Kentucky, as too free and easy in her behavior, too wild in her ways.

What was clear in the years that had passed was that Lucy Hanks was strong and strange, loved love and loved babies, had married a man she wanted, Henry Sparrow, and nine children had come and they were all learning to read and write under her teaching. Since she had married, the talk about her running wild had let down. After she married Henry Sparrow her daughter Nancy went under the roof of Thomas Sparrow, a brother of Henry, and Elizabeth Hanks Sparrow, a sister of Lucy.

Tom Lincoln had seen Nancy Hanks living with the Sparrows and noticed she was shrewd and dark and lonesome. He had heard her tremulous voice and seen her shaken with sacred desires in church camp-meetings; he had seen her at preachings in cabins when her face stood out as a sort of picture in black against the firelights of the burning logs. He knew she could read the Bible, and had read in other books. She had seen a few newspapers and picked out pieces of news and read her way through.

Her dark skin, dark brown hair, keen little gray eyes, outstanding forehead, somewhat accented chin and cheekbones, body of slender build, weighing about 130 pounds—these formed the outward shape of a woman carrying something strange and cherished along her ways of life. She was sad with sorrows like dark stars in blue mist. The hope

[1] *Tom Lincoln:* the father of Abraham Lincoln.

[2] *Wilderness Road:* a famous route used by pioneers headed West.

[3] *thee:* you. "Thee" is the objective form of "thou," the archaic second person singular. "Thy" is the possessive form of "thou."

was burned deep in her that beyond the harsh clay paths, the everyday scrubbing, washing, patching, fixing, the babble and the gabble[4] of today, there are pastures and purple valleys of song.

She had seen tall hills there in Kentucky. She had seen the stark backbone of Mulraugh's Hill become folded in thin evening blankets with a lavender mist sprayed by sunset lights, and for her there were the tongues of promises over it all.

She believed in God, in the Bible, in mankind, in the past and future, in babies, people, animals, flowers, fishes, in foundations and roofs, in time and the eternities outside of time; she was a believer, keeping in silence behind her gray eyes more beliefs than she spoke. She knew . . . so much of what she believed was yonder—always yonder. Every day came scrubbing, washing, patching, fixing. There was so little time to think or sing about the glory she believed in. It was always yonder. . . .

The day came when Thomas Lincoln signed a bond in the courthouse at Springfield in Washington County, and the bond gave notice: "There is a marriage shortly intended between Thomas Lincoln and Nancy Hanks." It was June 10, 1806. Two days later, a man twenty-eight years old and a woman twenty-three years old came before the Reverend Jesse Head, who later gave the county clerk the names of Thomas Lincoln and Nancy Hanks as having been "joined together in the Holy Estate of Matrimony agreeable to the rules of the Methodist Episcopal Church."

After the wedding came "the infare," the Kentucky style wedding celebration. One who was there said, "We had bear meat, venison, wild turkey and ducks, eggs wild and tame, maple sugar lumps tied on a string to bite off for coffee or whisky, syrup in big gourds, peach-and-honey; a sheep that two families barbecued whole over coals of wood burned in a pit, and covered with green boughs to keep the juices in; and a race for the whisky bottle."

The new husband put his June bride on his horse and they rode away on the red clay road along the timber trails to Elizabethtown. A daughter was born and they named her Sarah. The Lincolns had a cabin of their own to live in. It stood among wild crab-apple trees. And the smell of wild crab-apple blossoms, and the low crying of all wild things, came keen that summer to the nostrils of Nancy Hanks. The summer stars that year shook out pain and warning, strange laughters, for Nancy Hanks.

The same year saw the Lincolns moved to a place on the Big South Fork of Nolin's Creek, about two and a half miles from Hodgenville. They were trying to farm a little piece of ground and make a home. The house they lived in was a cabin of logs cut from the timber near by.

[4] *the babble and the gabble*: unimportant talks and actions.

The floor was packed-down dirt. One door, swung on leather hinges, let them in and out. One small window gave a lookout on the weather, the rain or snow, sun and trees, and the play of the rolling prairie and low hills. A stick-clay chimney carried the fire smoke up and away.

One morning in February of this year, 1809, Tom Lincoln came out of his cabin to the road, stopped a neighbor and asked him to tell "the granny woman,"[5] Aunt Peggy Walters, that Nancy would need help soon.

On the morning of February 12, a Sunday, the granny woman was there at the cabin. And she and Tom Lincoln and the moaning Nancy Hanks welcomed into the world of battle and blood, of whispering dreams and wistful dust, a new child, a boy.

A little later that morning Tom Lincoln threw some extra wood on the fire and an extra bearskin over the mother, went out of the cabin, and walked two miles up the road to where the Sparrows, Tom and Betsy, lived. In his slow way of talking—he was a slow and a quiet man—Tom Lincoln told them, "Nancy's got a boy baby." A half-sheepish look was in his eyes, as though maybe more babies were not wanted in Kentucky just then. The boy, Dennis Hanks, took to his feet, down the road to the Lincoln cabin. There he saw Nancy Hanks on a bed of poles cleated to a corner of the cabin, under warm bearskins.

She turned her dark head from looking at the baby to look at Dennis and threw him a tired, white smile from her mouth and gray eyes. He stood by the bed, his eyes wide open, watching the even, quiet breaths of this fresh, soft red baby.

"What you goin' to name him, Nancy?" the boy asked.

"Abraham," was the answer, "after his grandfather."

Soon came Betsy Sparrow. She washed the baby, put a yellow petticoat and a linsey shirt on him, cooked dried berries with wild honey for Nancy, put the one-room cabin in better order, kissed Nancy and comforted her, and went home.

With the baby she called Abe in her arms, Nancy Hanks went to Rock Spring more than once, sitting with her child and her thoughts, looking at running water and green moss. The secrets of the mingled drone and hush of the place gave her reminders of Bible language, "Be ye comforted," or "Peace, be still."

Cooking, washing, sewing, spinning, weaving, helping keep a home for a man and two babies, besides herself, in a one-room cabin, took a good deal of her time. If there were flies creeping over the face of the baby Abe, she had to drop her work and shoo the flies away. There were few hours in the year she was free to sit with her child and her thoughts, listening to the changing drone and hush of Rock Spring saying, "Be ye comforted," or "Peace, be still."

[5] *granny:* a shortened form for grandmother. The phrase "granny woman" was used for midwife, one who helped at childbirth.

The baby grew, learning to sit up, to crawl over the dirt floor of the cabin; the gristle became bone; the father joked about the long legs getting longer; the mother joked about how quick he grew out of one shirt into another.

During the year 1817, little Abe Lincoln, eight years old, going on nine, had an ax put in his hands and helped his father cut down trees and notch logs for the corners of their new cabin, forty yards from the pole-shed[6] where the family was cooking, eating, and sleeping.

A few days of this year in which the cabin was building,[7] Nancy told Abe to wash his face and hands extra clean; she combed his hair, held his face between her two hands, smacked him a kiss on the mouth, and sent him to school—nine miles and back—Abe and Sally[8] hand in hand hiking eighteen miles a day. Tom Lincoln used to say Abe was going to have "a real eddication," explaining, "You air a-goin' to larn readin', writin', and cipherin'."[9]

Some neighbors said, "It's a pore make-out of a school."[10] and Tom complained it was a waste of time to send the children nine miles just to sit with a lot of other children and read out loud all day in a "blab" school.[11] But Nancy, as she cleaned Abe's ears in corners where he forgot to clean them, and as she combed out the tangles in his coarse, sandy black hair,[12] used to say, "Abe, you go to school now, and larn all you kin."[13] And he kissed her and said, "Yes, Mammy," and started with his sister on the nine-mile walk through timberland where bear, deer, coon, and wildcats ran wild.

Fall time came with its early frost and they were moved into the new cabin, when horses and a wagon came breaking into the clearing one day. It was Tom and Betsy Sparrow to cook and sleep in the pole-shed of the Lincoln family till they could locate land and settle. Hardly a year had passed, however, when both Tom and Betsy were taken down with the "milk sick,"[14] beginning with a whitish coat on the tongue. Both died and were buried in October on a little hill in a clearing in the timbers near by.

[6] *pole-shed:* a crude shelter open on one side to the fire. The Lincolns lived in this pole-shed while the cabin was being built.

[7] *A few days of this year in which the cabin was building:* from time to time during the year in which the cabin was being built.

[8] *Sally:* a diminutive of the name Sarah.

[9] Sandburg is attempting to represent the dialect of Abe's father: *eddication*: education; *air a-goin' to larn*: are going to learn; *readin', writin', and cipherin':* reading, writing, and ciphering—that is, arithmetic.

[10] *pore make-out of a school:* poor makeshift or substitute for a real school.

[11] *"blab" school:* a school in which children study their lessons aloud.

[12] *sandy black hair:* Lincoln's black hair probably looked reddish (sandy) in the light.

[13] *larn all you kin:* dialect for "learn all you can."

[14] *"milk sick":* a common sickness in pioneer days caused by the milk of cows that had fed on poisonous weeds.

Soon after, there came to Nancy Hanks Lincoln that white coating of the tongue; her vitals burned; the tongue turned brownish; her feet and hands grew cold and colder, her pulse slow and slower. She knew she was dying, called for her children, and spoke to them her last choking words. Sarah and Abe leaned over the bed. A bony hand of the struggling mother went out, putting its finger into the boy's sandy black hair; her fluttering guttural words seemed to say he must grow up and be good to his sister and father.

So, on a bed of poles cleated to the corner of the cabin, the body of Nancy Hanks Lincoln lay, looking tired . . . tired . . . with a peace settling in the pinched corners of the sweet, weary mouth, silence slowly etching away the lines of pain and hunger drawn around the gray eyes where now the eyelids closed down in the fine pathos of unbroken rest, a sleep without interruption settling about the form of the stooped and wasted shoulder-bones, looking to the children who tiptoed in, stood still, cried their tears of want and longing, whispered "Mammy, Mammy," and heard only their own whispers answering, looking to these little ones of her brood as though new secrets had come to her in place of the old secrets given up with the breath of life.

And Tom Lincoln took a log left over from the building of the cabin, and he and Dennis Hanks whipsawed the log into planks, planed the planks smooth, and made them of a measure for a box to bury the dead wife and mother in. Little Abe, with a jackknife, whittled pine-wood pegs.[15] And then, while Dennis and Abe held the planks, Tom bored holes and stuck the whittled pegs through the bored holes. This was the coffin, and they carried it the next day to the same little timber clearing near by, where a few weeks before they had buried Tom and Betsy Sparrow. It was in the way of the deer-run leading to the saltish water; light feet and shy hoofs ran over those early winter graves.

So the woman, Nancy Hanks, died, thirty-six years old, a pioneer sacrifice, with memories of monotonous, endless everyday chores, of mystic Bible verses read over and over for their promises, and with memories of blue wistful hills and a summer when the crab-apple blossoms flamed white and she carried a boy-child in the world.

She had looked on fields of blue-blossomed flax and hummed "Hey, Betty Martin, tiptoe, tiptoe"; she had sung of bright kingdoms by and by and seen the early frost leaf its crystals on the stalks of button-weed and redbud; she had sung:

> You may bury me in the east,
> You may bury me in the west,
> And we'll all rise together in that morning.

[15] *whittled pine-wood pegs:* Tom Lincoln did not have metal nails for making the coffin.

Comprehension

1. Why was Nancy called Nancy Hanks by some and Nancy Sparrow by others?
2. When was Nancy born? Where was she born?
3. Did Nancy's mother and father move to Kentucky?
4. What did people say when they talked about Nancy's mother?
5. Where did Nancy go after her mother married Henry Sparrow?
6. Where did Lucy Hanks's nine children learn to read?
7. Where did Tom Lincoln see Nancy?
8. What did Nancy look like?
9. Did Nancy have to work hard every day? What hope was "burned deep in her"?
10. When were Tom and Nancy married? How old were they when they were married?
11. What meat did they serve at the wedding celebration?
12. What was the name of the Lincolns' first child?
13. What kind of house did they live in when they moved to the South Fork of Nolin's Creek? What was the floor made of?
14. Who was their son named after?
15. Did Nancy have much free time?
16. How old was Abe when he helped his father build a new cabin?
17. How far did Abe and his sister have to walk to school?
18. Was Abe's mother anxious for him to have an education?
19. What did Nancy Hanks die of?
20. Who made her coffin?
21. How old was Nancy Hanks when she died?
22. Was Nancy Hanks a religious woman?

Toward Interpretation

1. Before deciding to marry her, what qualities had Lincoln's father noticed in Nancy Hanks?
2. What kind of life did Nancy Hanks lead when she was married to Tom Lincoln?
3. What kind of boyhood did Abraham Lincoln have? What kind of influence did his mother have upon him?
4. Why was Nancy Hanks called a "pioneer sacrifice"? What were the circumstances of her death and burial?

Address at Gettysburg
November 19, 1863
by Abraham Lincoln

Abraham Lincoln was President of the United States during the Civil War, when the North and South were deeply divided on many critical issues—the most important of which was slavery. Though Lincoln wrote a number of well-known speeches during the course of his long political career, the address at Gettysburg is perhaps the most widely quoted of them all. Since it was first printed, there has hardly been a child of school age in the United States who has not had to study and memorize it. Lincoln was preceded on the program by Edward Everett, whose speech was long and conventional, phrased in the highly ornate style then popular in oratory. Lincoln's speech, in contrast, was extremely short and simple. It had been composed on the train to Gettysburg and was written in pencil on the back of an envelope. Some historians say that the people were so moved by Lincoln's words that they did not applaud; they responded instead with a profound and respectful silence. Ironically enough, Lincoln himself felt that the speech had been a failure.

Four score and seven years ago our fathers brought forth on this continent a new nation, conceived in liberty, and dedicated to the proposition that all men are created equal.

Now we are engaged in a great civil war; testing whether that nation, or any nation so conceived and so dedicated, can long endure. We are met on a great battlefield of that war. We have come to dedicate a portion of that field as a final resting-place for those who here gave their lives that that nation might live. It is altogether fitting and proper that we should do this.

But, in a larger sense, we cannot dedicate—we cannot consecrate—we cannot hallow—this ground. The brave men, living and dead, who struggled here have consecrated it, far above our poor power to add or detract. The world will little note, nor long remember, what we say here, but it can never forget what they did here. It is for us the living, rather, to be dedicated here to the unfinished work which they who fought here have thus far so nobly advanced. It is rather for us to be here dedicated to the great task remaining before us—that from these honored dead we take increased devotion to that cause for which they gave the last full measure of devotion; that we here highly resolve that these dead shall not have died in vain; that this nation, under God, shall have a new birth of freedom; and that government of the people, by the people, for the people, shall not perish from the earth.

Comprehension

1. When was the new nation founded?
2. What proposition was the new nation dedicated to?
3. What war was the nation engaged in at the time of Lincoln's speech?
4. Why have the people met at Gettysburg?
5. Who does Lincoln say has consecrated the ground?
6. What should the living dedicate themselves to?
7. What resolution should the people make?
8. Lincoln says the government of his nation is a government ____ the people, ____ the people, and ____ the people.

Toward Interpretation

1. What aspects of this speech suggest the humility and modesty that were characteristic of Lincoln?

Appeal to America

by M. K. Gandhi

One of Mohandas Gandhi's most remarkable achievements was the development of the concept of satyagraha, *or "soul-force." This remarkable idea, which he developed while he was practicing law in South Africa, is a combination of the concepts of noncooperation and nonviolence. Preaching* ahimsa, *complete harmlessness to all living things, Gandhi urged his followers to go to jail rather than to obey the indecent decrees of segregation. In jail, his followers were to manifest joy in their captivity and love toward their captors. Soon, with jails already filled, the South African police were seeking ways to avoid arresting Gandhi's followers who, in turn, found ever more ingenious ways of getting arrested for noncooperation.*

Back in India, Gandhi preached the gospel of disobedience and nonviolence to his own people, who were trying to gain independence from British rule. The struggle was a long and painful one, but Gandhi never doubted that it would succeed. At one point in the struggle Gandhi sought to enlist the assistance and sympathies of the British people themselves. In 1931 he went to England to further the causes he had been fighting for, and to explain himself in person to the English people. On September 13, 1931, he was asked to speak over the radio to the American people.

He agreed, although with some trepidation. Without any prepared speech, he approached the microphone: "Do I have to speak into that thing?" he asked. He was already on the air, and those words were the first the American public at large ever heard him speak. When he was given the signal to stop speaking, he said with a sigh of relief, "Well, that's over." Since he was still on the air those words, too, crossed the Atlantic. But the American public paid little attention to these slips, for they were deeply moved by his words, simply and forcefully spoken, as he set forth once again the ideas that were central to his mission.

Gandhi lived to see India's independence in 1947, but in the following year he was shot to death by a political fanatic. After his death Gandhi was universally called Mahatma, Great Soul. The great soul, in Hindu thought, is that one which has most clearly realized its relation to God. The ethical man may give us a pattern of conduct, but only the godlike man expands our awareness and enlarges our souls. That is what Gandhi did.

In my opinion, the Indian struggle [for freedom] bears in its consequences not only upon India [and England] but upon the whole world. It contains one-fifth of the human race. It represents one of the most ancient civilizations. It has traditions handed down from tens of thousands of years, some of which, to the astonishment of the world, remain intact. No doubt the ravages of time have affected the purity of that civilization as they have that of many other cultures and many institutions.

If India is to revive the glory of her ancient past, she can only do so when she attains her freedom. The reason for the struggle having drawn the attention of the world I know does not lie in the fact that we Indians are fighting for our liberty, but in the fact the means adopted by us for attaining that liberty are unique and, as far as history shows us, have not been adopted by any other people of whom we have any record.

The means adopted are not violence, not bloodshed, not diplomacy as one understands it nowadays, but they are purely and simply truth and non-violence. No wonder that the attention of the world is directed toward this attempt to lead a successful bloodless revolution. Hitherto, nations have fought in the manner of the brute. They have wreaked vengeance upon those whom they have considered to be their enemies.

We find in searching national anthems adopted by great nations that they contain imprecations upon the so-called enemy. They have vowed destruction and have not hesitated to take the name of God and seek divine assistance for the destruction of the enemy. We in India have endeavored to reverse the process. We feel that the law that governs brute creation is not the law that should guide the human race. That law is inconsistent with human dignity.

I, personally, would wait, if need be, for ages rather than seek to attain the freedom of my country through bloody means. I feel in the innermost recesses of my heart, after a political experience extending over an unbroken period of close upon thirty-five years, that the world is sick unto death of blood-spilling. The world is seeking a way out, and I flatter myself with the belief that perhaps it will be the privilege of the ancient land of India to show the way out to the hungering world.

Comprehension

1. What does Gandhi say about the population of India?
2. Why did India's struggle for freedom draw "the attention of the world"?
3. What are the means that India adopted for achieving independence?
4. What objection does Gandhi make to "the law that governs brute creation"?
5. What is the world "sick unto death" of?

Toward Interpretation

1. What does Gandhi hope that India's struggle for freedom will show the world?
2. What does the phrase "hungering world" mean to you?

Delight
by J. B. Priestley

Delight *is a little book of personal essays in which J. B. Priestley (born 1894) seeks to atone for his habit of grumbling. "What, does the man enjoy nothing?" his friends sometimes ask.*

In the introduction to the book, Priestley admits that his friends' questions have some justification. For one thing, he was born and raised in a part of northern England whose inhabitants are said to be naturally glum and dour and to consider faultfinding a hearty, healthy response to life. For another, Priestley served during the First World War under a superior who was one of the worst grumblers in the British army, and so it is not surprising that his habits of faultfinding became more deeply ingrained. Even Priestley's appearance seems to fit him for the role of critic: he is a large man, deliberate in his speech and manners—the kind of person one takes seriously.

Yet he insists that he is not as serious as he seems. Surely his outward appearance does not reveal the inner man, as you will see for yourself in the following sketches about the many things in life that have brought him keen delight.

Dreams

Now and again I have had horrible dreams but not enough of them to make me lose my delight in dreams. To begin with, I like the idea of dreaming, of going to bed and lying still and then, by some queer magic, wandering into another kind of existence. As a child I could never understand why grown-ups took dreaming so calmly when they could make such a fuss about any holiday. This still puzzles me. I am mystified by people who say they never dream and appear to have no interest in the subject. It is much more astonishing than if they said they never went out for a walk. Most people—or at least most Western Europeans—do not seem to accept dreaming as part of their lives. They appear to see it as an irritating little habit, like sneezing or yawning. I have never understood this. My dream life does not seem as important as my waking life, if only because there is far less of it, but to me it is important. As if there were at least two extra continents added to the world, and lightning excursions running to them at any moment between midnight and breakfast. Then again, the dream life, though queer and bewildering and unsatisfactory in many respects, has its own advantages. The dead are there, smiling and talking. The past is there, sometimes all broken and confused but occasionally as fresh as a daisy. And perhaps, as Mr. Dunne[1] tells us, the future is there too, winking at us. This dream life is often overshadowed by huge mysterious anxieties, with luggage that cannot be packed and trains that refuse to be caught; and both persons and scenes there are not as dependable and solid as they are in waking life, so that Brown and Smith merge into one person while Robinson splits into two,[2] and there are thick woods outside the bathroom door and the dining room is somehow part of a theater balcony; and there are moments of desolation or terror in the dream world that are worse than anything we have known under the sun. Yet this other life has its interests, its gaieties, its satisfactions, and, at certain rare intervals, a serene low or a sudden ecstasy, like glimpses of another form of existence altogether, that we cannot match with open eyes. Daft or wise, terrible or exquisite, it is a further helping of experience, a bonus after dark, another slice of life cut differently, for which, it seems to me, we are never sufficiently

[1] *Mr. Dunne:* J. W. Dunne, an English scientist who wrote *An Experiment with Time* (1927). In his book Dunne attempts to explain how and why dreams, when remembered in detail, tend to predict actual events in the waking world.

[2] *Brown, Smith, Robinson:* These names refer to any people one might meet in dreams. As names, they have no further significance.

grateful. Only a dream! Why only? It was there, and you had it. "If there were dreams to sell," Beddoes[3] inquires, "what would you buy?" I cannot say offhand, but certainly rather more than I could afford.

Transport in Films[1]

Nobody ever mentions it—but what delights me most in the unreal world of the films is the transport in that world, so different from ours. These transport arrangements and facilities seem to me far more fascinating than the faces and figures of the female stars. Travel in the film world is so smooth, punctual, speedy and effortless. Down here on earth,[2] where objects are both heavy and malicious, we move around with difficulty. Our cars refuse to start—or, when started, shake and bump us. Taxis are not always to be found, and when found, often behave badly. Trains are frequently late in both arriving and departing. Once on the run, then they rattle and roar and may give us headaches. Ships mostly set sail some hours after the proper time; they smell of paint, cabbage, oilskins and bilge water; they shiver and roll and pitch; and arrive on Thursday evening instead of Tuesday morning. As for air travel, it mostly consists of long waits in sheds haunted by stale cigars or on bleak windy landing grounds. And always, by air, sea or rail, there is the misery of luggage, the malice of heavy objects. But in the phantasmagoric world of the moving pictures, cars start up at once, taxis appear promptly, and all of them glide away like gondolas; trains arrive or depart within two seconds; and no sooner has any important character wandered on to an airfield than a suitable aircraft comes roaring up, lets down its steps, whisks him or her inside, and takes off before you can say "Metro-Goldwyn-Mayer."[3] Except in the comic films, which are closer to our world, the luggage problem does not exist, huge cabin trunks being magically projected into distant hotel suites. What these film characters say and do at the end of a journey often inspires nothing in me but a sour derision. I do not envy them their love affairs, the work they never do, the fun they are supposed to be having, their clothes and their parties, the roast sirloin and the ice pudding they order but never eat. But I delight in their transport facilities which are such stuff as dreams are made on. . . .[4]

[3] *Beddoes:* Thomas Lovell Beddoes, an English poet.

[1] *Transport:* The verb "transport," with stress on the second syllable, is commonly used in Great Britain and the United States. The noun "transport," however, is primarily British. The preferred American word in this context would be "transportation."

[2] *Down here on earth:* This phrase suggests the opposite of "up there in the world of films."

[3] *"Metro-Goldwyn-Mayer":* a well-known motion-picture-producing firm.

[4] This is a partial quotation from Shakespeare's famous lines in *The Tempest:*

We are such stuff
As dreams are made on, and our little life
Is rounded with a sleep.

Reading in Bed about Foul Weather

There is a peculiar delight, which I can still experience though I knew it best as a boy, in cozily reading about foul weather when equally foul weather is beating hard against the windows, when one is securely poised between the wind and rain and sleet outside and the wind and rain and sleet that leap from the page into the mind. The old romancers must have been aware of this odd little bonus of pleasure for the reader, and probably that is why so many of their narratives, to give them a friendly start, began with solitary horsemen, cloaked to the eyebrows, riding through the night on urgent business for the Duke,[1] sustained by nothing more than an occasional and dubious *ragout* or pasty and a gulp or two of sour wine (always fetched by surly innkeepers or their scowling slatterns), on sideroads deep in mire, with wind, rain, thunder and lightning, sleet, hail, snow, all turned on at the full. With the windows rattling away and hailstones drumming at the paper in the fireplace, snug in bed except for one cold elbow, I have traveled thousands and thousands of mucky miles with these fellows, braving the foulest nights, together crying "Bah!"[2]

Moments in the Morning

There are mornings even now when I arrive in my study like a demigod[1] who has been given a planet to play with. Outside my high windows the sunlight falls lovingly on all green and growing things. The paper on my desk looks as if it could be conjured almost without effort into a masterpiece. The keyboard of the typewriter glitters invitingly. The old tin box of paper fasteners, which somehow has survived all moves and changes, looks like some battered faithful sergeant who has been at my side in a hundred battles and sieges. The work, when we get down to it, will be wonderful. And brighter than the gilt along the book-shelves are the illusions of the moment . . . critics are kind and wise . . . readers and audiences are enchanted . . . income tax is sixpence in the pound[2] . . . the United Nations consists of united nations . . . and high and shining in the regard of all good folk everywhere is that sagacious, witty, tender, profound writer . . . who, now waking from his daydream, sits down, a fat grumpy fellow, to slog away[3] until lunchtime.

[1] This is a typical situation to be found in the old romances—"the Duke" standing for any important man on whose business a "solitary horseman" rides "through the night."

[2] *Bah!:* an exclamation of scorn. That is, the riders care nothing for the storm.

[1] *demigod:* a person whose father is a god and whose mother is a mortal. In other words, Priestley feels almost godlike in this magic mood.

[2] *sixpence in the pound:* This would be a very low income tax.

[3] *slog away:* work persistently and hard. In other words, the writing will not be "without effort" as Priestley in his earlier mood seems to think.

Making Stew

It is not often I am allowed to do this; and indeed my great stew-making time was during the darker hours of the war, when anything was about to happen. But I am always delighted to make stew. And it is unusually good stew. You might travel from Truro to Inverness,[1] even today, and be offered nothing better than or as good as my stew. One of my children, without any prompting from me, once ate four large helpings of it. My stew is thick, nourishing and wonderfully tasty. It has meat in it, but almost any kind of meat will do. I add all vegetables that are in season and in the house. And when I am in the mood I toss in exquisite little dumplings. After hours of simmering and thickening and thinning, for I never rush the business and keep peering into the pan, tasting, muttering a spell[2] or two, I add any red wine that I can lay my hands on, and then, at the last moment, drop in a spoonful of honey. The stew is then ready. The very smell is princely. All men and all children gobble my stew gratefully. The women, who hate us to master their little arts, pretend to taste dubiously, arch their brows,[3] wrinkle their noses, ask what is in it, complain about the mess in the kitchen; but nevertheless they contrive in a rather absent-minded manner to eat their share of the noble dish. How can they help it? Here is a stew that has been seasoned with many onions, red wine and honey—and my delight.

Giving Advice

Giving advice, especially when I am in no position to give it and hardly know what I am talking about. I manage my own affairs with as much care and steady attention and skill as—let us say—a drunken Irish tenor.[1] I swing violently from enthusiasm to disgust. I change policies as a woman changes hats. I am here today and gone tomorrow. When I am doing one job, I wish I were doing another. I base my judgments on anything—or nothing. I have never the least notion what I shall be doing or where I shall be in six months time. Instead of holding one thing steadily, I try to juggle with six. I cannot plan, and if I could I would never stick to the plan. I am a pessimist in the morning and an optimist at night, am defeated on Tuesday and insufferably victorious by Friday. But because I am heavy, have a deep voice and smoke a pipe, few people realize that I am a flibber-

[1] *Truro to Inverness:* Truro is in Cornwall, which is located in the southwestern tip of the island of Britain. Inverness is in the north of Scotland. From Truro to Inverness would be a way of saying from one end of Britain to the other.

[2] *muttering a spell:* exerting magic over the bubbling stew to make it good as folklore says witches and magicians do.

[3] *arch their brows:* raise their eyebrows to show doubt.

[1] *drunken Irish tenor:* A drunken singer is not in control of himself. Priestley is suggesting that he manages his own affairs badly.

tigibbet on a weathercock.[2] So my advice is asked. And then, for ten minutes or so, I can make Polonius[3] look a trifler. I settle deep in my chair, two hundred pounds of portentousness, and with some first-rate character touches in the voice and business with pipe,[4] I begin: "Well, I must say that in your place—" And inside I am bubbling with delight.

Departing Guests

I am more of a host than a guest. I like people to stay with me but do not much care about staying with them, and usually say I am too busy. The only people we ask to stay with us are people we like—I do not believe in business hospitality, which has the seed of corruption[1] in it—and all Fridays I work in a pleasant glow just because I know some nice people are coming down by the last train. I am genuinely glad to see them. But I suspect that I am still more delighted when they go, and the house is ours again. It is not that I feel that I have been mistaken in these guests, though this has happened of course at times. After the week end I may like them more than ever, having discovered new virtues and unsuspected charms. Nevertheless, I am delighted to see them go. They leave more room in which to live properly. Meals are quicker and easier. There is no more hanging about, no more sight-seeing, no further necessity for bright talk. My mind, like my body, puts on its old clothes again. I enjoy hard work (my own kind) and foolish play, and both are difficult when you are cluttered up with guests. I like to think about life in this world, and it is not easy to do this when animated and talkative pieces of it[2] are all over the place. With guests about I am conscious of myself as a solid, but as soon as they have gone I expand into a gas again.[3] And a gas can have more delight than a solid. So—*Good-by! . . . Good-by! . . . Good—*

[2] *flibbertigibbet on a weathercock:* A flibbertigibbet is a frivolous and giddy person. A weathercock is a wooden or metal rooster that turns on top of a building and shows the direction of the wind. The whole expression suggests a very undependable person.

[3] *Polonius:* a character in Shakespeare's *Hamlet,* noted for giving advice.

[4] In other words, a large man ("two hundred pounds") using an impressive voice and using impressive gestures with his pipe ("some first-grade character touches") gives grave ("portentous") advice. This is a humorous description of the author's pose.

[1] In other words, since it may not be sincere and may be offered for selfish reasons, "business hospitality" has the possibility (seed planted in it) of becoming corrupt, or spoiled.

[2] *animated and talkative pieces of it:* "Pieces of it" means "pieces of life," a way of referring to the author's guests.

[3] An amusing reference to the author's shift from a heavy and unresponsive mood (like a solid) to a light and gay one (like a gas).

Dreams

Comprehension

1. How often has Priestley had horrible dreams?
2. What does he like about dreaming?
3. What kind of people mystify Priestley?
4. How does the past appear in his dreams?
5. What are the people in his dreams like?
6. What occurs at "certain rare intervals"?
7. If dreams were sold, how many would Priestley buy?

Toward Interpretation

1. How does Priestley describe the advantages and disadvantages of dreaming?

Transport in Films

Comprehension

1. What is travel in the film world like?
2. What happens to cars, taxis, and trains in the real world?
3. What happens to cars, taxis, and trains in films?
4. What doesn't Priestley envy the film characters?
5. What does he take delight in?

Toward Interpretation

1. Does Priestley delight in the realism, or lack of it, to be found in films?

Reading in Bed about Foul Weather

Comprehension

1. What does Priestley like to read about when there is foul weather outside?
2. What scene do many of the "old romancers" begin with?

Toward Interpretation

1. Why do the solitary horseman and Priestley cry "Bah!" together?

Moments in the Morning

Comprehension

1. What does Priestley say his work will be like when he gets down to it?
2. What bright momentary illusions does he have about critics, income tax, and the United Nations?
3. How long does Priestley's daydream last?

Toward Interpretation

1. Compare the way Priestley feels when he arrives in his study and the way he feels when he awakes from his daydream and sits down to work.

Making Stew

Comprehension

1. Does Priestley make stew often?
2. Priestley says his stew is thick. What other two adjectives does he use to describe it?
3. What does Priestley do as the stew is cooking?
4. Priestley doesn't say that men and children *eat* his stew gratefully. What verb does he use?
5. Do the women eat much of the stew?

Toward Interpretation

1. Why do the women of the family pretend they do not like Priestley's stew? By what signs does he recognize their pretense?

Giving Advice

Comprehension

1. How does Priestley manage his own affairs?
2. Does he plan ahead?
3. Do people ask Priestley for his advice?
4. Does he give advice readily?

Toward Interpretation

1. Why is Priestley secretly delighted when people ask him for advice?

Comprehension

1. Does Priestley prefer to be a host or a guest?
2. Does Priestley entertain business acquaintances?
3. Why does Priestley work on Fridays "in a pleasant glow"?
4. Is he sad to see his guests leave?

Toward Interpretation

1. When guests are about, Priestley thinks of himself as a "solid." How does he think of himself after they leave? What change of state does he undergo?

A Most Forgiving Ape
by Alan Moorehead

In 1957, a book entitled No Room in the Ark *was enthusiastically received by the naturalists and sportsmen who were concerned with the fast-diminishing wildlife in Africa. Its Australian author, Alan Moorehead (born in 1910), reminded the world that unless something were done then, many of the great animals of the African plain and jungle would soon become extinct. The following chapter from the book presents an unforgettable picture of the mountain gorilla, one of the species in danger of being wiped out.*

According to his own statement, Africa is in the author's blood. He has made many journeys in southern, eastern, and central Africa and has come to love its people and its animals. He is an excellent observer and a distinguished writer with the power not only to convey facts but to evoke in the imagination of his readers the sights and sounds and smells of Africa.

Just south of the equator, in the extreme south-western corner of Uganda, a chain of eight volcanoes rises to a height of 15,000 feet and straggles in a ragged line across the border into the Belgian Congo. This is one of the more grandiose spectacles in Central Africa, and it is in many ways a strange and disturbing place. Approaching it from the Uganda side you emerge quite suddenly on to the crest of a mountain pass, and there, all at once, the scene breaks out before you with the theatricality of a curtain lifted from a stage. Mount Muhavura, the first of the volcanoes, is a perfect cone with thick green jungle on its sides, and beyond this one glimpses the outlines of other, loftier peaks, usually with their tops neatly cut off by a bank of heavy cloud. The last two volcanoes on the Congo side are still active, and all the floor of the valley below them is dotted with black forbidding patches of lava. This is a region of landslides and earth tremors and nothing seems secure. Indeed, in recent years still another volcano has burst out of a stretch of level plain and has now risen to a height of six hundred feet.

For the most part the local African tribesmen live in a damp soporific heat around the lakes at the foot of the volcanoes, and they seldom go up into the cold jungles and the cloudy heights above; that area, the temperate and sub-alpine zone, has become the refuge of one of the rarest of all wild animals in Africa, the mountain gorilla.

The gorilla is something of a paradox in the African scene. One thinks one knows him very well. For a hundred years or more he has been killed, captured and imprisoned in zoos. His bones have been mounted in natural history museums everywhere, and he has always exerted a strong fascination upon scientists and romantics alike. He is the stereotyped monster of the horror films and the adventure books, and an obvious (though not perhaps strictly scientific) link with our ancestral past.

Yet the fact is we know very little about gorillas. No really satisfactory photograph has ever been taken of one in a wild state, no zoologist, however intrepid, has been able to keep the animal under close and constant observation in the dark jungles in which it lives. Carl Akeley, the American naturalist, led two expeditions to these volcanoes in the nineteen-twenties, and now lies buried here among the animals he loved so well. But even he was unable to discover how long the gorilla lives, or how or why it dies, nor was he able to define the exact social pattern of the family groups, or indicate the final extent of their intelligence. All this and many other things remain almost as much a mystery as they were when the French explorer Du Chaillu first described the animal to the civilized world a century ago. The Abominable Snowman[1] who haunts the imagination of climbers in the Himalayas is hardly more elusive.

[1] *The Abominable Snowman:* a strange creature that is said to live in the Himalayan Mountains. According to the stories, it is half-human. In this respect it resembles the gorilla, whose "human-ness" the author finds appealing.

The little that is known about gorillas certainly makes you want to know a great deal more. Sir Julian Huxley[2] has recorded that thrice in the London Zoo he saw an eighteen-month-old specimen trace the outline of its own shadow with its finger. "No similar artistic initiative," he writes, "has been recorded for any other anthropoid, though we all know now that young chimpanzees will paint 'pictures' if provided with the necessary materials." Huxley speaks too of a traveller seeing a male gorilla help a female up a steep rock-step on Mount Muhavura, and gallantry of that kind is certainly not normal among animals. It is this "human-ness" of the gorilla which is so beguiling. According to some observers he courts and makes love in the same way that humans do. Once the family is established it clings together. It feeds in a group in the thick bamboo jungles on the mountainside in the daytime, each animal making a tidy pile of its food—wild celery, bamboo shoots and other leaves—and squatting down to eat it; and by night each member of the family makes its own bed by bending over and interlacing the bamboo fronds so as to form a kind of oval-shaped nest which is as comfortable and springy as a mattress. The father tends to make his bed just a foot or two from the ground, the mother a little higher, and the children (perhaps two or three of them) safely lodged in the branches up above.

When he walks (and usually a family will travel about half a mile a day), the gorilla takes the main weight on his short legs and rests lightly on the knuckles of his hands at the end of his very long arms. When he stands upright a full-grown male rises to six foot, but with that immense chest he is far heavier than any normal man could ever be. Six hundred pounds is not uncommon. His strength is incredible—certainly great enough to enable him to take a man in his hands and wrench his head off. The female is much smaller and lighter.

Miss J. H. Donisthorpe, who recently made a study of gorillas in the Muhavura area, says that the animals have a strong smell which she describes as a mixture of human sweat, manure and charred wood. They have good eyesight but are probably deficient in both hearing and smelling. They appear to talk to one another, Miss Donisthorpe says, in high-pitched voices, not unlike that of a woman, or by smacking their lips or striking their cheeks, and the female, if alarmed, will scream. The male, on the other hand, is capable of making a frightening demonstration in the face of danger. He stays behind while his family gets away, rising to his feet and uttering a terrifying roar. Sometimes he will drum on his chest and shake the trees around him with every appearance of uncontrollable fury. In extremity he will charge.

But all this, Miss Donisthorpe assured us, is no more than shadow boxing[3] as a general rule, for the gorilla is a gentle, kindly creature, a most

[2] *Sir Julian Huxley:* a famous British scientist.

[3] *shadow boxing:* boxing with one's shadow; hence, merely pretending to be fierce.

forgiving ape who lives at peace with all the other animals, and his reputation for savagery and belligerence is nothing but a myth. When the animal charges the thing to do is to stand your ground and look him in the eye. Then he will turn aside and slip away through the undergrowth.

Nobody knows how many gorillas are left among the volcanoes or whether they are decreasing or increasing, but the numbers are very small, probably something between fifty and two hundred. Nowadays they are protected after a fashion[4] and no one may legally shoot or capture them, but this still does not prevent the local tribesmen from killing them. If the gorillas spoil their crops (and the crops are being pushed steadily further up the mountainsides), or loot the honey from the wild beehives which the tribesmen have placed in the trees, then spearsmen track them to their lairs and take reprisals. Nine gorillas were butchered in this way just before I myself arrived in the area earlier this year.

It was, I must confess, only by chance that I found myself there at all, for I had been heading in a quite different direction from Tanganyika northwards to the valley of the upper Nile. I knew something about the gorilla sanctuary among the volcanoes, but had never planned to go there since the animals have grown very timid and difficult to get at, and few people ever manage to see them. It happened, however, that our safari (a modest one consisting of myself, a companion and a Swahili[5] boy all travelling together with our food and bedding in a single truck) had arrived at Kabale, the southernmost town in Uganda, and here we had decided to rest in comfortable surroundings for a couple of days.

Kabale is quite a landmark in central Africa. It possesses a delightful English inn set among lawns and terraced gardens. There is a well-kept golf course just outside the grounds, and within the immediate neighbourhood of the hotel itself one can play tennis, badminton, croquet, bowls, table tennis and possibly squash as well (though I never verified this). In the evening one drinks French wine at dinner, reads the magazines in the lounge, plays bridge and listens to the radio. Very rightly the European inhabitants of East Africa take their holidays in this cool green place, for it bears a striking resemblance to any of the lusher golfing resorts in southern England, Sunningdale perhaps. It is not, however, the Africa that the traveller comes to see. Changing for dinner the night we arrived I remembered the gorillas. They lay only half a day's drive away through the mountains, and despite the heavy rain that had been falling the road, I discovered, was passable. Next morning we were on our way. It was not that we expected to see a gorilla any more than an amateur deep-sea fisherman will count on hooking a marlin or a sailfish at his first attempt; we were simply glad to be back in primitive Africa again and in an atmosphere where the unexpected might just possibly happen.

[4] *after a fashion:* in some ways.
[5] *Swahili:* The Swahili are a Moslem Bantu people from Zanzibar and the neighboring coasts.

We came over the crest of the mountains and followed the sweep of the eagles far down into the valley below, to the little village of Kisoro at the foot of Muhavura and its neighbouring cone, Mount Mgahinga. Here one stays with the game warden, Mr. M. W. Baumgartel, a man who, like Carl Akeley before him, devotes his life to the gorillas. Mr. Baumgartel was not unoptimistic. If we rose early on the following morning, he said, he would give us guides to take us up the mountains. It would mean climbing to at least ten thousand feet and we would be walking all day, without any definite prospect of success; the very best we could hope for was one fleeting glimpse of a gorilla through the undergrowth.

Now I cannot, by any sort of indulgence,[6] pretend that the climb we made on the following day was in any way exceptional. Many people have done it before and are still doing it. Miss Donisthorpe during her three months research on the gorillas used to make the ascent almost every day. I merely wish to record that for any middle-aged person of sedentary habits it is a considerable ordeal, and that only a sort of vanity or pig-headedness will keep him going; having once embarked on this enterprise he will feel no doubt, as I did, that he must keep on. A curious optimism intervenes; suddenly it becomes not only possible but imperative to clamber up every new height which would have seemed impossible at the outset of the journey. Having never given wild gorillas more than a passing thought in my life before, it now became absolutely essential that I should see one.

Our two guides turned out to be thin little Africans wearing battered suits and hats and anything less like mountaineers could hardly have been imagined. In point of fact, as we soon discovered, they were experts with hypersensitive powers of sight and smell and hearing. They were as indefatigable as the gorilla himself, and like all highly-trained trackers they appeared to feel their way through the bush as though they were moved by some sixth sense which attuned them to their quarry's instincts,[7] so that they knew exactly which path to follow and where to stop and change direction. Certainly it would have been impossible to find the gorillas without them.

We drove first to the foot of the mountains, and then with one guide in front and the other behind we set off on foot, along an uncompromising track that led directly upwards to the saddle between Muhavura and Mgahinga. A watercourse rushed down the mountain beside us, a bright hot sun burst through the clouds, and as we climbed the valley behind us spread out marvellously below; beyond it range after range of hills rolled away towards the Congo. But after the first few minutes I gave up looking at any of these splendid things. Instead I kept my head

[6] *by any sort of indulgence:* Here the author means "even though I would like to."
[7] *attuned them to their quarry's instincts:* told them how the hunted animals were likely to act.

resolutely downwards, concentrating upon the next step ahead. It seemed at times that we were climbing almost perpendicularly. Pretty soon we were in the bamboo belt. Bamboo grows on these central African mountains in thin stalks from ten to twenty feet high, and so thickly that it is often impenetrable. One of the guides took his panga, a broad hooked blade about eighteen inches long, and cut me a walking stick. I suppose it helped, but already I was getting beyond caring.

Then at last after some two hours or more we came out on a clearing and rested. We were now just below 8,000 feet, and all around us unexpected things were growing, banks of huge nettles, orchids sprouting from the grass, plants like bulrushes and those bright flame-coloured flowering reeds which as children we used to call red-hot pokers. The bamboo here had thinned out a little, and on the heights of the two mountains above we could see the curious productions of the alpine zones, giant heather, giant groundsel and giant lobelias. Everything here was giant size but reduced to the appearance of littleness by the tremendous space around us. A vast cloud, shot through with sunlight, was tearing off the crest of Muhavura.

I remember Baumgartel telling me that at this height elephants, leopards and hyenas roamed about as well as the gorilla, but I could see no sign of movement anywhere along the mountain slopes, and in the sky only the long circular sweeps of the eagles sailing by. The silence seemed absolute.

Presently, when my companion and I had gathered our breath a little, the guides indicated that we must go on again. This, for me, had I only known it, was where the impossible began. Hitherto we had at least proceeded on our feet in an upright position. Now we headed into a thick scrub of mingled bamboo and hypericum trees and often the only possible method of getting ahead was on all fours like a gorilla. The guides would not at this stage cut us a path with their pangas lest the noise should alarm the animals, and so it was necessary to haul oneself bodily through the undergrowth, and always we kept going upward.

By midday we had passed the ten thousand foot mark, but I am not really able to recall the incidents of these hours, for red lights had long since begun to dance in front of my eyes and however quickly I gasped for breath it never seemed possible to get enough air into my lungs.[8] The guides kept casting about in different directions and disappearing into the scrub, but then they would call to one another with an insistent bell-like whistle and that was the only sound I heard except for the noise created by my own beastly wallowing in the thickets. We seemed to be following some sort of a trail, since I saw gorilla droppings on the ground at intervals, and finally we came up with a group of their nests. There they all were, the big ones and the little ones, exactly as they

[8] *air into my lungs:* As Moorehead climbs higher and higher, he begins to feel the effects of the altitude.

had been described. I had an impulse to climb up and try one of those springy beds, but that would have meant using up more energy when I had none to spare, and anyway the nests were fouled with droppings. I stared dully at a little pile of shavings on the ground; obviously a gorilla had sat here peeling the bark off a twig before he ate it, and I looked at one of the guides interrogatively. But he shook his head. This was an old nesting place and the gorilla family had long since moved on. We started our crawling climb again.

Once or twice, I recall, I experienced a moment of fear and it was fear bordering on panic. What on earth was there to protect us if a gorilla suddenly appeared out of the bushes only a yard or two away? We had no rifle. It would be quite impossible to run away in this scrub. I did not now for one instant believe all those stories about how the gorilla was always more frightened of human beings than they were of him. Here was I in the jungle, a human being, or at any rate what was left of one, and I knew, with that certainty that only a profound searching of the heart can reveal, that I was more frightened than any gorilla could ever be. There was no question whatever of my standing my ground and looking him firmly in the eye. I was going to stiffen into paralysis with my eyes tightly shut and wait for my head to be torn off.

But then fatigue created a kind of mental anæsthetic. We had been climbing now for more than four hours and were evidently getting nowhere. Suddenly it became more important to stop and lie down than to see a gorilla, and fear was overwhelmed by the sheer physical pain in my chest and legs. Let the others go on and see all the gorillas they wanted. I was going to stop here and now. As I subsided on to a patch of open ground I called to the others and waved them on. A little surprisingly, I felt, they did go on and left me alone. But then what did it matter? Let all the gorillas in the world come and get me: I really did not care.

The next ten minutes were as timeless as only the amnesia of utter exhaustion could make them, and it seemed that I had been resting there in a daze for an hour at least when I opened my eyes and saw my companions standing above me excitedly urging me to get up. They had come on a fresh gorilla track at last, an entire family on the move just ahead of us. And indeed as we scrambled on again I saw fresh droppings on the ground and broken branches that clearly had only recently been wrenched from the trees. But it was no good. After twenty minutes my legs had turned to water again and against the evident displeasure of the guides I demanded lunch.

In the earlier part of our journey through Africa my friend and I had always chosen a pleasant place with a view or beside some stream in which to eat our lunch. Here, however, we sank down on to the earth where we were and dully stuffed the food into our mouths. There was no view anywhere, nothing but the oppressive and silent scrub. The two guides watched us impatiently, squatting a yard or two away. Yet it was amazing what those hunks of bread and meat did: life and hope began to flow through the blood again, and a cup of sweet coffee from a thermos flask accelerated the process. I rose groggily to my feet and faced the impossible once more. We fell into line again with myself drawing up in the rear.

The guides now adjured us to keep the strictest silence, and in fact it was this silence that dominated all the last moments of our climb. It closed around one with a thick palpable drug-like heaviness, almost as if one's ears were stuffed with cotton wool or one's sense of hearing had suddenly failed; layer on layer of silence. And this void, this nothingness of sound, was suddenly torn apart by a single high-pitched bellowing scream. It was bizarre to the point of nightmare. It was as if one had received a sudden unexpected blow on the back of the head. As I stood there, heart thumping, transfixed with shock, one of the guides grabbed me by the arm and half dragged and half pushed me through the undergrowth towards a little rise where the others were standing. I looked at the point where they were staring and I remember calling out aloud, 'Oh my God, how wonderful!'

And the truth is he was wonderful. He was a huge shining male, half crouching, half standing, his mighty arms akimbo. I had not been prepared for the blackness of him; he was a great craggy pillar of gleaming blackness, black crew-cut hair on his head, black deep-sunken eyes glaring towards us, huge rubbery black nostrils and a black beard. He shifted his posture a little, still glaring fixedly upon us, and he had the dignity and majesty of prophets.[9] He was the most distinguished and splendid animal I ever saw and I had only one desire at that moment: to go forward towards him, to meet him and to know him: to communicate. This experience (and I am by no means the only one to feel it in the presence of a gorilla) is utterly at variance with one's reactions to all other large wild animals in Africa. If the lion roars, if you get too close to an elephant and he fans out his ears, if the rhinoceros lowers his head and turns in your direction, you have, if you are unarmed and even sometimes if you are, just one impulse and that is to run away. The beast you feel is savage, intrinsically hostile, basically a murderer. But with the gorilla there is an instant sense of recognition. You might be badly frightened, but in the end you feel you will be able to make some gesture, utter some sound, that the animal will recognize and understand. At all events you do not have the same instinct to turn and bolt.

Afterwards I remembered another thing. Normally, when you come up against a rare wild animal in Africa, you grab your binoculars or your camera at once. It is a simple reflex action. This gorilla was thirty yards away and divided from us by tangled undergrowth and might not perhaps have made a very good photograph, but we could certainly have

[9] *dignity and majesty of prophets:* The gorilla looked like an inspired religious leader.

seen him more clearly through glasses. Yet none of us moved. In my own case (and I suspect in the case of my friend as well) I felt that there was not a second to be lost of this contact, not even the few instants required to put the binoculars to my eyes. I wanted to see him naturally and I wanted to see him whole.

And now abruptly he rose to his full height. Had I really been about to give expression to my sub-conscious desire to move towards him I expect that, at this moment, I would have paused, for he was tremendous in his great height and strength. It was a question now as to whether or not he would beat on his chest and charge, so as to give his family (unseen by us but certainly lurking somewhere there in the bush) further time to get away, but, in fact, he did neither of these things. He lifted his head and gave vent to another of those outlandish and terrifying barking-screams. Once again it seemed to bring every living thing in the bush, including one's own heart, to a full stop. Then he dropped on to his hands and melted away. There was, of course, no chance of following him; despite his size he could travel many times faster than we could.

That was the end of the show, and it had lasted I suppose a couple of hundred seconds. Yet still, after much wandering through Africa in the last few years, I rate this as the most exciting encounter that has come my way; and I remember how, no longer any need for silence, the guides with their pangas slashed a path for us to return through the bush, and how they grinned and were pleased because we were pleased, and how I went down the mountain like a young gazelle in two hours straight, never a touch of fatigue, never a thought for my blistered feet after such a happy day.

Comprehension

1. Does the gorilla live in a temperate or a tropical area? Does he live at the foot of the volcanoes or higher up in the mountains?
2. Do we know very much about gorillas?
3. What examples does Moorehead give of the gorilla's "human-ness"?
4. How tall is a male gorilla? How much does he weigh? How strong is he?
5. Can the male gorilla act ferocious? Is he really savage and belligerent? What should you do if a gorilla charges?
6. How many gorillas are left? Are they protected?
7. Had the author planned to make a trip especially to see the gorillas?
8. The author stayed at an inn in Kabale. What is this inn like? Is it typically African or English?
9. Did the author expect to see gorillas on his trip up the mountains? What did Mr. Baumgartel say was the best he could hope for?
10. Was the climb up the mountain an easy one? What kept the author going?

11. What were the two guides like?
12. What was the bamboo belt like?
13. What was the next stage of the climb like? Why didn't the guides cut a path through the vegetation?
14. How high had they climbed by midday? What signs did they see that gorillas had been nearby?
15. Why was the author frightened? What did he think he would do if a gorilla charged?
16. How was his fear overcome?
17. What did the author do that caused the guides to be displeased?
18. Did the lunch help the author to go on?
19. What was the gorilla's scream like? How did the author react to the scream?
20. What did the author say when he saw the gorilla?
21. What did the gorilla look like?
22. What desire did the author have when he looked at the gorilla? Did he react as one usually reacts when he is close to a large wild animal?
23. Why didn't the author take a picture or use his binoculars?
24. What did the gorilla do?
25. How long did the "show" last?
26. How did the author compare this experience with others he had had in Africa?
27. What was his trip down the mountain like?

Toward Interpretation

1. What facts about the mountain gorilla were known to the author before he set out to invade their mountain sanctuary among the volcanoes of central Africa? How had he learned them?
2. Why is the gorilla "something of a paradox" in the African scene?
3. What were the circumstances under which the author caught his first glimpse of a mountain gorilla? What was the "show" that lasted only "a couple of hundred seconds"?
4. How did the author react when he saw the gorilla? What was there about the gorilla that made him unique, that made him different from other wild animals?

BARRIE

Section Three
Drama

Ideally we should meet a play as we meet a piece of music—in performance. If we are to read it, we must learn to interpret the script, as a musician does the printed score: we must imagine that we can see and hear the characters in action. Some playwrights (Barrie and Saroyan are among them) add detailed *stage directions* when they publish their plays. These stage directions may define the time and place. They may also describe the characters and sometimes even analyze them for us. But the stage directions can do only a small part of our work: if we are to understand a play, we must depend mainly on what the characters say and do. Reading a play requires a lively cooperating imagination, quick to take hints and follow clues, ready to see with the inner eye and hear with the inner ear.

The playwright has special restrictions not imposed on the novelist or short-story writer. He is firmly restricted in time by the patience and endurance of an audience. He is restricted in space by the physical limitations of the stage and the kind of visual backgrounds his theater affords. And he is restricted in subject matter by the interests and capacities of his audience. He must catch his audience's attention at once and hold it steadily. However casual a speech may seem, every word must count. Every speech not only reveals character but hints at something to come or carries the situation forward.

From the very first line, the playwright must put his story into motion. At the same time, he gives the audience the information that is necessary for an understanding of what is happening—who the people are, how they are related to each other, and what problems they are going to face. But these detailed explanations cannot be dull and routine. They must come easily to the surface as the action progresses. The *exposition* must be presented with great skill. In *The Will,* Barrie sets his play in motion in a scene which centers around a lost letter. Robert Devizes, who has lost the letter which explained the purpose of a young couple's visit to his father's law office, tries to bluff his way through an interview with them. Rather than admit the loss, he tries to arrive indirectly at the contents of the letter. Thus, while the audience is watching for young Robert to make a slip, it learns what it needs to know about the characters and the situation.

To hold the attention of the audience, the playwright expresses what he has to say in *action.* Barrie, for instance, wishing to show how lives may be progressively dominated by greed, dramatizes the action of making a will—an action that naturally and easily gives a man a chance to estimate what he wants, what he has, what it means to him, and what he can do with it. He shows the making of a will on three occasions, twenty and ten years apart. Thus he compresses a lifetime into minutes and provides three key points from which we can plot the course of the lives of a young couple from the beginning of their marriage to its end. In this way, Barrie reveals with shocking clarity the progress of a moral degeneration so gradual that the characters themselves are hardly aware of it.

To present an illusion of life, the playwright must root his play firmly in a particular time and place. The *environment* in which the characters move must be clearly and specifically sketched in. Frequently a playwright depends on the painted scenery to tell the audience about the social background—the design and furnishings of a room can define instantaneously the social class, the kind of family, the amount of money they have, the sort of life they lead. The clothing the characters wear, the kind of language they use, and the way they walk, sit down, and handle common objects can also fix time and place. This is how Barrie introduces us so quickly to the world of English middle-class prosperity and acquisitiveness.

The playwright must introduce his characters in such a way as to stir in the audience both recognition of what the characters are like and curiosity to know more about them. Thus the author creates *suspense* at the same time that he is providing information, for what people will do and what will happen to them depends on what sort of people they are. This curiosity about what will happen next holds an audience and draws it into the *conflict* that is the heart of any play. Sometimes the conflict is head-on—the conflict of a man against his fate, the conflict of a man against a tyrant. Sometimes it is mostly psychological, as in *The Will*, where generosity and love are defeated by selfish ambition and greed. Sometimes it is even more vague and generalized, as in *My Heart's in the Highlands*, where aspiring man is in conflict with the complex circumstances of time, place, and society that close him in.

The conflict becomes clearer as the play moves ahead in a series of waves, each crest a little higher than the one before. At each peak something is decided, something lost or won. Only at the *climax* of the play, the highest peak of all, when interest and uncertainty are at their greatest, does the outcome of the conflict become sure. When the story is over, we are able to see what it all amounts to, what the playwright has been gradually disclosing throughout the play. Only then can we define and assess the *theme*.

The playwright does not discuss man and his condition in abstract moral principles. He presents men, alive and walking, embodied in a story or action which expresses the theme more fully than any statement could. Barrie does not philosophize about what time does to men. Instead, he shows us people changing with time and becoming more intensely and obviously the image of their limited inner selves. And he reinforces the meaning of the action by a typical dramatic device: He shows us a physical analogy for a spiritual condition. We see how the small black spot of cancer, grown out of control before it was recognized, made a sick and dying man of Surtees. At the end of the play, we need only a reminder to understand that something like that has happened in the lives of Philip and Emily.

Saroyan, writing of man's nostalgia for the home he can never return to, devises a less tidy play that at first does not seem to be going anywhere. But by the end of the story we have seen a poet and his son making a home out of nothing but loving kindness, and an old man who finds with them a substitute for home in which he can take at least temporary refuge. And at last we see the family ejected from the home to which their hearts will in longing return. If we see all this fully, and hear the characters as they speak, we need not worry about phrasing the theme: it will find its way to us through the open door of our understanding.

The Will
by J. M. Barrie

Sir James Matthew Barrie (1860–1937) first made himself known through novels and short stories in which he depicted Scottish life and character accurately and with affectionate humor. He was a small, acutely shy man, whose mischievous wit played above a profound melancholy. His view of human nature, with its infinite powers of sentimental self-deception, was wry and disillusioned and basically sad.

But Barrie's greatest and most lasting reputation was made through a series of highly successful plays that were shrewd, witty, and consistently entertaining. Some of them were realistic, like What Every Woman Knows. *Others were fantastic, like* Peter Pan. *But they all demonstrated his remarkable control of the realistic conventions of the early twentieth-century English theater. Barrie was unexcelled at inventing stage actions which were at once amusing and directly expressive of his meanings, and he knew how to put these actions together tightly and economically. Interest never flags and forward motion never ceases. Yet the plays move so gracefully and easily that the careful craftsmanship is concealed.*

The Will, *one of Barrie's more brilliant achievements in the difficult one-act form, illustrates most of his qualities as a dramatist: quickly and sharply, in three short scenes all acted out in a single room, it sums up the lives of two people. The judgment the play passes on the final achievement of these lives is stern and unrelenting. But it is also kindly: gently but ruefully, Barrie shows us what our prized feelings of loving generosity only too often come to.*

Characters

MR. DEVIZES, SENIOR
MR. DEVIZES, JUNIOR
SURTEES, *a clerk*
PHILIP ROSS
EMILY ROSS, *Philip's wife*
SENNET, *a clerk*
CREED, *a clerk*

The scene is any lawyer's office. It may be, and no doubt will be, the minute reproduction of some actual office, with all the characteristic appurtenances thereof, every blot of ink in its proper place; but for the purpose in hand any bare room would do just as well. The only thing essential to the room, save the two men sitting in it, is a framed engraving on the wall of Queen Victoria, which dates sufficiently the opening scene, and will be changed presently to King Edward, afterward to King George, to indicate the passing of time.[1] *No other alteration is called for. Doubtless different furniture came in, and the tiling of the fireplace was renewed, and at last someone discovered that the flowers in the window box were dead, but all that is as immaterial to the action as the new bluebottles; the succession of monarchs will convey allegorically the one thing necessary, that time is passing, but that the office of Devizes, Devizes, & Devizes goes on.*

The two men are DEVIZES SENIOR *and* JUNIOR. SENIOR, *who is middle-aged, succeeded to a good thing years ago, and as the curtain rises we see him bent over his table making it a better thing. It is pleasant to think that before he speaks he adds another thirteen and fourpence, say, to the fortune of the firm.*

JUNIOR *is quite a gay dog,*[2] *twenty-three, and we catch him skillfully balancing an office ruler on his nose. He is recently from Oxford*[3]*—*

> If you show him in Hyde Park, lawk, how they will stare,
> Tho' a very smart figure in Bloomsbury Square.[4]

[1] Queen Victoria reigned from 1837 to 1901. King Edward (Edward VII) reigned from 1901 to 1910. King George (George V) reigned from 1910 to 1936.
[2] *gay dog:* slang for lively fellow.
[3] *Oxford:* a famous university in England.
[4] Hyde Park is a fashionable district in London, contrasting with Bloomsbury Square, a less fashionable district. The exclamation "lawk" is a softened form of "Lord."

Perhaps JUNIOR *is a smarter figure in the office (among the clerks) than he was at Oxford, but this is one of the few things about him that his shrewd father does not know.*

There moves to them by the only door into the room a middle-aged clerk called SURTEES, *who is perhaps worth looking at, though his manner is that of one who has long ceased to think of himself as of any importance to either God or man. Look at him again, however (which few would do), and you may guess that he has lately had a shock—touched a living wire—and is a little dazed by it. He brings a card to* MR. DEVIZES, SENIOR, *who looks at it and shakes his head.*

MR. DEVIZES "Mr. Philip Ross." Don't know him.

SURTEES (*Who has an expressionless voice.*) He says he wrote you two days ago, sir, explaining his business.

MR. DEVIZES I have had no letter from a Philip Ross.

ROBERT Nor I.

[*He is more interested in his feat with the ruler than in a possible client, but* SURTEES *looks at him oddly.*]

MR. DEVIZES Surtees looks as if he thought you had.

[ROBERT *obliges by reflecting in the light of* SURTEES'S *countenance.*[5]]

ROBERT Ah, you think it may have been that one, Surty?

MR. DEVIZES (*Sharply.*) What one?

ROBERT It was the day before yesterday. You were out, Father, and Surtees brought me in some letters. His mouth was wide open. (*Thoughtfully.*) I suppose that was why I did it.

MR. DEVIZES What did you do?

ROBERT I must have suddenly recalled a game we used to play at Oxford. You try to fling cards one by one into a hat. It requires great skill. So I cast one of the letters at Surtees's open mouth, and it missed him and went into the fire. It may have been Philip Ross's letter.

MR. DEVIZES (*Wrinkling his brows.*) Too bad, Robert.

ROBERT (*Blandly.*) Yes, you see I am out of practice.

SURTEES He seemed a very nervous person, sir, and quite young. Not a gentleman of much consequence.[6]

ROBERT (*Airily.*) Why not tell him to write again?

MR. DEVIZES Not fair.

SURTEES But she—

ROBERT She? Who?

SURTEES There is a young lady with him, sir. She is crying.

ROBERT Pretty?

SURTEES I should say she is pretty, sir, in a quite inoffensive way.

[5] In other words, Robert, seeing the look on Surtee's face, thinks back (reflects) on the incident.

[6] *Not a gentleman of much consequence:* not a very important man.

ROBERT (*For his own gratification.*) Ha!

MR. DEVIZES Well, when I ring show them in.

ROBERT (*With roguish finger.*) And let this be a lesson to you, Surty, not to go about your business with your mouth open. (SURTEES tries to smile as requested, but with poor success.) Nothing the matter, Surty? You seem to have lost your sense of humor.

SURTEES (*Humbly enough.*) I'm afraid I have, sir. I never had very much, Mr. Robert.

[*He goes quietly. There has been a suppressed emotion about him that makes the incident poignant.*]

ROBERT Anything wrong with Surtees, Father?

MR. DEVIZES Never mind him. I am very angry with you, Robert.

ROBERT (*Like one conceding a point in a debating society.*) And justly.

MR. DEVIZES (*Frowning.*) All we can do is to tell this Mr. Ross that we have not read his letter.

ROBERT (*Bringing his knowledge of the world to bear.*) Is that necessary?

MR. DEVIZES We must admit that we don't know what he has come about.

ROBERT (*Tolerant of his father's limitations.*) But don't we?

MR. DEVIZES Do you?

ROBERT I rather think I can put two and two together.

MR. DEVIZES Clever boy! Well, I shall leave them to you.

ROBERT Right.

MR. DEVIZES Your first case, Robert.

ROBERT (*Undismayed.*) It will be as good as a play to you to sit there and watch me discovering before they have been two minutes in the room what is the naughty thing that brings them here.

MR. DEVIZES (*Dryly.*) I am always ready to take a lesson from the new generation. But of course we old fogies could do that also.

ROBERT How?

MR. DEVIZES By asking them.

ROBERT Pooh. What did I go to Oxford for?

MR. DEVIZES God knows. Are you ready?

ROBERT Quite.

[MR. DEVIZES *rings.*]

MR. DEVIZES By the way, we don't know the lady's name.

ROBERT Observe me finding it out.

MR. DEVIZES Is she married or single?

ROBERT I'll know at a glance. And mark me, if she is married, it is our nervous gentleman who has come between her and her husband; but if she is single, it is little Wet Face who has come between him and his wife.

MR. DEVIZES A Daniel![7]

[7] *Daniel:* In the Bible, Daniel was able to interpret dreams. Here Mr. Devizes is teasing Robert.

[*A young man and woman are shown in: very devoted to each other, though* ROBERT *does not know it. Yet it is the one thing obvious about them; more obvious than his cheap suit, which she presses so carefully beneath the mattress every night, or than the strength of his boyish face. Thinking of him as he then was by the light of subsequent events one wonders whether, if he had come alone, something disquieting could have been read in that face which was not there while she was by. Probably not; it was certainly already there, but had not yet reached the surface. With her, too, though she is to be what is called changed before we see them again, all seems serene; no warning signals; nothing in the way of their happiness in each other but this alarming visit to a lawyer's office. The stage direction might be "Enter two lovers." He is scarely the less nervous of the two, but he enters stoutly in front of her as if to receive the first charge. She has probably nodded valiantly to him outside the door, where she let go his hand.*]

ROBERT (*Master of the situation.*) Come in, Mr. Ross. (*And he bows reassuringly to the lady.*) My partner—indeed my father.

[MR. DEVIZES *bows but remains in the background.*]

PHILIP (*With a gulp.*) You got my letter?

ROBERT Yes—yes.

PHILIP I gave you the details in it.

ROBERT Yes, I have them all in my head. (*Cleverly.*) You will sit down, Miss—I don't think I caught the name.

[*As much as to say, "You see, Father, I spotted that she was single at once."*]

MR. DEVIZES (*Who has also formed his opinion.*) You didn't ask for it, Robert.

ROBERT (*Airily.*) Miss—?

PHILIP This is Mrs. Ross, my wife.

[ROBERT *is a little taken aback, and has a conviction that his father is smiling.*]

ROBERT Ah yes, of course. Sit down, please, Mrs. Ross.

[*She sits as if this made matters rather worse.*]

PHILIP (*Standing guard by her side.*) My wife is a little agitated.

ROBERT Naturally. (*He tries a "feeler."*) These affairs—very painful at the time—but one gradually forgets.

EMILY (*With large eyes.*) That is what Mr. Ross says, but somehow I can't help—(*The eyes fill.*) You see, we have been married only four months.

ROBERT Ah—that does make it—yes, certainly. (*He becomes the wife's champion, and frowns on* PHILIP.)

PHILIP I suppose the sum seems very small to you?

ROBERT (*Serenely.*) I confess that is the impression it makes on me.

PHILIP I wish it was more.

ROBERT (*At a venture.*) You are sure you can't make it more?

PHILIP How can I?

ROBERT Ha!

EMILY (*With sudden spirit.*) I think it's a great deal.

PHILIP Mrs. Ross is so nice about it.

ROBERT (*Taking a strong line.*) I think so. But she must not be taken advantage of. And of course we shall have something to say as to the amount.

PHILIP (*Blankly.*) In what way? There it is.

ROBERT (*Guardedly.*) Hum. Yes, in a sense.

EMILY (*Breaking down.*) Oh dear!

ROBERT (*More determined than ever to do his best for this wronged woman.*) I am very sorry, Mrs. Ross. (*Sternly.*) I hope, sir, you realize that the mere publicity to a sensitive woman—

PHILIP Publicity?

ROBERT (*Feeling that he has got him on the run.*) Of course for her sake we shall try to arrange things so that the names do not appear. Still—

PHILIP The names?

[*By this time* EMILY *is in tears.*]

EMILY I can't help it. I love him so.

ROBERT (*Still benighted.*) Enough to forgive him? (*Seeing himself suddenly as a mediator.*) Mrs. Ross, is it too late to patch things up?

PHILIP (*Now in flame.*)[8] What do you mean, sir?

MR. DEVIZES (*Who has been quietly enjoying himself.*) Yes, Robert, what do you mean precisely?

ROBERT Really I—(*He tries browbeating.*) I must tell you at once, Mr. Ross, that unless a client gives us his fullest confidence we cannot undertake a case of this kind.

PHILIP A case of what kind, sir? If you are implying anything against my good name—

ROBERT On you honor, sir, is there nothing against it?

PHILIP I know of nothing, sir.

EMILY Anything against my husband, Mr. Devizes! He is an angel.

ROBERT (*Suddenly seeing that little Wet Face must be the culprit.*) Then it is you.

EMILY Oh, sir, what is me?

PHILIP Answer that, sir.

8 *(Now in flame)*: very angry.

ROBERT Yes, Mr. Ross, I will. (*But he finds he cannot.*) On second thoughts I decline. I cannot believe it has been all this lady's fault, and I decline to have anything to do with such a painful case.

MR. DEVIZES (*Promptly.*) Then I will take it up.

PHILIP (*Not to be placated.*) I think your son has insulted me.

EMILY Philip, come away.

MR. DEVIZES One moment, please. As *I* did not see your letter, may I ask Mr. Ross what is your business with us?

PHILIP I called to ask whether you would be so good as to draw up my will.

ROBERT (*Blankly.*) Your will! Is that all?

PHILIP Certainly.

MR. DEVIZES Now we know, Robert.

ROBERT But Mrs. Ross's agitation?

PHILIP (*Taking her hand.*) She feels that to make my will brings my death nearer.

ROBERT So that's it.

PHILIP It was all in the letter.

MR. DEVIZES (*Coyly.*) Anything to say, Robert?

ROBERT Most—ah—extremely—(*He has an inspiration.*) But even now I'm puzzled. You are Edgar Charles Ross?

PHILIP No, Philip Ross.

ROBERT (*Brazenly.*) Philip Ross? We have made an odd mistake, Father. (*There is a twinkle in* MR. DEVIZES'S *eye. He watches interestedly to see how his son is to emerge from the mess.*) The fact is, Mrs. Ross, we are expecting to-day a Mr. Edgar Charles Ross on a matter —well—of a kind—Ah me. (*With fitting gravity.*) His wife, in short.

EMILY (*Who has not read the newspapers in vain.*) How awful. How sad.

ROBERT Sad indeed. You will quite understand that professional etiquette[9] prevents my saying one word more.

PHILIP Yes, of course—we have no desire—But I did write.

ROBERT Assuredly. But about a will. That is my father's department. No doubt you recall the letter now, Father?

MR. DEVIZES (*Who if he won't hinder won't help.*) I can't say I do.

ROBERT (*Unabashed.*) Odd. You must have overlooked it.

MR. DEVIZES Ha. At all events, Mr. Ross, I am quite at your service now.

PHILIP Thank you.

ROBERT (*Still ready to sacrifice himself on the call of duty.*) You don't need me any more, Father?

[9] *professional etiquette*: here, the correct manners for a lawyer.

MR. DEVIZES No, Robert; many thanks. You run off to your club now and have a bit of lunch. You must be tired. Send Surtees in to me. (*To his clients.*) My son had his first case today.

PHILIP (*Politely.*) I hope successfully.

MR. DEVIZES Not so bad. He rather bungled it at first, but he got out of a hole rather cleverly. I think you'll make a lawyer yet, Robert.

ROBERT Thank you, Father. (*He goes jauntily, with a flower in his buttonhole.*)

MR. DEVIZES Now, Mr. Ross.

[*The young wife's hand goes out for comfort and finds* PHILIP'S *waiting for it.*]

PHILIP What I want myself is that the will would go into one sentence, "I leave everything of which I die possessed[10] to my beloved wife."

MR. DEVIZES (*Thawing to the romance of this young couple.*) Well, there have been many worse wills than that, sir.

[EMILY *is emotional.*]

PHILIP Don't give way, Emily.

EMILY It was those words, "of which I die possessed." (*Imploringly.*) Surely he doesn't need to say that—please, Mr. Devizes?

MR. DEVIZES Certainly not. I am confident I can draw up the will without mentioning death at all.

EMILY (*Huskily.*) Oh, thank you.

MR. DEVIZES At the same time, of course, in a legal document in which the widow is the sole—

[EMILY *again needs attention.*]

PHILIP (*Reproachfully.*) What was the need of saying "widow"?

MR. DEVIZES I beg your pardon, Mrs. Ross. I unreservedly withdraw the word "widow." Forgive a stupid old solicitor. (*She smiles gratefully through her tears.* SURTEES *comes in.*) Surtees, just take a few notes, please. (SURTEES *sits in the background and takes notes.*) The facts of the case, as I understand, Mrs. Ross, are these: Your husband (*Quickly.*)—who is in the prime of health—but knows life to be uncertain—

EMILY Oh!

MR. DEVIZES —though usually, as we learn from Holy Script itself, it lasts seven times ten years—and believing that he will in all probability live the alloted span,[11] nevertheless, because of his love

[10] *everything of which I die possessed:* everything owned at the time of death.

[11] *seven times ten years:* reference to Psalm 90 in the Old Testament: "The days of our years are threescore years and ten." A score is twenty. The man's lifetime (allotted span) would be three twenties plus ten, or seventy years.

of you thinks it judicious to go through the form—it is a mere form—of making a will.

EMILY (*Fervently.*) Oh, thank you.

MR. DEVIZES Any details, Mr. Ross?

PHILIP I am an orphan. I live at Belvedere, 14 Tulphin Road, Hammersmith.

EMILY (*To whom the address has a seductive sound.*) We live there.

PHILIP And I am a clerk in the employ of Curar and Gow, the foreign coaling agents.

MR. DEVIZES Yes, yes. Any private income?

[*They cannot help sniggering a little at the quaint question.*]

PHILIP Oh, no!

MR. DEVIZES I see it will be quite a brief will.

PHILIP (*To whom the remark sounds scarcely worthy of a great occasion.*) My income is a biggish one.

MR. DEVIZES Yes?

EMILY (*Important.*) He has a hundred and seventy pounds a year.

MR. DEVIZES Ah.

PHILIP I began at sixty pounds. But it is going up, Mr. Devizes, by leaps and bounds. Another fifteen pounds this year.

MR. DEVIZES Good.

PHILIP (*Darkly.*) I have a certain ambition.

EMILY (*Eagerly.*) Tell him, Philip.

PHILIP (*With a big breath.*) We have made up our minds to come to three hundred and sixty-five pounds a year before I—retire.

EMILY That is a pound a day.

MR. DEVIZES (*Smiling sympathetically on them.*) So it is. My best wishes.

PHILIP Thank you. Of course the furnishing took a good deal.

MR. DEVIZES It would.

EMILY He insisted on my having the very best. (*She ceases. She is probably thinking of her superb spare bedroom.*)

PHILIP But we are not a penny in debt, and I have two hundred pounds saved.

MR. DEVIZES I think you have made a brave beginning.

EMILY They have the highest opinion of him in the office.

PHILIP Then I am insured for five hundred pounds.

MR. DEVIZES I am glad to hear that.

PHILIP Of course I would like to leave her a house in Kensington and a carriage and pair.[12]

MR. DEVIZES Who knows, perhaps you will.

EMILY Oh!

[12] *a carriage and pair (of horses):* a symbol of wealth.

MR. DEVIZES Forgive me.

EMILY What would houses and horses be to me without him!

MR. DEVIZES (*Soothingly.*) Quite so. What I take Mr. Ross to mean is that when he dies—if he ever should die—everything is to go to his—his spouse.

PHILIP (*Dogged.*) Yes.

EMILY (*Dogged.*) No.

PHILIP (*Sighing.*) This is the only difference we have ever had. Mrs. Ross insists on certain bequests. You see, I have two cousins, ladies, not well off,[13] whom I have been in the way of helping a little. But in my will, how can I?

MR. DEVIZES You must think first of your wife.

PHILIP But she insists on my leaving fifty pounds to each of them. (*He looks appealingly to his wife.*)

EMILY (*Grandly.*) A hundred pounds.

PHILIP Fifty pounds.

EMILY Dear, a hundred pounds.

MR. DEVIZES Let us say seventy-five pounds.

PHILIP (*Reluctantly.*) Very well.

EMILY No, a hundred pounds.

PHILIP She'll have to get her way. Here are their names and addresses.

MR DEVIZES Anything else?

PHILIP (*Hurriedly.*) No.

EMILY The convalescent home, dear. He was in it a year ago, and they were so kind.

PHILIP Yes, but—

EMILY Ten pounds. (*He has to yield, with a reproachful, admiring look.*)

MR. DEVIZES Then if that is all, I won't detain you. If you look in tomorrow, Mr. Ross, about this time, we shall have everything ready for you.

[*Their faces fall.*]

EMILY Oh, Mr. Devizes, if only it could all be drawn up now, and done with.

PHILIP You see, sir, we are screwed up to it today.[14]

[*"Our fate is in your hands," they might be saying, and the lawyer smiles to find himself such a power.*]

MR. DEVIZES (*Looking at his watch.*) Well, it certainly need not take long. You go out and have lunch somewhere, and then come back.

[13] *not well off:* not prosperous.
[14] *screwed up to it today:* They have screwed up their courage—that is, they have tried hard to be brave and are ready to act today.

EMILY Oh, don't ask me to eat.

PHILIP We are too excited.

EMILY Please may we just walk about the street?

MR. DEVIZES (*Smiling.*) Of course you may, you ridiculous young wife.

EMILY I know it's ridiculous of me, but I am so fond of him.

MR. DEVIZES Yes, it is ridiculous. But don't change, especially if you get on in the world, Mr. Ross.

PHILIP No fear!

EMILY (*Backing from the will, which may now be said to be in existence.*) And please don't give us a copy of it to keep. I would rather not have it in the house.

MR. DEVIZES (*Nodding reassuringly.*) In an hour's time. (*They go, and the lawyer has his lunch, which is simpler than* ROBERT'S: *a sandwich and a glass of wine. He speaks as he eats.*) You will get that ready, Surtees. Here are the names and addresses he left. (*Cheerily.*) A nice couple.

SURTEES (*Who is hearing another voice.*)[15] Yes, sir.

MR. DEVIZES (*Unbending.*) Little romance of its kind. Makes one feel quite gay.

SURTEES Yes, sir.

MR. DEVIZES (*Struck perhaps by the deadness of his voice.*) You don't look very gay, Surtees.

SURTEES I'm sorry, sir. We can't all be gay. (*He is going out without looking at his employer.*) I'll see to this, sir.

MR. DEVIZES Stop a minute. Is there anything wrong? (SURTEES *has difficulty in answering, and* MR. DEVIZES *goes to him kindly.*) Not worrying over that matter we spoke about? (SURTEES *inclines his head.*) Is the pain worse?

SURTEES It's no great pain, sir.

MR. DEVIZES (*Uncomfortably.*) I'm sure it's not—what you fear. Any specialist would tell you so.

SURTEES (*Without looking up.*) I have been to one, sir—yesterday.

MR. DEVIZES Well?

SURTEES It's—that, sir.

MR. DEVIZES He couldn't be sure.

SURTEES Yes, sir.

MR. DEVIZES An operation—

SURTEES Too late, he said, for that. If I had been operated on long ago there might have been a chance.

MR. DEVIZES But you didn't have it long ago.

SURTEES Not to my knowledge, sir; but he says it was there all the

[15] *hearing another voice:* Surtees is thinking about someone else's words. He is not really paying attention to Mr. Devizes.

same, always in me, a black spot, not so big as a pin's head, but waiting to spread and destroy me in the fullness of time. All the rest of me as sound as a bell. (*That is the voice that* SURTEES *has been hearing.*)

MR. DEVIZES (*Helpless.*) It seems damnably unfair.

SURTEES (*Humbly.*) I don't know, sir. He says there's a spot of that kind in pretty nigh all of us, and if we don't look out it does for us in the end.

MR. DEVIZES (*Hurriedly.*) No, no, no.

SURTEES He called it the accursed thing. I think he meant we should know of it and be on the watch. (*He pulls himself together.*) I'll see to it at once, sir.

[*He goes out.* MR. DEVIZES *continues his lunch.*]

The curtain falls here for a moment only, to indicate the passing of a number of years. When it rises we see that the engraving of Queen Victoria has given way to one of King Edward.

ROBERT *is discovered, immersed in affairs. He is now a middle-aged man who has long forgotten how to fling cards into a hat. To him comes* SENNET, *a brisk clerk.*

SENNET Mrs. Philip Ross to see you, sir.

ROBERT Mr. Ross, don't you mean, Sennet?

SENNET No, sir.

ROBERT Ha. It was Mr. Ross I was expecting. Show her in. (*Frowning.*) And, Sennet, less row in the office, if you please.

SENNET (*Glibly.*) It was these young clerks, sir—

ROBERT They musn't be young here, or they go. Tell them that.

SENNET (*Glad to be gone.*) Yes, sir.

[*He shows in* MRS. ROSS. *We have not seen her for twenty years and would certainly not recognize her in the street. So shrinking her first entrance into this room, but she sails in now a galleon.*[16] *She is not so much dressed as richly upholstered. She is very sure of herself. Yet she is not a different woman from the* EMILY *we remember; the pity of it is that somehow this is the same woman.*]

ROBERT (*Who makes much of his important visitor and is also wondering why she has come.*) This is a delightful surprise, Mrs. Ross. Allow me. (*He removes her fine cloak with proper solicitude, and* EMILY *walks out of it in the manner that makes it worth possessing.*) This chair, alas, is the best I can offer you.

EMILY (*Who is still a good-natured woman if you attempt no nonsense with her.*) It will do quite well.

ROBERT (*Gallantly.*) Honored to see you in it.

[16] *galleon:* a heavy sailing ship of the fifteenth to eighteenth centuries, used in commerce and in battle.

EMILY (*Smartly.*) Not you. You were saying to yourself, "Now what brings the woman here?"

ROBERT Honestly, I—

EMILY And I'll tell you. You are expecting Mr. Ross, I think?

ROBERT (*Cautiously.*) Well—ah—

EMILY Pooh. The cunning of you lawyers. I know he has an appointment with you, and that is why I've come.

ROBERT He arranged with you to meet him here?

EMILY (*Preening herself.*) I wouldn't say that. I don't know that he will be specially pleased to find me here when he comes.

ROBERT (*Guardedly.*) Oh?

EMILY (*Who is a woman that goes straight to her goal.*) I know what he is coming about. To make a new will.

ROBERT (*Admitting it.*) After all, not the first he has made with us, Mrs. Ross.

EMILY (*Promptly*) No, the fourth.

ROBERT (*Warming his hands at the thought.*) Such a wonderful career. He goes from success to success.

EMILY (*Complacently.*) Yes, we're big folk.

ROBERT You are indeed.

EMILY (*Sharply.*) But the last will covered everything.

ROBERT (*On guard again.*) Of course it is a matter I cannot well discuss even with you. And I know nothing of his intentions.

EMILY Well, I suspect some of them.

ROBERT Ah.

EMILY And that's why I'm here. Just to see that he does nothing foolish.

[*She settles herself more comfortably as* MR. ROSS *is announced. A city magnate walks in. You know he is that before you see that he is* PHILIP ROSS.]

PHILIP (*Speaking as he enters.*) How do, Devizes, how do. Well, let's get at this thing at once. Time is money, you know, time is money. (*Then he sees his wife.*) Hello, Emily.

EMILY (*Unperturbed.*) You didn't ask me to come, Philip, but I thought I might as well.

PHILIP That's all right.

[*His brow had lowered at first sight of her, but now he gives her cleverness a grin of respect.*]

EMILY It is the first will you have made without taking me into your confidence.

PHILIP No important changes. I just thought to save you the—unpleasantness of the thing.

EMILY How do you mean?

PHILIP (*Fidgeting.*) Well, one can't draw up a will without feeling for the moment that he is bringing his end nearer. Is that not so, Devizes?

ROBERT (*Who will quite possibly die intestate.*) Some do have that feeling.

EMILY But what nonsense. How can it have any effect of that kind one way or the other?

ROBERT Quite so.

EMILY (*Reprovingly.*) Just silly sentiment, Philip. I would have thought it would be a pleasure to you handling such a big sum.

PHILIP (*Wincing.*) Not handling it, giving it up.

EMILY To those you love.

PHILIP (*Rather shortly.*) I'm not giving it up yet. You talk as if I was on my last legs.

EMILY (*Imperturbably.*) Not at all. It's you that are doing that.

ROBERT (*To the rescue.*) Here is my copy of the last will. I don't know if you would like me to read it out?

PHILIP It's hardly necessary.

EMILY We have our own copy at home and we know it well.

PHILIP (*Sitting back in his chair.*) What do you think I'm worth today, Devizes?

[*Everyone smiles. It is as if the sun had peeped in at the window.*]

ROBERT I daren't guess.

PHILIP An easy seventy thou.[17]

EMILY And that's not counting the house and the country cottage. We call it a cottage. You should see it!

ROBERT I have heard of it.

EMILY (*More sharply, though the sun still shines.*) Well, go on, Philip. I suppose you are not thinking of cutting me out of anything.

PHILIP (*Heartily.*) Of course not. There will be more to you than ever.

EMILY (*Coolly.*) There's more to leave.

PHILIP (*Hesitating.*) At the same time—

EMILY Well? It's to be mine absolutely of course. Not just a life interest.

PHILIP (*Doggedly.*) That is a change I was thinking of.

EMILY Just what I have suspected for days. Will you please to say why?

ROBERT (*Whose client after all is the man.*) Of course it is quite common.

EMILY I didn't think my husband was quite common.[18]

ROBERT I only mean that as there are children—

PHILIP That's what I mean too.

EMILY And I can't be trusted to leave my money to my own children! In what way have I ever failed them before?

PHILIP (*Believing it, too.*) Never, Emily, never. A more devoted mother—if you have one failing it is that you spoil them.

EMILY Then what's your reason?

PHILIP (*Less sincerely.*) Just to save you worry when I'm gone.

EMILY It's no worry to me to look after my money.

PHILIP (*Bridling.*) After all, it's my money.

EMILY I knew that was what was at the back of your mind.

PHILIP (*Reverently.*) It's such a great sum.

EMILY One would think you were afraid I would marry again.

PHILIP (*Snapping.*) One would think you looked to my dying next week.

EMILY Tuts.[19]

[PHILIP *is unable to sit still.*]

PHILIP My money. If you were to invest it badly and lose it . . . I tell you, Devizes, I couldn't lie quiet in my grave if I thought my money was lost by injudicious investments.

EMILY (*Coldly.*) You are thinking of yourself, Philip, rather than of the children.

PHILIP Not at all.

[17] *thou:* short for thousand.

[18] *common:* Emily is playing on words. Robert used common with its meaning of "usual." Emily uses the word with its meaning of "vulgar."

[19] *Tuts:* an exclamation of annoyance or impatience.

ROBERT (*Hastily.*) How are the two children?

EMILY Though I say it myself, there never were better. Harry is at Eton, you know, the most fashionable school in the country.

ROBERT Doing well, I hope.

PHILIP (*Chuckling.*) We have the most gratifying letters from him. Last Saturday he was caught smoking cigarettes with a lord. (*With pardonable pride.*) They were sick together.

ROBERT And Miss Gwendolen? She must be almost grown up now.

[*The parents exchange important glances.*]

EMILY Should we tell him.

PHILIP Under the rose,[20] you know, Devizes.

ROBERT Am I to congratulate her?

EMILY No names, Philip.

PHILIP No, no names—but she won't be a plain Mrs.,[21] no sir.

ROBERT Well done, Miss Gwendolen. (*With fitting jocularity.*) Now I see why you want a new will.

PHILIP Yes, that's my main reason, Emily.

EMILY But none of your life interests for me, Philip.

PHILIP (*Shying.*) We'll talk that over presently.

ROBERT Will you keep the legacies as they are?

PHILIP Well, there's that five hundred pounds for the hospitals.

EMILY Yes, with so many claims on us, is it necessary?

PHILIP (*Becoming stouter.*) I'm going to make it a thousand pounds.

EMILY Philip!

PHILIP My mind is made up. I want to make a splash[22] with the hospitals.

ROBERT (*Hurrying to the next item.*) There is fifty pounds a year each to two cousins, ladies.

PHILIP I suppose we'll keep that as it is, Emily?

EMILY It was just gifts to them of a hundred pounds each at first.

PHILIP I was poor at that time myself.

EMILY Do you think it's wise to load them with so much money? They'll not know what to do with it.

PHILIP They're old.

EMILY But they're wiry. Seventy-five pounds a year between them would surely be enough.

PHILIP It would be if they lived together, but you see they don't. They hate each other like cat and dog.

EMILY That's not nice between relatives. You could leave it to them on condition that they do live together. That would be a Christian action.

20 *Under the rose:* a translation of the Latin phrase *sub rosa.* Anything told *sub rosa* is told confidentially. The rose was a symbol of silence.

21 *a plain Mrs.:* In other words, some title of rank, like Lady, will precede her name.

22 *make a splash:* slang for make an impression. He intends to leave a large amount to the hospitals.

PHILIP There's something in that.

ROBERT Then the chief matter is whether Mrs. Ross—

EMILY Oh, I thought that was settled.

PHILIP (*With a sigh.*) I'll have to give in to her, sir.

ROBERT Very well. I suppose my father will want to draw up the will. I'm sorry he had to be in the country today.

EMILY (*Affable now that she has gained her point.*) I hope he is wearing well?[23]

ROBERT Wonderfully. He is away playing golf.

PHILIP (*Grinning.*) Golf. I have no time for games. (*Considerately.*) But he must get the drawing-up of my will. I couldn't deprive the old man of that.

ROBERT He will be proud to do it again.

PHILIP (*Well satisfied.*) Ah! There's many a one would like to look over your father's shoulder when he's drawing up my will. I wonder what I'll cut up for[24] in the end. But I must be going.

EMILY Can I drop you anywhere? I have the grays[25] out.

PHILIP Yes, at the club. (*Now* MRS. ROSS *walks into her cloak.*) Good-day, Devizes. I won't have time to look in again, so tell the old man to come to me.

ROBERT (*Deferentially.*) Whatever suits you best. (*Ringing.*) He will be delighted. I remember his saying to me on the day you made your first will—

PHILIP (*Chuckling.*) A poor little affair that.

ROBERT He said to me you were a couple whose life looked like being a romance.

PHILIP And he was right—eh, Emily?—though he little thought what a romance.

[*They make a happy departure, and* ROBERT *is left reflecting.*]

The curtain again falls, and rises immediately, as the engraving shows, on the same office in the reign of King George. It is a foggy morning and a fire burns briskly. MR. DEVIZES, SENIOR, *arrives for the day's work just as he came daily for over half a century. But he has no right to be here now. A year or two ago they got him to retire, as he was grown feeble; and there is an understanding that he does not go out of his house alone. He has, as it were, escaped today, and his feet have carried him to the old office that is the home of his mind. He was portly when we saw him first, but he has become little again and as light as the schoolboy whose deeds are nearer to him than many of the events of later years. He arrives at the office, thinking it is old times, and a clerk surveys him uncomfortably from the door.*

[23] *wearing well:* in other words, in good health.
[24] *what I'll cut up for:* how much money I'll leave.
[25] *the grays:* The reference here is to her carriage, drawn by a pair of gray horses.

CREED (*Not quite knowing what to do.*) Mr. Devizes has not come in yet, sir.

MR. DEVIZES (*Considering.*) Yes I have. Do you mean Mr. Robert?

CREED Yes, sir.

MR. DEVIZES (*Querulously.*) Always late. Can't get that boy to settle down. (*Leniently.*) Well, well, boys will be boys—eh, Surtees?

CREED (*Wishing* MR. ROBERT *would come.*) My name is Creed, sir.

MR. DEVIZES (*Sharply.*) Creed? Don't know you. Where is Surtees?

CREED There is no one of that name in the office, sir.

MR. DEVIZES (*Growing timid.*) No? I remember now. Poor Surtees! (*But his mind cannot grapple with troubles.*) Tell him I want him when he comes in. (*He is changing, after his old custom, into an office coat.*)

CREED That is Mr. Dev—Mr. Robert's coat, sir.

MR. DEVIZES He has no business to hang it there. That is my nail.

CREED He has hung it there for years, sir.

MR. DEVIZES Not at all. I must have it. Why does Surtees let him do it? Help me into my office coat, boy.

[CREED *helps him into the coat he has taken off, and the old man is content.*]

CREED (*Seeing him lift up the correspondence.*) I don't think Mr. Devizes would like you to open the office letters, sir.

MR. DEVIZES (*Pettishly.*) What's that? Go away, boy. Send Surtees.

[*To the relief of* CREED, ROBERT *arrives, and, taking in the situation, signs to the clerk to go. He has a more youthful manner than when last we saw him, has* ROBERT, *but his hair is iron-gray. He is kindly to his father.*]

ROBERT You here, Father?

MR. DEVIZES (*After staring at him.*) Yes, you are Robert. (*A little frightened.*) You are an old man, Robert.

ROBERT (*Without wincing.*) Getting on, Father. But why did they let you come? You haven't been here for years.

MR. DEVIZES (*Puzzled.*) Years? I think I just came in the old way, Robert, without thinking.

ROBERT Yes, yes. I'll get someone to go home with you.

MR. DEVIZES (*Rather abject.*) Let me stay, Robert. I like being here. I won't disturb you. I like the smell of the office, Robert.

ROBERT Of course you may stay. Come over to the fire. (*He settles his father by the fire in the one armchair.*) There, you can have a doze by the fire.

MR. DEVIZES A doze by the fire. That is all I'm good for now. Once—but my son hangs his coat there now. (*Presently he looks up fearfully.*) Robert, tell me something in a whisper: Is Surtees dead?

ROBERT (*Who has forgotten the name.*) Surtees?

MR. DEVIZES My clerk, you know.

ROBERT Oh. Why, he has been dead this thirty years, Father.

MR. DEVIZES So long! Seems like yesterday.

ROBERT It is just far-back times that seem clear to you now.

MR. DEVIZES (*Meekly.*) Is it?

[ROBERT *opens his letters, and his father falls asleep.* CREED *comes.*]

CREED Sir Philip Ross.

[*The great* SIR PHILIP ROSS *enters, nearly sixty now, strong of frame still, but a lost man. He is in mourning, and carries the broken pieces of his life with an air of braggadocio. It should be understood that he is not a "sympathetic" part, and any actor who plays him as such will be rolling the play in the gutter.*][26]

ROBERT (*On his feet at once to greet such a client.*) You, Sir Philip.

PHILIP (*Head erect.*) Here I am.

ROBERT (*Because it will out.*) How are you?

[26] *a "sympathetic" part . . . rolling the play in the gutter:* The actor should not attempt to make the audience feel sorry for Philip. If they sympathize with him, the effect of the play will be spoiled.

PHILIP (*As if challenged.*) I'm all right—great. (*With defiant jocularity.*) Called on the old business.

ROBERT To make another will?

PHILIP You've guessed it—the very first time. (*He sees the figure by the fire.*)

ROBERT Yes, it's my father. He's dozing. Shouldn't be here at all. He forgets things. It's just age.

PHILIP (*Grimly.*) Forgets things. That must be fine.

ROBERT (*Conventionally.*) I should like, Sir Philip, to offer you my sincere condolences. In the midst of life we are—How true that is. I attended the funeral.

PHILIP I saw you.

ROBERT A much-esteemed lady. I had a great respect for her.

PHILIP (*Almost with relish.*) Do you mind,[27] when we used to come here about the will, somehow she—we—always took for granted I should be the first to go.

ROBERT (*Devoutly.*) These things are hid from mortal eyes.

PHILIP (*With conviction.*) There's a lot hid. We needn't have worried so much about the will if—Well, let us get at it. (*Fiercely.*) I haven't given in, you know.

ROBERT We must bow our heads—

PHILIP Must we? Am I bowing mine?

ROBERT (*Uncomfortably.*) Such courage in the great hour—yes—and I am sure Lady Ross—

PHILIP (*With the ugly humour that has come to him.*) She wasn't that.

ROBERT The honor came so soon afterward—I feel she would like to be thought of as Lady Ross. I shall always remember her as a fine lady richly dressed who used—

PHILIP (*Harshly.*) Stop it. That's not how I think of her. There was a time before that—she wasn't richly dressed— (*He stamps upon his memories.*) Things went wrong, I don't know how. It's a beast of a world. I didn't come here to talk about that. Let us get to work.

ROBERT (*Turning with relief from the cemetery.*) Yes, yes, and after all life has its compensations. You have your son who—

PHILIP (*Snapping.*) No I haven't. (*This startles the lawyer.*) I'm done with him.

ROBERT If he has been foolish—

PHILIP Foolish! (*Some dignity comes into the man.*) Sir, I have come to a pass when "foolish" as applied to my own son would seem to me a very pretty word.

ROBERT Is it as bad as that?

PHILIP He's a rotter.[28]

[27] *Do you mind:* Here, this means "do you remember."
[28] *rotter:* slang for a worthless person.

ROBERT It is very painful to me to hear you say that.

PHILIP More painful, think you, than for me to say it? (*Clenching his fists.*) But I've shipped him off. The law had to wink at it,[29] or I couldn't have done it. Why don't you say I pampered him and it serves me right? It's what they are all saying behind my back. Why don't you ask me about my girl? That's another way to rub it in.

ROBERT Don't, Sir Philip. I knew her. My sympathy—

PHILIP A chauffeur, that is what he was. The man who drove her own car.

ROBERT I was deeply concerned—

PHILIP I want nobody's pity. I've done with both of them, and if you think I'm a broken man you're much mistaken. I'll show them. Have you your papers there? Then take down my last will. I have everything in my head. I'll show them.

ROBERT Would it not be better to wait till a calmer—

PHILIP Will you do it now, or am I to go across the street?

ROBERT If I must.

PHILIP Then down with it. (*He wets his lips.*) I, Philip Ross, of 77 Bath Street, W., do hereby revoke all former wills and testaments,[30] and I leave everything of which I die possessed—

ROBERT Yes?

PHILIP Everything of which I die possessed—

ROBERT Yes?

PHILIP I leave it—I leave it— (*The game is up.*) My God, Devizes, I don't know what to do with it.

ROBERT I—I—really—come—

PHILIP (*Cynically.*) Can't you make any suggestions?

ROBERT Those cousins are dead, I think?

PHILIP Years ago.

ROBERT (*Troubled.*) In the case of such a large sum—

PHILIP (*Letting all his hoarded gold run through his fingers.*) The money I've won with my blood. God in heaven! (*Showing his teeth.*) Would that old man[31] like it to play with? If I bring it to you in sacks, will you fling it out of the window for me?

ROBERT Sir Philip!

PHILIP (*Taking a paper from his pocket.*) Here, take this. It has the names and addresses of the half-dozen men I've fought with most for gold; and I've beaten them. Draw up a will leaving all my money

[29] *wink at it:* In other words, Philip did something that was not strictly legal, while the law "closed its eyes."

[30] *revoke all former wills and testaments:* cancel all previous wills and statements relating to the disposal of property.

[31] Philip is referring to Mr. Devizes, Senior, who sits by the fire.

to be divided among them, with my respectful curses, and bring it to my house and I'll sign it.

ROBERT (*Properly shocked.*) But really I can't possibly—

PHILIP Either you or another. Is it to be you?

ROBERT Very well.

PHILIP Then it's settled. (*He rises with a laugh. He regards* MR. DEVIZES *quizzically.*) So you weren't in at the last will after all, old Sleep-by-the-Fire.

[*To their surprise the old man stirs.*]

MR. DEVIZES What's that about a will?

ROBERT You are awake, Father?

MR. DEVIZES (*Whose eyes have opened on* PHILIP'S *face.*) I don't know you, sir.

ROBERT Yes, yes, Father, you remember Mr. Ross. He is Sir Philip now.

MR. DEVIZES (*Courteously.*) Sir Philip? I wish you joy, sir, but I don't know you.

ROBERT (*Encouragingly.*) Ross, Father.

MR. DEVIZES I knew a Mr. Ross long ago.

ROBERT This is the same.

MR. DEVIZES (*Annoyed.*) No, no. A bright young fellow he was, with such a dear, pretty wife. They came to make a will. (*He chuckles.*) And bless me, they had only twopence halfpenny. I took a fancy to them, such a happy pair.

ROBERT (*Apologetically.*) The past is clearer to him than the present nowadays. That will do, Father.

PHILIP (*Brusquely.*) Let him go on.

MR. DEVIZES Poor souls, it all ended unhappily, you know.

PHILIP (*Who is not brusque to him.*) Yes, I know. Why did things go wrong, sir? I sit and wonder, and I can't find the beginning.

MR. DEVIZES That's the sad part of it. There was never a beginning. It was always there. He[32] told me all about it.

ROBERT He is thinking of something else, I don't know what.

PHILIP Quiet. What was it that was always there?

MR. DEVIZES It was always in them—a spot no bigger than a pin's head, but waiting to spread and destroy them in the fullness of time.

ROBERT I don't know what he has got hold of.

PHILIP He knows. Could they have done anything to prevent it, sir?

MR. DEVIZES If they had been on the watch. But they didn't know, so they weren't on the watch. Poor souls.

PHILIP Poor souls.

MR. DEVIZES It's called the accursed thing. It gets nearly everybody in

[32] Now Mr. Devizes is thinking of Surtees.

the end, if they don't look out. (*He sinks back into his chair and forgets them.*)

ROBERT He is just wandering.

PHILIP The old man knows. (*He slowly tears up the paper he had given* ROBERT.)

ROBERT (*Relieved.*) I am glad to see you do that.

PHILIP A spot no bigger than a pin's head. (*A wish wells up in him, too late perhaps.*) I wish I could help some young things before that spot has time to spread and destroy them as it has destroyed me and mine.

ROBERT (*Brightly.*) With such a large fortune—

PHILIP (*Summing up his life.*) It can't be done with money, sir.

[*He goes away, God knows where.*]

Comprehension

1. In the stage directions before the play begins, Barrie introduces three of the central characters. Refer to these directions to answer the following questions:
   a. How old is Devizes, Senior? Has he been a successful lawyer?
   b. How old is Devizes, Junior? Where was he educated? Is he a serious young man? By what action is he characterized for the audience when the curtain rises?
   c. How old is Surtees the clerk? If you looked at him carefully, what might you guess?
2. What happened to Philip Ross's letter? Is Robert sorry about his mistake? Does he apologize for destroying the letter?
3. How does Surtees describe Philip Ross?
4. Mr. Devizes suggests that they tell Philip Ross the truth—that they haven't read his letter. Does Robert agree? What does he mean by "I can put two and two together"?
5. In his stage directions Barrie describes Philip Ross and his wife before they enter the office. What are they like? Are they in love? Do they have much money?
6. What does Robert assume the Rosses have come to his office about? What is the real reason for the Rosses' visit to the law office?
7. Why is Mrs. Ross upset about her husband making out a will? Is she superstitious?
8. What does Devizes, Senior, say about his son's first case? What does he mean by saying, "He got out of a hole rather cleverly"?
9. What phrase does Emily object to when Mr. Devizes first begins talking about the will?
10. Why does Mr. Devizes say, "I see it will be quite a brief will"?

11. Emily insists that her husband leave some money to others. Who are they?
12. Why does Mr. Devizes call Emily "ridiculous"? Does he approve of her behavior? Does he hope that Philip and Emily will always love each other in the same way?
13. Why has Surtees been looking so dispirited?
14. Why does the curtain fall? How is the passage of time conveyed to the audience?
15. How old is Robert now? Is he still a "gay dog"? How does Barrie convey to the audience Robert's change in personality?
16. How has Emily changed during the twenty years? Does Barrie approve of the change?
17. Why has Emily come to the law office?
18. What change would Philip like to make in the will? What is a "life interest"?
19. Why is Philip worried about leaving his money to his wife to manage?
20. What is revealed about the Rosses' sense of values through the remarks they make about their two children?
21. Why does Philip want to leave more money to the hospitals? Does his wife agree with him?
22. What condition does Emily suggest should be attached to the bequest of the two cousins?
23. What does Philip say when he hears that Devizes, Senior, is out playing golf?
24. Is Philip going to return to the office to sign the new will?
25. What happens at the beginning of the third scene? How has Devizes, Senior, changed? Why has he come to the office?
26. How does Robert behave toward his father? Does he let his father stay?
27. How old is Philip in the third scene? What is his title? Is he a happy man?
28. What did Philip and his wife take for granted when they used to come to the office about his will?
29. What has happened to Philip's children?
30. To whom does Philip eventually decide to leave his money?
31. What does Mr. Devizes talk about after he wakes up?
32. What does Philip do after listening to the old man? What does he wish he could do?

Toward Interpretation

1. Like all skillful playwrights, Barrie gives hints early in the play that prepare the audience for its eventual outcome. In *The Will* this is accomplished toward the end of the first scene by a comment

made by Mr. Devizes in response to Mrs. Ross's fear that she is being "ridiculous." What is this comment, and how does it foreshadow future developments?

2. Good playwrights also try to make every scene count—to make it contribute in some way to the development of plot or character. How is the scene between Mr. Devizes and Surtees made use of at the end of the play?
3. Scene 2 closes with a reference to "romance." How does this reference tie together the first and second scenes? How do you interpret Philip's remark—"though he little thought what a romance"?
4. How does Philip reveal that he has become, in Barrie's words, "a lost man"? How does he reveal his true feelings toward his dead wife? Toward his children?
5. In the last line of the play, Philip finally reveals that he has discovered his fatal mistake, a mistake that destroyed his own life and the lives of his family. What is that mistake?

My Heart's in the Highlands

by William Saroyan

Like Johnny's father in the play, William Saroyan is a genius. He himself has been loudly admitting it for many years now. But unlike Johnny's father, Saroyan is a genius who got his writing published. Born in 1908 in the California town of Fresno—his parents were Armenian immigrants—he grew up in hardship and poverty, sure of his gifts and longing for fame and success. Largely self-taught as a writer, impatient of discipline and restraint, he stubbornly went his own way and wrote a great many short stories straight from the heart, with only occasional and minimal interference from the mind. When he published the first volume of them in 1934, the critics were puzzled, for the stories had no exact structure and seemed to go nowhere in particular. Yet these casual, almost shapeless little pieces amused and touched their readers, bringing to most of them a delight that was difficult to define or justify.

Saroyan's plays were as casually improvised as his stories. Unlike Barrie's plays—where the story sets a course and unswervingly follows it—

Saroyan's are a series of little, loosely connected scenes. Each scene is a pleasing miniature in which the characters, through odd actions and strangely irrelevant dialogue, make an impression on each other and on the audience. Yet when one looks back on the play, the little scenes fit into place like the pieces of a mosaic: a picture of life has been put together, a simple story has been told.

Regarded logically, Saroyan's dialogue seems wayward and even a little silly, for the characters communicate more through feelings than ideas. They respond not to what is said but to what is intended. Johnny talks to the grocer about hunger in faraway China, but the grocer knows that he is really talking about a specific need for bread and cheese in California. Two little boys establish a fleeting but satisfying friendship while one is giving the other a lesson in whistling—and the friendship is expressed as much by the rhythmic bouncing of the ball between them as by their conversation. Johnny may not understand all of his grandmother's rapid Armenian, but he understands her. In short, Saroyan's people, because they are kind and affectionate as well as lonely and lost, can reach out and touch each other across barriers of age and backgrounds and even language.

Saroyan's world has no villains and little malice. But it is not free from evil. As Johnny says when the family is setting out from the home that is no longer theirs, "something's wrong somewhere." If something is wrong, it is not in these beautiful people, whose hearts are always back in the idealized home they will long for and never find—except as they create it for themselves each day.

The People

JOHNNY
HIS FATHER, BEN ALEXANDER, *the poet*
JOHNNY'S GRANDMOTHER
JASPER MacGREGOR, *the man with the heart in the highlands*
MR. KOSAK, *the grocer*
ESTHER, *his beautiful daughter*
RUFE APLEY, *the carpenter*
PHILIP CARMICHAEL, *the young man from the Old People's Home*
HENRY, *the morning paper route carrier*
MR. WILEY, *the mailman*
MR. CUNNINGHAM, *the real estate agent*
THE YOUNG HUSBAND AND WIFE, AND THEIR BABY
GOOD FRIENDS AND NEIGHBORS
A DOG

The Place

A house on San Benito Avenue in Fresno, California, Mr. Kosak's grocery store.

The Time

August and November, 1914

An old white, broken-down, frame house with a front porch, on San Benito Avenue in Fresno, California. There are no other houses near by, only a desolation of bleak land and red sky. It is late afternoon of a day in August 1914. The evening sun is going down.

JOHNNY, *aged nine, but essentially ageless, is sitting, dynamic and acrobatic, on the steps of the porch, dead to the world and deep in thought of a high and holy order. Far away a train whistle cries mournfully. He listens eagerly, cocking his head on one side like a chicken, trying to understand the meaning of the cry and at the same time to figure out everything. He doesn't quite make it and when the cry ends he stops being eager. A fourteen-year-old boy on a bicycle, eating an ice-cream cone and carrying newspaper bags, goes by on the sidewalk in silence, oblivious of the weight on his shoulders and of the contraption on which he is seated, because of the delight and glory of ice cream in the world.* JOHNNY *leaps to his feet and waves to the boy smiling in a big humanitarian way, but is ignored. He sits down again and listens to a small overjoyed but angry bird. After making a brief forceful speech of no meaning, the bird flies away.*

From inside the house is heard the somber voice of JOHNNY'S FATHER *reciting poetry of his own composition.*

JOHNNY'S FATHER The long silent day journeys through the sore solemn heart, and—(*Bitter pause.*) And—(*Quickly.*) The long silent day journeys through the sore solemn heart, and—(*Pause.*) No. (*He roars and begins again.*) Crippled and weeping, time stumbles through the lone lorn heart.

[*A table or chair is pushed over in anger. A groan. Silence. The boy listens. He gets up and tries to stand on his head, fails, tries again, fails, tries again, and succeeds. While he is standing on his head he hears the loveliest and most amazing music in the world: a solo on a bugle. The music is "My Heart's in the Highlands." The bugler, a very old man, finishes the solo in front of the house. The boy leaps to his feet and runs up to the old man, amazed, delighted and bewildered.*]

JOHNNY I sure would like to hear you play another song.

MACGREGOR Young man, could you get a glass of water for an old man whose heart is not here, but in the highlands?

JOHNNY What highlands?

MACGREGOR The Scotch Highlands. Could you?

JOHNNY What's your heart doing in the Scotch Highlands?

MACGREGOR My heart's grieving there. Could you get me a glass of cool water?

JOHNNY Where's your *mother?*

MACGREGOR (*Inventing for the boy.*) My mother's in Tulsa, Oklahoma, but her heart isn't.

JOHNNY Where *is* her heart?

MACGREGOR (*Loud.*) In the Scotch Highlands. (*Soft.*) I'm very thirsty, young man.

JOHNNY How come the members of your family are always leaving their hearts in the highlands?

MACGREGOR (*In the Shakespearean manner.*) That's the way we are. Here today and gone tomorrow.[1]

JOHNNY (*Aside.*) Here today and gone tomorrow? (*To* MACGREGOR.) How do you figure?[2]

MACGREGOR (*The philosopher.*) Alive one minute and dead the next.

JOHNNY Where's your *mother's mother?*

MACGREGOR (*Inventing, but angry.*) *She's* up in Vermont, in a little town called White River, but her heart isn't.

JOHHNY Is her poor old withered heart in the highlands, too?

MACGREGOR Right smack in[3] the highlands. Son, I'm dying of thirst.

[JOHNNY'S FATHER *comes out of the house in a fury, as if he has just broken out of a cage, and roars at the boy like a tiger that has just awakened from evil dreams.*]

JOHNNY'S FATHER Johnny, get the hell away from that poor old man. Get him a pitcher of water before he falls down and dies. Where the hell are your manners?

JOHNNY Can't a fellow try to find out something from a traveler once in a while?

JOHNNY'S FATHER Get the old man some water, God damn it. Don't stand there like a dummy. Get him a drink, I tell you, before he falls down and dies.

JOHNNY *You* get him a drink. You're not doing anything.

JOHNNY'S FATHER Not doing anything? Why, Johnny, you *know* I'm getting a new poem arranged in my mind.

JOHNNY How do you figure I know? You're just standing there on the porch with your sleeves rolled up.

JOHNNY'S FATHER (*Angry.*) Well, you ought to know. (*Roaring.*) You're my son. (*Amazed.*) If you shouldn't know, who should?

MACGREGOR (*Blithely.*) Good afternoon. Your son has been telling me how clear and cool the climate is in these parts.

1 *Here today and gone tomorrow:* This is a common saying. It means life is short.
2 *How do you figure?:* What do you mean?
3 *Right smack in:* right in the middle of.

JOHNNY (*Bewildered, but eager to learn. Aside.*) Holy Moses,[4] I didn't say anything about the climate. Where's he getting that stuff from?

JOHNNY'S FATHER (*The aristocrat, grandly.*) How do you do? Won't you come in for a little rest? We should be honored to have you at our table for a bit of supper.

MACGREGOR (*The realist.*) Sir, I'm starving. I shall come right in. (*He moves to enter the house.* JOHNNY *gets in his way, looking up at him.*)

JOHNNY (*The romantic.*) Can you play "Drink to Me Only with Thine Eyes"?[5] I sure would like to hear you play that song on the bugle. That song is my favorite. I guess I like that song better than any song in the world.

MACGREGOR (*The disillusioned.*) Son, when you get to be my age you'll know songs aren't important, bread's the thing.

JOHNNY (*The faithful.*) Anyway, I sure would like to hear you play that song.

[MACGREGOR *goes up on the porch and shakes hands with* JOHNNY'S FATHER.]

MACGREGOR (*History in the making.*) My name is Jasper MacGregor. I am an actor.

JOHNNY'S FATHER (*Delighted.*) I'm mighty glad to make your acquaintance. (*The imperial giver of orders.*) Johnny, get Mr. MacGregor a pitcher of water. (JOHNNY *runs around the house.*)

MACGREGOR (*Dying of thirst, sighing, but telling the truth nevertheless.*) Charming boy.

JOHNNY'S FATHER (*Ordinary statement.*) Like myself, he's a genius.

MACGREGOR (*Roaring from fatigue.*) I suppose you're very fond of him?

JOHNNY'S FATHER (*Delighted to be alive.*) We are the same person—He is the heart of my youth— Have you noticed his eagerness?

MACGREGOR (*Delighted to be still alive.*) I should say I have.

JOHNNY'S FATHER (*Proudly and with anger.*) I'm the same way myself, although older and less brilliant.

[JOHNNY, *running, returns with a pitcher of water which he hands to the old man. The old man throws back his shoulders, lifts his head, his nostrils expand, he snorts, his eyes widen, he lifts the pitcher of water to his lips and drinks all the water in one long swig, while* JOHNNY *and his* FATHER *watch with amazement and admiration. The old man breathes deeply, looks around at the landscape and up at the sky and to the end of San Benito Avenue where the evening sun is going down.*]

MACGREGOR (*Reflection, sadly; weariness, softly.*) I reckon I'm five thou-

[4] *Holy Moses:* a mild oath, now seldom used.

[5] *"Drink to Me Only with Thine Eyes":* a poem by Ben Jonson, who lived in the late sixteenth and early seventeenth century. The poem was set to music and has long been popular among English-speaking people.

sand miles from home. Do you think we could eat a little bread and cheese to keep my body and spirit together?

JOHNNY'S FATHER (*Napoleon.*) Johnny, run down to the grocer's and get a loaf of French bread and a pound of cheese.

JOHNNY (*The voice of doom.*) Give me the money.

JOHNNY'S FATHER (*Statistics, poetic, with pride.*) You know I haven't got a *penny*, Johnny. Tell Mr. Kosak to give us credit.

JOHNNY (*The unwilling dutiful son.*) He won't do it. He's tired of giving us credit. He says we don't work and never pay our bills. We owe him forty cents.

JOHNNY'S FATHER (*Impatient, irritated.*) Go on down there and argue it out with him. You know that's your job.

JOHNNY (*Defending his rights.*) He won't listen to reason. He says he doesn't know anything about anything. All he wants is the forty cents.

JOHNNY'S FATHER (*Napoleon.*) Go on down there and make him give you a loaf of bread and a pound of cheese. (*Gently, pleading, flattering.*) You can do it, Johnny.

MACGREGOR (*Impatient and hungry.*) Go on down there and tell Mr. Kosak to give you a loaf of bread and a pound of cheese, son.

JOHNNY'S FATHER Go ahead, Johnny. You've never failed to leave that store with something or other. You'll be back here in ten minutes with food fit for a King. (*For his own amusement.*) Or at least a Duke of some kind.

JOHNNY I don't know. Mr. Kosak says we are trying to give him the merry run-around.[6] He wants to know what kind of work you do.

JOHNNY'S FATHER (*Furiously.*) Well, go ahead and tell him. (*The hero.*) I have nothing to conceal. I write poetry, night and day.

JOHNNY (*Giving in at last.*) All right, but I don't think he'll be impressed. He says you never go out and look for work. He says you're lazy and no good.

JOHNNY'S FATHER (*Roaring.*) You go down there and tell that great-hearted Slovak he's crazy, Johnny. You go on down there and tell that splendid scholar and gentleman your father is one of the greatest unknown poets living.

JOHNNY He won't care, Pa, but I'll go. I'll do my best. Haven't we got anything in the house?

JOHNNY'S FATHER (*Mock-tragically, roaring.*) Only popcorn. (*To* MACGREGOR.) We've been eating popcorn four days in a row now. Johnny, you've got to get bread and cheese if you expect me to finish that long poem.

JOHNNY I'll do my best.

[6] *the merry run-around:* a series of excuses.

MACGREGOR Don't take too long, Johnny. I'm five thousand miles from home.

JOHNNY I'll run all the way, Mr. MacGregor.

JOHNNY'S FATHER (*For the amusement of the good Lord.*) If you find any money on the way, remember we go fifty-fifty.[7]

JOHNNY (*Delighted with the comedy.*) All right, Pa. (JOHNNY *runs down the street.*)

The inside of Mr. Kosak's Grocery Store. MR. KOSAK *is sleeping on his folded arms when* JOHNNY *runs into the store.* MR. KOSAK *lifts his head. He is a fine, gentle, serious man with a big, blond, old-fashioned mustache. He shakes his head trying to waken.*

JOHNNY (*The diplomat, as it were.*) Mr. Kosak, if you were in China and didn't have a friend in the world and no money, you'd expect somebody over there to give you a pound of rice, wouldn't you?

MR. KOSAK What do you want?

JOHNNY I just want to talk a little. You'd expect some member of the Aryan race to help you out a little, wouldn't you, Mr. Kosak?[8]

MR. KOSAK How much money you got?

JOHNNY It's not a question of money, Mr. Kosak. I'm talking about being in China.

MR. KOSAK I don't know nothing[9] about nothing.

JOHNNY How would you feel in China that way, Mr. Kosak?

MR. KOSAK I don't know, Johnny. What would I be doing in China?

JOHNNY Well, you'd be visiting there. You'd be hungry and five thousand miles from home and not a friend in the world. You wouldn't expect *everybody* to turn you away without even a pound of rice, would you, Mr. Kosak?

MR. KOSAK I guess not, but you ain't in China, Johnny, and neither is your Pa. You or your Pa's got to go out and work sometime in your lives, so you might as well start now. I ain't going to give you no more groceries on credit because I know you won't pay me.

JOHNNY Mr. Kosak, you misunderstand me. This is 1914, not 1913. I'm not talking about a few groceries. I'm talking about all them heathen people around you in China and you hungry and dying.

MR. KOSAK This ain't China. You got to get out and make your living in this country. Everybody's got to work in America.

JOHNNY Mr. Kosak, suppose it was a loaf of bread and a pound of cheese

[7] *go fifty-fifty:* a slang expression meaning to divide evenly.

[8] Johnny is trying to get credit from Mr. Kosak by persuading him that members of the same race should help each other out.

[9] *I don't know nothing:* nonstandard for "I don't know anything." Throughout this scene, Johnny's careful, imaginative language is in contrast to Mr. Kosak's.

you needed to keep you alive in the world, would you hesitate to ask a Christian *missionary* for these things?

MR. KOSAK Yes, I would. I would be ashamed to ask.

JOHNNY Even if you knew you would give him back *two* loaves of bread and *two* pounds of cheese instead of one loaf and one pound? Even then, Mr. Kosak?

MR. KOSAK Even then.

JOHNNY Don't be that way, Mr. Kosak. That's defeatist talk, and you know it. Why, the only thing that would happen to you would be death. You'd *die* out there in China, Mr. Kosak.

MR. KOSAK I wouldn't care if I would. You and your Pa have got to pay for bread and cheese. Why don't your Pa go out and get a job?

JOHNNY (*Swift abandonment of the intellectual attack for the human one.*) Mr. Kosak, how are you?

MR. KOSAK I'm fine, Johnny. How are *you*?

JOHNNY Couldn't be better, Mr. Kosak. How are the children?

MR. KOSAK They're all fine, Johnny. Stephan is beginning to walk now.

JOHNNY That's great. How's Angela?

MR. KOSAK Angela's beginning to sing. How's your Grandmother?

JOHNNY She's fine. She's beginning to sing too. She says she'd rather be an opera singer than Queen of England. How's your wife Martha, Mr. Kosak?

MR. KOSAK Oh, swell.

JOHNNY I can't tell you how glad I am to hear that everything is fine at your house. I know Stephan is going to be a great man some day.

MR. KOSAK I hope so. I'm going to send him to high school and see that he gets every chance I didn't get. I don't want *him* to have trouble all *his* life, too.

JOHNNY I have great faith in Stephan, Mr. Kosak.

MR. KOSAK What do you want, Johnny, and how much money you got?

JOHNNY Mr. Kosak, you know I didn't come here to buy anything. You know I enjoy a quiet philosophical chat with you every now and then. (*Quickly, pleading.*) Let me have a loaf of French bread and a pound of cheese.

MR. KOSAK You got to pay cash, Johnny.

JOHNNY And Esther? How is your beautiful daughter Esther?

MR. KOSAK She's all right, Johnny, but you got to pay cash. You and your Pa are the worst citizens in this county.

JOHNNY I'm glad Esther's all right, Mr. Kosak. Jasper MacGregor is visiting our house. He's a great actor.

MR. KOSAK Never heard of him.

JOHNNY And a bottle of beer for Mr. MacGregor.

MR. KOSAK I can't give you a bottle of beer.

JOHNNY Sure, you can.

MR. KOSAK I can't. I'll let you have one loaf of French bread and a pound of cheese, but that's all. What kind of work does your Pa do *when* he works, Johnny?

JOHNNY My father writes poetry, Mr. Kosak. That's the only work my father does. He's one of the greatest writers of poetry in the world.

MR. KOSAK When does he get any money?

JOHNNY He *never* gets any money. You can't have your cake and eat it too.[10]

MR. KOSAK I don't like that kind of work. Why doesn't your Pa work like everybody else, Johnny?

JOHNNY He works harder than everybody else. My father works twice as hard as the average man.

[MR. KOSAK *hands* JOHNNY *a loaf of French bread and a pound of cheese.*]

MR. KOSAK Well, that's fifty-five cents you owe me, Johnny. I'll let you have some stuff this time, but never again.

JOHNNY (*At the door.*) Tell Esther I love her. (JOHNNY *runs out of the store.* MR. KOSAK *swings at a fly, misses, swings again, misses, and, objecting to the world in this manner, he chases the fly all around the store, swinging with all his might.*)

The house. JOHNNY'S FATHER *and the old man are looking down the street to see if* JOHNNY *is coming back with food. His* GRANDMOTHER *is standing on the porch also eager to know if there is to be food.*

MacGREGOR I think he's got some food with him.

JOHNNY'S FATHER (*With pride.*) Of course he has. (*He waves at the old lady on the porch who runs into the house to set the table.* JOHNNY *runs to his* FATHER *and* MacGREGOR.) I knew you'd do it.

MacGREGOR So did I.

JOHNNY He says we got to pay him fifty-five cents. He says he's not going to give us any more stuff on credit.

JOHNNY'S FATHER That's *his* opinion. What did you talk about?

JOHNNY First I talked about being hungry and at death's door in China. Then I inquired about the family.

JOHNNY'S FATHER How is everyone?

JOHNNY Fine. I didn't find any money, though. Not even a *penny*.

JOHNNY'S FATHER Oh, that's all right. Money isn't everything. (*They go into the house.*)

The living room. They are all at the table after supper. MacGREGOR *finds crumbs here and there which he places delicately in his mouth. He looks around the room to see if there isn't something more to eat.*

[10] *have your cake and eat it too:* This is a common expression used when people want two things but can have only one or the other. Johnny is saying that a person cannot be a poet and make money also.

MACGREGOR That green can up there, Johnny. What's in there?

JOHNNY Marbles.

MACGREGOR That cupboard, Johnny. Anything *edible* in there?

JOHNNY Crickets.

MACGREGOR That big jar in the corner there, Johnny. What's delectable in there?

JOHNNY I got a gopher snake in that jar.

MACGREGOR Well, I could go for[11] a bit of boiled gopher snake in a big way, Johnny.

JOHNNY (*Defiantly, protector of animals.*) Nothing doing, Mr. MacGregor.

MACGREGOR Why not, Johnny? Why the hell not, son? I hear of fine Borneo natives eating snakes and grasshoppers. You haven't got a half dozen fat grasshoppers around, have you, Johnny?

JOHNNY Only four.

MACGREGOR Well, trot them out, son, and after we've had our fill, I'll play "Drink to Me Only with Thine Eyes" for you. I'm mighty hungry, Johnny.

JOHNNY So am I, but I don't want anybody killing them innocent animals.[12] They got rights the same as anybody else.

JOHNNY'S FATHER (*To* MACGREGOR.) How about a little music? I think the boy would be delighted.

JOHNNY (*Leaping to his feet.*) I sure would, Mr. MacGregor.

MACGREGOR All right, Johnny. Bread. Bread. My God, how savagely it quarrels with the heart. (MACGREGOR *gets up and begins to blow into the bugle. He blows louder and more beautifully and mournfully than anybody ever blew into a bugle. Eighteen* NEIGHBORS *gather in front of the house and cheer when he finishes the solo: "Drink to Me Only with Thine Eyes."*)

JOHNNY'S FATHER (*Delighted, for amusement.*) I want you to meet your public. (*They go out on the porch.*)

The house. The crowd is looking up at JOHHNY'S FATHER, MACGREGOR *and* JOHNNY.

JOHNNY'S FATHER Good neighbors, and friends, I want you to meet Jasper MacGregor, the greatest Shakespearean actor of our day. (*Pause.*) I believe.

MACGREGOR (*The actor.*) I remember my first appearance in London in 1851 as if it was yesterday. I was a boy of fourteen from the slums of Glasgow. My first part was a courier in a play, the title of which I have unfortunately forgotten. I had no lines to speak, but moved about a good deal, running from officer to officer, and from lover to his beloved, and back again, over and over again.

[11] *go for:* a slang expression meaning to enjoy.

[12] *them innocent animals:* those innocent animals. For Johnny, this is a rare slip in grammar.

RUFE APLEY, THE CARPENTER (*Regretfully interrupting the great speech.*) How about another song, Mr. MacGregor?

MACGREGOR Have you got an egg at your house?

RUFE APLEY I sure have. I've got a *dozen* eggs at my house.

MACGREGOR Would it be convenient for you to go and get one of them dozen eggs? When you return I'll play a song that will make your heart leap with joy and grief.

RUFE APLEY I'm on my way already. (*He goes.*)

MACGREGOR (*To the crowd.*) My friends, I should be delighted to play another song for you on this golden-throated bugle, but time and distance from home find me weary. If you will be so good as to go, each of you to his home, and return in a moment with some morsel of food, I shall be proud to gather my spirit together and play a song I know will change the course of each of your lives, and change it, mind you, for the better. (*The people go. The last to go is* ESTHER KOSAK, *who hears the speech out, then runs.* MACGREGOR, JOHNNY'S FATHER, *and* JOHNNY *sit on the steps and remain in silence, and one by one the people return, bringing food to* MACGREGOR: *an egg, a sausage, a dozen green onions, two kinds of cheese, butter, two kinds of bread, boiled potatoes, fresh tomatoes, a melon, tea, and many other good things to eat.)* Thank you, my friends, thank you. (*He stands solemnly, waiting for absolute silence, straightens himself, looks about him furiously, lifts the bugle to his lips and is irritated by the swift and noisy return of* ESTHER KOSAK, *bringing an eggplant. When there is silence, he plays "My Heart's in the Highlands, My Heart is not Here." The* PEOPLE *weep, kneel, sing the chorus, and go away.* MACGREGOR *turns to the father and son. Grandly.*) Sir, if it is all the same to you I should like to dwell in your house for a long time to come.

JOHNNY'S FATHER (*Delighted and amazed.*) Sir, my house is your house. (*They go into the house.*)

The living room. Eighteen days later, MACGREGOR *is lying on the floor, face up, asleep. Johnny is walking about quietly in the room, looking at everybody. His* FATHER *is at the table, writing poetry. His* GRANDMOTHER *is sitting in the rocking chair, rocking. There is a knock on the door. Everybody but* MACGREGOR *jumps up and runs to it.*

JOHNNY'S FATHER (*At the door.*) Yes?

YOUNG MAN I am looking for Jasper MacGregor, the actor.

JOHNNY'S FATHER What do you want?

JOHNNY Well, ask him in anyway, Pa.

JOHNNY'S FATHER Yes, of course. Excuse me. Won't you please come in? (*The* YOUNG MAN *enters.*)

YOUNG MAN My name is Philip Carmichael. I am from the Old People's Home. I have been sent to bring Mr. MacGregor home.

MACGREGOR (*Wakening and sitting up.*) Home? Did someone mention home? (*Roaring.*) I'm five thousand miles from home, always have been, and always will be. Who is this young man?

YOUNG MAN Mr. MacGregor, I'm Philip Carmichael, from the Old People's Home. They've sent me to bring you back. We are putting on our annual show in two weeks and need you for the leading role.

MACGREGOR (*Getting up with the help of* JOHNNY'S FATHER *and* JOHNNY.) What kind of a part is it? I can't be playing young adventurers any longer.

YOUNG MAN The part is King Lear,[13] Mr. MacGregor. It is perfect for you.

MACGREGOR (*The actor, with a job again.*) Good-by, my beloved friends. (*He returns from the porch.*) In all the hours of my life, in all the places I have visited, never and nowhere have I had the honor and pleasure

[13] *King Lear:* the tragic old man in Shakespeare's play of the same name.

to commune with souls loftier, purer, or more delightful than yours. Good-by. (*The* OLD MAN *and the* YOUNG MAN *leave the house. There is a moment of silence, full of regret and loneliness.*)

JOHNNY'S FATHER (*Hungry, loudly.*) Johnny, go on down to Mr. Kosak's store and get a little something to eat. I know you can do it, Johnny. Get *anything.*

JOHNNY (*Hungry, loudly, and angry.*) Mr. Kosak wants eighty-five cents. He won't give us anything more without money.

JOHNNY'S FATHER Go on down there, Johnny. You know you can get that fine Slovak gentleman to give us a little something to eat.

JOHNNY (*With despair.*) Aw, Pa.

JOHNNY'S FATHER (*Amazed, roaring.*) What? You, *my son,* in a mood like that. Come on. I fought the world this way before you were born. After you were born we fought it together, and we're going to go on fighting it. The people love poetry but don't know it, that's all. Nothing is going to stop us, Johnny. Go on down there now and get us something to eat.

JOHNNY All right, Pa. I'll do my best. (*He runs to the door.*)

The house. It now has a large sign: "For Rent." It is a moment before daybreak of a day early in November, 1914. There is a suggestion of Winter coming. High in the sky a flock of geese flying south make their call. JOHNNY *is sitting on the steps of the front porch with his chin in his hand. He hears the geese, listening carefully, leaps to his feet and looks into the sky for them. The sound decreases, then ends.* JOHNNY *goes back to the steps of the porch and sits down. As the sun rises, a big solemn smile comes over his face. He looks out of the corner of his eye at the morning's light as if it were a quiet friend with whom he was on terms of perfect understanding. As the light increases, this play between* JOHNNY *and the sun grows, like a theme of music, bringing him to his feet, turning his face to the light. He lifts his arms, and very solemnly begins turning somersaults. He then runs around the house lickety-split and returns on the other side, almost dancing.*

A freight train goes by not far enough away not to make the earth tremble. The light of morning increases.

A newspaper route carrier arrives on foot, whistling. He is the typical small-town morning route carrier: about thirteen years old. He is in that somber and dignified state which comes over men who have done their work. His paper bags are empty. Night is over. His daily wage has been earned. The papers have been left at the doors of the readers. Another day has come to the world. He has walked two hours through dark streets to morning. The song he is whistling is soft and full of understanding. It is a song of his own composition, a morning song.

JOHNNY (*Running down the steps.*) Hello.

THE BOY (*Stopping.*) Hello.

JOHNNY What was that song?

THE BOY What song?

JOHNNY That you were whistling?

THE BOY Was I whistling?

JOHNNY Sure. Didn't you know?

THE BOY I guess I'm always whistling.

JOHNNY What was it?

THE BOY I don't know.

JOHNNY I wish I could whistle.

THE BOY Anybody can whistle.

JOHNNY I can't. How do you do it?

THE BOY There's no *how* to it. You just whistle.

JOHNNY How?

THE BOY Like this. (*He whistles a moment, obviously improvising a tour de force of technique.*)[14]

JOHNNY (*With admiration.*) I wish I could do that.

THE BOY (*Pleased and eager to make an even better impression.*) That was nothing. Listen to this. (*He gives the melody a sort of counterpoint, two tones, and a bit of syncopation.*)

JOHNNY Can't you teach me to do that?

THE BOY You can't teach whistling. You just do it. This is another way. (*He whistles a little melody, the loud newsboy's style, but he keeps it soft.*)

JOHNNY (*Trying to whistle.*) Like that?

THE BOY That's the way to start. Keep it up and after a while your mouth'll take the right shape and you'll be whistling before you know it.

JOHNNY Honest?

THE BOY Sure.

JOHNNY Is your mother dead?

THE BOY How did you know?

JOHNNY My mother's dead too.

THE BOY Yeah?

JOHNNY (*With a sigh.*) Yeah. She died.

THE BOY I don't remember my mother. Do you remember your mother?

JOHNNY I don't exactly remember her. Sometimes I dream about her, though.

THE BOY I used to, too.

JOHNNY Don't you any more?

THE BOY (*Disillusioned.*) Naaaah. What good does that do you?

JOHNNY My mother sure is beautiful.

THE BOY Yeah, I know. I remember. You got a father?

[14] *improvising a tour de force of technique: Tour de force* is a French expression meaning an act showing great skill. Here the boy is making up (improvising) a tune showing great musical skill.

JOHNNY (*Proudly.*) Oh, sure. He's in the house *now*, sleeping.

THE BOY My *father's* dead, too.

JOHNNY Your *father*, too?

THE BOY (*Matter-of-fact.*) Yeah. (*They begin bouncing an old tennis ball back and forth to each other.*)

JOHNNY Haven't you got anybody?

THE BOY I got an aunt, but she ain't really my aunt. I was brought up in an orphanage. I'm adopted.

JOHNNY What's an orphanage?

THE BOY That's a kind of place where kids that ain't got any mothers and fathers live until somebody adopts them.

JOHNNY What do you mean, adopts?

THE BOY Somebody who wants a boy or girl comes to the orphanage and looks everybody over and goes away with whoever they like. If they pick you, you go and stay with them.

JOHNNY Do you like that?

THE BOY It's all right. (THE BOY *puts away the ball.*)

JOHNNY What's your name?

THE BOY Henry. What's yours?

JOHNNY Johnny.

THE BOY Do you want a paper? There's a War in Europe.

JOHNNY I haven't got any money. We aren't rich. We don't work. My father writes poetry.

THE BOY (*Giving* JOHNNY *the extra.*) Oh, that's all right. Don't you *ever* have any money?

JOHNNY Sometimes. I found a quarter once. It was lying on the sidewalk, right in front of me. Once my father got a check for ten dollars from New York, too. We bought a chicken and a lot of stamps and paper and envelopes. The chicken wouldn't lay eggs, though, so my grandmother killed it and cooked it for us. Did you ever eat chicken?

THE BOY Sure. I guess I've eaten chicken six or seven times.

JOHNNY What are you going to do when you grow up?

THE BOY Shucks. I don't know. I don't know what I'll do.

JOHNNY (*Proudly.*) I'm going to be a poet, like my father. He said so.

THE BOY I guess I'll carry a paper route for a while. (*He moves to go.*) Well. So long.

JOHNNY Won't you come here again?

THE BOY I go by here every morning about this time. I ain't never seen you up before, though.

JOHNNY (*Smiling.*) I had a dream and then I woke up and didn't want to sleep any more. I wanted to get up and come out here. I saw my mother.

THE BOY Maybe I'll see you again some morning when you can't sleep.

JOHNNY I hope so. So long.

THE BOY So long. Just keep trying and you'll be whistling before you know it.

JOHNNY Thanks. (THE BOY *goes, whistling.* JOHNNY *tosses the folded paper up on the porch, and sits down again on the steps. His* GRANDMOTHER *comes out on the porch with a broom and begins to sweep.*)

JOHNNY'S GRANDMOTHER (*In Armenian, which is the only language she speaks, with the exception of Turkish, Kurdish, and a little Arabic, which nobody around seems to know.*) How are you, my heart?

JOHNNY (*Who understands Armenian, but hardly ever speaks it; in English.*) Fine.

JOHNNY'S GRANDMOTHER How's your Papa?

JOHNNY I don't know. (*Calling loudly to his Father.*) Oh, Pa. How are you? (*Pause. Louder.*) Pa. (*Pause. Silence.*) I guess he's sleeping.

JOHNNY'S GRANDMOTHER Is there any money?

JOHNNY Money? (*Shaking his head.*) No.

JOHNNY'S FATHER (*From inside the house.*) Johnny?

JOHNNY (*Jumping to his feet.*) Pa?

JOHNNY'S FATHER Did you call?

JOHNNY Yeah. How are you?

JOHNNY'S FATHER Fine, Johnny. How are you?

JOHNNY Fine, Pa.

JOHNNY'S FATHER Is that all you woke me up for?

JOHNNY (*To his* GRANDMOTHER.) He's fine. (*Louder to his* FATHER.) The old lady wanted to know.

JOHNNY'S FATHER (*In Armenian, to the old lady.*) Good night, Ma. (*To Johnny, in English.*) What do you mean, old? She's not so old.

JOHNNY I don't mean old. You know what I mean.

[JOHNNY'S FATHER *comes out on the porch, buttoning his shirt, nods to the old lady, looks out of the corner of his eye at the sun, exactly the same way* JOHNNY *did, smiling the same way, stretches all over, faces the sun, leaps down the steps and turns one somersault, not so good. The somersault leaves him flat on his back.*]

JOHNNY You ought to get a little more exercise, Pa. You're always sitting down.

JOHNNY'S FATHER (*On his back.*) Johnny, your father is a great poet. I may not be able to turn a somersault as well as you, but if you want to know what kind of an athlete I am, just read the poetry I wrote yesterday.

JOHNNY Is it really good, Pa?

JOHNNY'S FATHER Good? (*He leaps to his feet, like an acrobat.*) It's *great.* I'm going to send it to *The Atlantic Monthly*[15] too.

[15] *The Atlantic Monthly:* a periodical that publishes distinguished prose and poetry.

JOHNNY Oh, I forgot, Pa. There's a paper on the porch.

JOHNNY'S FATHER (*Going up to the porch.*) You mean a morning paper, Johnny?

JOHNNY Yeah.

JOHNNY'S FATHER Well, that's a pleasant surprise. Where in the world did you get it?

JOHNNY Henry gave it to me.

JOHNNY'S FATHER Henry? Who's Henry?

JOHNNY He's a boy who hasn't got a mother or a father, either. He sure can whistle, too.

JOHNNY'S FATHER (*Picking up the paper, opening it.*) That was certainly nice of him. (*He loses himself in the headlines.*)

JOHNNY'S GRANDMOTHER (*To both of them, to herself, and to the world.*) Where's that man?

JOHNNY'S FATHER (*Deep in the news.*) Hmmm?

JOHNNY Who?

JOHNNY'S GRANDMOTHER You know. That old man who blew the horn. (*She pantomimes the blowing of a horn.*)

JOHNNY Oh. Mr. MacGregor? They took him back to the Old People's Home.

JOHNNY'S FATHER (*Reading the paper.*) Austria. Germany. France. England. Russia. Zeppelins. Submarines. Tanks. Machine guns. Bombs. (*Shaking his head.*) They've gone crazy again.

JOHNNY'S GRANDMOTHER (*To* JOHNNY, *reproachfully.*) Why don't you speak Armenian, boy?

JOHNNY I can't talk Armenian.

JOHNNY'S FATHER (*To* JOHNNY.) What's the matter?

JOHNNY She wants to know about Mr. MacGregor.

JOHNNY'S GRANDMOTHER (*To* JOHNNY'S FATHER.) Where is he?

JOHNNY'S FATHER (*In Armenian.*) He's back in the Old People's Home.

JOHNNY'S GRANDMOTHER (*Shaking her head sadly.*) Ahkh, ahkh, the poor old prisoner.

JOHNNY Is it like a prison, Pa?

JOHNNY'S FATHER I don't know for sure, Johnny.

JOHNNY'S GRANDMOTHER (*Furiously, the way her son and grandson speak when they are irritated.*) Why doesn't he come back and stay here where he belongs? (*She goes into the house.*)

JOHNNY That's right, Pa. Why doesn't Mr. MacGregor come back and stay here? Does he have to stay in that place?

JOHNNY'S FATHER If you're an old, old man, Johnny, and haven't got any people, and no money, I guess you do.

JOHNNY I sure get lonesome for him sometimes. Don't you, Pa?

JOHNNY'S FATHER To tell you the truth, Johnny, I do.

JOHNNY I'm always remembering him, especially the music. And the way he drinks water.

JOHNNY'S FATHER He's a great man.

JOHNNY Is his heart really in the highlands like he said, Pa?

JOHNNY'S FATHER Not exactly.

JOHNNY Is he really five thousand miles from home, too?

JOHNNY'S FATHER At least that many.

JOHNNY Do you think he'll ever get home again some day?

JOHNNY'S FATHER He's an old man, Johnny. He will.

JOHNNY You mean he'll take a train and a boat and get back where the highlands are?

JOHNNY'S FATHER Not that, Johnny. It's a little different from that. He'll *die*.

JOHNNY Is that the only way a man gets home?

JOHNNY'S FATHER That's the only way.

[*All this time, of course,* JOHNNY'S FATHER *has been turning the pages of the morning paper, and* JOHNNY *has been going through various kinds of acrobatics, walking on the porch railing, leaping down, turning somersaults, standing on his head, and so forth. Some of his questions have been asked while he has been standing on his head. A sharp whistle is heard in the distance.*]

JOHNNY (*Eagerly.*) It's Mr. Wiley, the mailman, Pa. (JOHNNY'S FATHER *jumps to his feet, dropping the paper.*)

JOHNNY Do you think maybe we'll get a letter from New York with a check in it maybe?

JOHNNY'S FATHER I don't know, Johnny.

[MR. WILEY, *riding a bicycle, arrives. He is almost knocked off the bicycle by* JOHNNY'S FATHER.]

MR. WILEY (*Getting off the bicycle as if it were a horse.*) Good morning, Mr. Alexander.

JOHNNY'S FATHER Good morning, Mr. Wiley.

JOHNNY Any mail for us, Mr. Wiley?

MR. WILEY (*Bringing a packet of letters from his bag, loosening the strap, and looking them over.*) Well, now, let me see, Johnny. I think I've got something here for your father.

JOHNNY Is it from New York?

MR. WILEY (*Holding a flat envelope.*) Yes, it is, Johnny. Well, Mr. Alexander, it looks like Winter's coming again. The geese were flying this morning.

JOHNNY'S FATHER (*Excited, tense, yet eager to be casual.*) Yes, I know. (*To himself.*) I know. I know.

JOHNNY If *I* ever get a letter from New York I'm going to save it up.

MR. WILEY (*He wants to talk.*) How are things, Mr. Alexander?

JOHNNY'S FATHER I've been lucky in my work, thank you, Mr. Wiley.

JOHNNY My father was in New York once. Weren't you, Pa?

JOHNNY'S FATHER Yes, I was, Johnny. How is your family, Mr. Wiley?

MR. WILEY All fine, except the littlest one, Joe. He's always crying. That's one thing I can't stand either, a baby crying all the time. I don't know what it does to me, but it makes me lose all faith in everything. When Joe cries I say to myself, Aw, what's the use?

JOHNNY I guess I'll reach New York some day before I die.

JOHNNY'S FATHER It's nothing, Mr. Wiley. He'll stop crying after a while.

MR. WILEY Well, I hope so, and the sooner the better. (*He goes off with the envelope.*) Good-by, Mr. Alexander. Good-bye, Johnny.

JOHNNY'S FATHER Mr. Wiley.

[MR. WILEY *hands over the envelope. They say good-by, and* MR. WILEY *rides off.* JOHNNY'S FATHER *holds the envelope before him, obviously eager to open it, yet fearful to do so.*]

JOHNNY (*Impatient.*) All right, Pa. Go ahead; open it. What are you waiting for?

JOHNNY'S FATHER (*Angry; roaring.*) Johnny, I'm scared. I can't understand how I, your father, can be so scared.

JOHNNY You don't sound scared, Pa. Who's it from?

JOHNNY'S FATHER It's from *The Atlantic Monthly* all right. You remember them poems I wrote after Mr. MacGregor was here?

JOHNNY Maybe they've bought the poems.

JOHNNY'S FATHER Bought them, my eye. They don't buy *poetry*, Johnny. They *scare* you to death. (*Reading his name and address with great solemnity, awful tenderness and terrible rage.*) Ben Alexander, 2226 San Benito Avenue, Fresno, California.

JOHNNY It's for you all right, Pa. Why don't you open it?

JOHNNY'S FATHER (*Roaring.*) I'm scared, I tell you. I'm scared and ashamed. *Those poems were great.* How can it be that I'm scared?

JOHNNY (*Also defiant.*) Don't be scared, Pa.

JOHNNY'S FATHER (*Angry.*) Why do they clamor for all things but the best? Why do they destroy themselves running after things of death, and thrust aside all things of life? I can't understand it. There's no hope for *anybody*.

JOHNNY Sure there is, Pa. (*Furiously.*) Who the hell is *The Atlantic Monthly?*

JOHNNY'S FATHER (*Angry.*) Johnny, go away. Go away. Please go away.

JOHNNY (*Angry, too.*) All right, Pa. (JOHNNY *goes around the house, reappears, looks at his father a moment, and then knows he must stay out of the way.*)

[*It is obvious that* JOHNNY'S FATHER *knows* The Atlantic Monthly *has sent back the poems. It is equally obvious that he can't believe the poems have come back. It is obvious too that the poems are great, because the man is. He paces about like a tiger. He seems to be speaking to the world, even though his lips are set. At last he tears the envelope open, in a fury. The envelope falls. He unfolds the manuscript of poems. A slip of white, heavy paper falls to the floor of the porch. He stands, very tall, and very proud, and reads the poems to himself, turning the pages swiftly.*]

JOHNNY'S FATHER (*Furiously.*) Ah, you crazy, miserable fools. (*He sits on the steps of the porch and buries his face in his hands. The manuscipt of poems is on the steps. After several minutes he kicks the poems off the steps of the porch onto the ground and takes up the morning paper again, looking at the headlines. Quietly, with deep fury, his voice mounting in intensity.*) Go ahead, kill *everybody*. Declare *War* on one another. Take the people by the thousands and mangle them. Their poor hearts and their poor spirits and their poor bodies. Give them ugliness. Pollute their dreams. Horrify them. Distort them with hatred for one another. Befoul the legend of the living, you maniacs whose greatness is measured by the number you destroy. (JOHNNY *appears at the side of the house, unseen. He stands in a trance, listening to his father. The sky begins to darken.*) You frauds of the world. You wretched and ungodly. (*He stands and points a finger, as if across the world.*) Go ahead. *Fire* your feeble guns. You won't kill *anything*. (*Quietly, smiling.*) There will always be poets in the world.

[*Lightning flashes silently.*]

The house. The sky is dark, as at the beginning of a storm. An occasional deep and faraway roar of thunder is heard, and a flash of lightning is seen. JOHNNY'S FATHER *is on the steps of the porch, smiling: a foolish, tragic, desolate, lonely smile. Everything is the same; the manuscript of poems is on the ground; the envelope is on the porch. The newspaper too. It is several hours later.*

JOHNNY'S FATHER (*Shaking his head foolishly, unable to accept the truth.*) Johnny. (*Pause. A little louder.*) Johnny. (*Pause, softer this time.*) Johnny. (*Roaring.*) Johnny. (*The boy comes around the house shyly and stands before his father. His father looks up, fire in his eye, defiant, bitter, stubborn, powerful.*)

JOHNNY'S FATHER (*Tenderly, but with tremendous power.*) Have you had your breakfast?

JOHNNY (*Shyly.*) I'm not hungry, Pa.

JOHNNY'S FATHER You go inside now and eat.

JOHNNY I'm not hungry.

JOHNNY'S FATHER You do what I tell you.

JOHNNY I won't eat unless you do.

JOHNNY'S FATHER You do what I tell you.

JOHNNY I won't eat unless you do.

JOHNNY'S FATHER I'm not hungry.

JOHNNY I'll go down to Mr. Kosak's and see if I can get something.

JOHNNY'S FATHER (*Humiliated. Taking the boy's arm.*) No, Johnny. (*He pauses, obviously trying to find words with which to explain about themselves and the grocer.*) Johnny? I thought we'd be getting some money. I didn't think it would be this way. Now, go on inside and eat.

JOHNNY (*Going up the stairs.*) You got to eat, too. (*He goes into the house.*)

[*There is a silent flash of lightning.* A MAN *in a business suit, and a young* HUSBAND *and* WIFE *with a* BABY *in the mother's arms, come up.*]

THE REAL ESTATE MAN This is the house. The rent's six dollars a month. It's not exactly fancy, but it'll keep out the rain and cold.

[JOHNNY'S FATHER *has been staring at the people, his vision frozen.*]

THE REAL ESTATE MAN (*Coming up to* JOHNNY'S FATHER, *extending his hand, while the others stand back in a group.*) Remember me? I put up the "For Rent" sign.

JOHNNY'S FATHER (*Rising.*) I remember. How do you do.

THE REAL ESTATE MAN (*Embarrassed.*) Well. Mr. Corey, the owner of the house, is out of town, and these people are looking for a house. *Right away.*

JOHNNY'S FATHER Of course. I can leave any time. Have they furniture?

THE REAL ESTATE MAN (*Turning to the poor family.*) Have you furniture?

THE HUSBAND No.

JOHNNY'S FATHER (*To the family.*) You can have my furniture. There isn't much of it, but it'll do. There's a pretty good stove.

THE WIFE (*With the diginity of the poor.*) We wouldn't want to take *your* furniture.

JOHNNY'S FATHER That's all right. I haven't paid rent for three months. I'll leave the furniture for the rent. (THE REAL ESTATE MAN *tries to speak.*)

JOHNNY'S FATHER It's all right. I'm sorry I haven't the $18. The furniture's worth about that much. You can let these people have it till Mr. Corey gets back. (*To the family.*) Do you want to go through the house?

THE HUSBAND It looks all right.

THE REAL ESTATE MAN (*Going.*) Then that's settled. (*To the people.*) The rent's six dollars a month. We pay the water.[16]

JOHNNY'S FATHER (*To the people.*) You can move in any time.

THE HUSBAND Thank you very much. We'll be back this afternoon or tomorrow. (*They are going as* JOHNNY *comes out with a plate containing two slices of bread and a small bunch of grapes.*)

JOHNNY Who were those people?

JOHNNY'S FATHER Just some people walking by.

JOHNNY What were you talking about?

[16] *We pay the water:* The six dollars for rent includes the charge for water.

JOHNNY'S FATHER Just talking, Johnny.

JOHNNY (*Shouting; very angry.*) Don't feel bad, Pa.

JOHNNY'S FATHER (*Turning and looking at the boy with love, amazement, admiration, and delight, laughing suddenly.*) I don't feel bad, Johnny. Let the world be the world, and God love everyone.

JOHNNY (*Bantering.*) All right then. Let's eat. (*He puts the plate on the top step and they sit down together and begin to eat. They eat in silence, looking at one another, the boy looking at his father out of the corner of his eye as he had looked at the sun; the father looking at the boy the same way. The boy begins to smile. The father begins to smile too.*)

JOHNNY Do you like grapes, Pa?

JOHNNY'S FATHER Of course I like grapes.

JOHNNY Pa?

JOHNNY'S FATHER Yes?

JOHNNY Is it really like a prison?[17]

JOHNNY'S FATHER Sometimes I'm *sure* it is. Sometimes I *know* it never can be.

JOHNNY What, Pa?

JOHNNY'S FATHER I guess it's fifty-fifty, Johnny. You know. It's both.

JOHNNY I mean, do you think he gets homesick sometimes?

JOHNNY'S FATHER I'm sure he does.

JOHNNY I wish he'd come back.

JOHNNY'S FATHER I'd like to see him again.

JOHNNY I remember him all the time.

JOHNNY'S FATHER I do too. I'll always remember him.

JOHNNY So will I. Did he *have* to go back, Pa?

JOHNNY'S FATHER I guess he did.

JOHNNY He seemed like a nice young man.

JOHNNY'S FATHER You mean the young man who came and got him?

JOHNNY Yeah, you know. That young man who talked so sharp, like he was speaking in front of an audience.

JOHNNY'S FATHER He was all right. (*There is one more grape on the plate.*)

JOHNNY Go ahead, Pa. Take it.

JOHNNY'S FATHER (*Blithely.*) No, that's yours, Johnny. I counted.

JOHNNY All right, Pa. (*He takes the last grape and eats it.*) Is it stealing, Pa?

JOHNNY'S FATHER (*Comically.*) Well, some say it is and some say it isn't. (*Dramatically.*) *I* say it isn't. (*Shouting.*) You took them off the vines, didn't you?

JOHNNY I took them off the vines all right, Pa.

JOHNNY'S FATHER (*Comically.*) Then it couldn't very well be stealing.

JOHNNY When would it be stealing?

JOHNNY'S FATHER (*Tossing it off like nothing.*) The way I see it, Johnny,

[17] Johnny is bringing the conversation back to Mr. MacGregor. His grandmother has previously called Mr. MacGregor a "prisoner" in the Old People's Home.

stealing is where there's unnecessary damage or cruelty to an innocent one, so that there may be undeserved profit or power to one who is not innocent.

JOHNNY Oh. (*Pause.*) Well, if it isn't stealing, Pa, I guess I'll go get some more. (*He gets up.*) They'll all be gone pretty soon. (*Goes off.*)

JOHNNY'S FATHER (*When the boy is gone, laughing.*) My son John. My God, how fortunate I have been. How grateful I am. (*He picks up the manuscript of poems, puts it in his coat pocket, and walks down the street.*)

The inside of Mr. Kosak's Grocery Store. Again MR. KOSAK *is sleeping on his folded arms. The store looks more poverty-stricken than before. The family apparently has been eating the stock.* JOHNNY'S FATHER *comes into the store quietly, almost shyly.* MR. KOSAK *lifts his head, blinks his eyes, stands.*

JOHNNY'S FATHER (*Almost guiltily.*) I'm Johnny's father.

[*The two men stand staring at one another a moment, each of them delighted, embarrassed, impressed, pleased, and angry about the same things in the world: greed, deceit, unkindliness, disproportion. They each begin to smile, then shake hands warmly.*]

MR. KOSAK I recognize you. Johnny has told me about you. It is an honor.

JOHNNY'S FATHER You are a kind man.

MR. KOSAK I do not know.

JOHNNY'S FATHER (*Slowly.*) I have come to say good-by. To apologize. To thank you.

MR. KOSAK (*Swiftly.*) You're not going away?

JOHNNY'S FATHER I'm sorry, yes.

MR. KOSAK We shall all miss Johnny.

JOHNNY'S FATHER I have no money. I am in debt to you.

MR. KOSAK It is nothing.

JOHNNY'S FATHER I may not see you again. (*He brings the manuscript of poems from his pocket. Powerfully.*) *I* am a poet. *These* are some of my poems. (*Swiftly.*) I am not offering them to you in place of the money I owe you. Money is another thing. (*Pleading.*) Will you keep them for your kindness?

MR. KOSAK (*Sincerely.*) I cannot take your poems. (*Pause.*)

JOHNNY'S FATHER I hope you have been prospering.

MR. KOSAK The people have no money. I do not know how I am going to put in new stock.

JOHNNY'S FATHER I'm sorry.

MR. KOSAK In the Winter it is worse. The packing-houses are closed. There are no jobs. I would give them something if I could, but this Winter I have no money for new stock. I may have to close the store. There is hardly enough for my family.

JOHNNY'S FATHER (*Touched and angry.*) These poems. Let me tell you they are the finest I have ever written. I want to leave them with you.

[*Mr. Kosak's daughter,* ESTHER, *a beautiful girl of seven, comes into the store, from the back.*]

MR. KOSAK This is my daughter Esther. Esther, this is Johnny's father.

JOHNNY'S FATHER Johnny's told me about you.

ESTHER (*Really pleased, but shy.*) How do you do.

MR. KOSAK They're going away.

ESTHER (*Shocked.*) Oh.

JOHNNY'S FATHER Johnny will miss you.

[*The girl's lips tremble, tears come to her eyes. She turns and runs out of the store.*]

MR. KOSAK Everything is like that.

JOHNNY'S FATHER They are children.

MR. KOSAK Yes, but it's that way from the beginning and it never changes. Only women never learn to believe it.

JOHNNY'S FATHER Won't you give *her* these poems?

MR. KOSAK Please. It's nothing. She will cry for a while, but it is nothing.

JOHNNY'S FATHER Here. (*Giving* MR. KOSAK *the poems.*) You will be doing me a kindness by keeping them. (*Loudly, to God and the world.*) Don't you see, poetry must be *read* to be poetry. It may be that one reader is all that I deserve. If this is so, I want that reader to be you.

MR. KOSAK I thank you. I am unworthy.

JOHNNY'S FATHER (*Smiling.*) Good-by.

MR. KOSAK Good-by.

[JOHNNY'S FATHER *goes out of the store. The grocer takes his glasses out of his pocket, puts them on, unfolds the manuscript, and standing in the middle of the store, begins to read, softly, to himself, moving his lips. The expression of his face begins to change. Rain begins to fall. His daughter* ESTHER *comes back into the store.*]

MR. KOSAK (*Reading from one of the poems, in a quiet voice.*) Deep in the bowels of the earth, and far dispersed into the green waters of the sea, and held tight within the hardness of rock, I thee remember, love, remember me. (*The girl begins to sob aloud, and the father turns and goes to her.*)

The living room of the house. Some time later. JOHNNY'S FATHER *is at his table, looking over a stock of manuscripts. It is still raining. Every once in a while he gets up and goes to the window.*

JOHNNY'S FATHER What the hell's happened to him? (*He goes back to his manuscripts and looks over some poems, grows irritated with them, throws them down, and goes to the window again. Then begins to walk back and forth, waiting. At last* JOHNNY *tears up the front porch stairs,*[18] *bursts into the house, closes the door quickly, and bolts it. He is breathless and scared. You know he is one who has been pursued. He has four medium-sized bunches of purple-red Emperors;*[19] *a half dozen black figs, and two pomegranates.*)

JOHNNY (*Excited and breathless.*) Where shall I hide them, Pa?

JOHNNY'S FATHER What's the matter, Johnny?

JOHNNY You said it wasn't stealing, Pa.

JOHNNY'S FATHER (*With furious irritation.*) Well, it isn't.

JOHNNY What about the farmer's dog, then?

JOHNNY'S FATHER What are you talking about? What farmer's dog?

JOHNNY The farmer's dog that chased me all the way here.

JOHNNY'S FATHER Dog? Do you mean to tell me a dog chased you? What kind of a dog?

JOHNNY I didn't get a chance to take a good look, but I guess it's a great big one.

JOHNNY'S FATHER (*Very angry at this awful humiliation.*) Did the God damn thing try to bite you or anything, Johnny?

JOHNNY I don't think so, Pa, but I thought it was going to any minute.

JOHNNY'S FATHER Did it growl at you?

JOHNNY It wasn't exactly a growl.

JOHNNY'S FATHER What happened?

JOHNNY I just ran all the way, with the dog right behind me.

JOHNNY'S FATHER Where is it now?

JOHNNY It's *outside*, I think, Pa. Are you sure it isn't stealing?

JOHNNY'S FATHER (*Very angry, eating three or four grapes.*) Of course it isn't stealing. I'll take care of the dog. No man or beast can scare your father, Johnny. Always remember that. (*He goes cautiously to the window and peeks out.*)

JOHNNY Is it out there, Pa?

JOHNNY'S FATHER There's a little dog out there, Johnny. It's asleep, I think.

JOHNNY (*Jumping bitterly.*) *I knew it.* It's the farmer's dog, waiting for me.

JOHNNY'S FATHER It's not a very big dog, Johnny.

JOHNNY Yeah, but if it's stealing—if it's the *farmer's* dog—what about that?

JOHNNY'S FATHER Why, that little bitty dog doesn't belong to anybody, Johnny. That little dog is looking for a friend, I bet.

JOHNNY It chased me all the way. Are you sure, Pa?

[18] *tears up the front porch stairs:* runs up the stairs very fast.
[19] *Emperors:* a variety of grape.

JOHNNY'S FATHER Sure I'm sure, Johnny. I'm no poet for nothing. I understand things. (*The dog begins to growl and bark.* JOHNNY'S FATHER *jumps back from the window, frightened.* JOHNNY *jumps tense and speechless.*)

JOHNNY (*Whispering.*) What is it, Pa?

JOHNNY'S FATHER Somebody's coming, I think.

JOHNNY You see, Pa? *It is stealing.* It's the farmer. (*He runs to the table and gathers the fruit into his arms. His* GRANDMOTHER *comes running into the room.*)

JOHNNY'S GRANDMOTHER (*In Armenian.*) What's all the hullabaloo, in the rain?

JOHNNY'S FATHER Shhhh. (JOHNNY *takes the fruit out of the living room; returns, scared to death. The dog is still growling and barking.* JOHNNY'S FATHER *is even more scared than* JOHNNY.)

JOHNNY (*Sore, and now defiant.*) God damn it, Pa. Now look at the mess we're in.

JOHNNY'S FATHER I wish I had a cigarette.

JOHNNY (*Now worrying about his father; to his grandmother, in Armenian.*) Are there cigarettes? (JOHNNY'S GRANDMOTHER *runs into the next room. The dog stops growling.*)

JOHNNY You see, Pa? It's the farmer. Where shall I hide? Don't open the door.

JOHNNY'S FATHER *Open the door?* Help me with this table. (*They push the table up against the door, and tiptoe back to the center of the room.* JOHNNY'S GRANDMOTHER *runs back with one cigarette and one match which she hands to* JOHNNY'S FATHER, *who lights the cigarette, inhales deeply, and straightens up.*)

JOHNNY'S FATHER (*Dramatically.*) *I* am the one who took the fruit, understand, Johnny?

JOHNNY Don't open the door, Pa. (JOHNNY'S FATHER *picks up a small stool, takes it quietly to the table up against the door, places it on the table, to make it heavier.* JOHNNY *picks up a chair and puts it on the table. The* OLD LADY *puts a vase on the table.* JOHNNY'S FATHER *adds three books to the barricade. In fact, as the knocks continue, the family little by little puts all the household goods up against the door.*)

JOHNNY'S FATHER Don't be afraid, Johnny.

JOHNNY He can't get in, can he, Pa?

JOHNNY'S FATHER I don't think so.

[*The* GRANDMOTHER, *the* FATHER *and the* SON *stand together in the bare room, defying the world. There is a long pause, full of mingling of awful fear and furious defiance. After half a minute the silence is broken. It is a solo on the bugle: "My Heart's in the Highlands." The sun comes out.*]

JOHNNY (*Shouting.*) It's Mr. MacGregor.

JOHNNY'S FATHER (*Running to the window, lifting it, and shouting out to

MacGREGOR.) Welcome, Mr. MacGregor. Johnny, rearrange the furniture. (JOHNNY'S FATHER *returns to the barricade and helps* JOHNNY *and his* GRANDMOTHER *rearrange the furniture. At last everything is out of the way.* JOHNNY'S FATHER *swings open the door.* JASPER MacGREGOR, *still playing the solo, preceded by the dog, which is a very small street dog, comes in. The dog runs around playfully, all excited.* MacGREGOR'S *eyes are full of grief and joy.* JOHNNY *begins making trips to the kitchen, returning with the fruit, on a plate, and a pitcher of water.* MacGREGOR *finishes the solo. There is a moment when everybody stands stockstill, including the dog.* JOHNNY *offers* MacGREGOR *the pitcher of water.*)

MacGREGOR (*Weary.*) Not this time, Johnny.

JOHNNY'S FATHER Welcome, my friend.

MacGREGOR I've run away. They're after me now, but I won't go back. They stole my bugle. They tried to keep me in bed. They said I was sick. I'm not sick; I'm old. I know my days on earth are numbered. I want them to be with you. Don't let them take me back.

JOHNNY'S FATHER I won't. (*He draws out a chair for the old man.*) Please sit down. (*They all sit down.* MacGREGOR *looks around at everybody.*)

MacGREGOR It's good to see you again.

JOHNNY Is your heart still in the highlands?

MacGREGOR (*Nodding.*) In the highlands, son.

JOHNNY'S FATHER (*Angry.*) *Johnny.*

JOHNNY (*Sore, too.*) What?

JOHNNY'S FATHER Shut up.

JOHNNY Why?

JOHNNY'S FATHER *Why?* What do you get so dumb for every once in a while? Can't you see Mr. MacGregor is weary?

JOHNNY (*To* MacGREGOR.) Are you?

MacGREGOR (*Nods.*) But where's your mother, son?

JOHNNY She's dead.

MacGREGOR (*Almost to himself.*) Not dead, Johnny. (*He shakes his head.*) In the highlands.

JOHNNY'S GRANDMOTHER (*To his father.*) What's he saying?

JOHNNY'S FATHER (*Shaking his head.*) Nothing. (*To* MacGREGOR.) Won't you eat?

MacGREGOR (*Looking at the plate.*) One grape. No more. (*He plucks a grape off a bunch, puts it in his mouth. Suddenly turns, startled.*) Are they coming?

JOHNNY'S FATHER Don't be afraid, my friend. Lie down and rest. (JOHNNY'S FATHER *takes the* OLD MAN *to the couch. The* OLD MAN *stretches out, face up.* JOHNNY'S FATHER *returns to the table. Nobody is eating. The* OLD MAN *jumps up suddenly. It's nothing again. He gets up and returns to the table.*)

MACGREGOR You won't let them take me back, will you?

JOHNNY'S FATHER No. (*He breaks open a pomegranate and hands* MACGREGOR *half.*) Try to eat something.

MACGREGOR Thank you, my friend. (*He eats some of the pomegranate. There's a knock on the door,* MACGREGOR *leaps to his feet, furiously.*)

MACGREGOR (*Roaring.*) You'll not take me back. I warn you. I'll fall down and die. I belong here, with these people.

JOHNNY'S FATHER (*Scared.*) Shall we open the door?

JOHNNY (*Also scared.*) Shall we?

MACGREGOR (*Powerfully.*) Of course we'll open the door. (*He goes to the door, opens it. It is* RUFE APLEY, *the carpenter, who is a little shaken up by* MACGREGOR'S *fury.*)

RUFE APLEY Hello, Mr. MacGregor.

JOHNNY Who is it?

RUFE APLEY It's Rufe Apley.

MACGREGOR How do you do, Rufe?

JOHNNY'S FATHER (*At the door.*) Come in, Rufe. (RUFE *comes in. He has a loaf of bread, a sausage and two eggs in his hands.*)

RUFE I was sitting home doing nothing when I heard that song again. I was sure it was Mr. MacGregor.

MACGREGOR I'm delighted you remembered.

RUFE Nobody could ever forget that song, Mr. MacGregor. I brought these few things.

MACGREGOR (*Taking them and putting them on the table.*) Thank you, my friend, thank you.

[*There is another knock at the door. It is* SAM WALLACE; *he is a lineman, in full regalia: overalls, tools hanging all over him, tape, straps around his calves, spikes, everything. He has cheese and tomatoes and radishes with him.*]

WALLACE I *knew* it was Mr. MacGregor. I said to myself, I'll go over with a few things to eat.

MACGREGOR This is indeed a pleasant surprise.

RUFE (*Obviously trying hard to say something.*) Ah, Mr. MacGregor?

MACGREGOR Yes, my friend? Speak up. I'm a plain man, no different in any way from yourself.

RUFE My wife's sister and her family are outside. I know they'd like to hear you play again. There are some other people.

MACGREGOR (*Flattered.*) Of course I'll play. I'm over eighty and not long for this world. Before I go I'd like to become a part of you who shall live after I am dead. Are there children out there too?

RUFE Seven. My wife's sister's kids.

[*Three or four neighbors come in, bringing food.* MACGREGOR *takes up his bugle. Everybody follows him out of the room to the porch, except* JOHNNY'S FATHER. MACGREGOR *begins to play the solo again. This time he's too old and weak to really play, but he finishes the solo as well as he is able to.* JOHNNY'S FATHER

paces about the room, smiling, frowning, loving the place. The door to the kitchen opens quietly and ESTHER KOSAK *stands in the doorway.* JOHNNY'S FATHER *turns and sees her. She is no longer crying. She has something clutched in her fist.*]

JOHNNY'S FATHER (*Quietly.*) Hello, Esther.

ESTHER Where's Johnny?

JOHNNY'S FATHER I'll go get him. (*He goes out on the porch. The* GIRL *stands alone in terrible sadness and loneliness. After a moment* JOHNNY *comes rushing in, all excited, but calms down quickly when he begins to feel the mood of the girl.*)

JOHNNY Hello, Esther.

ESTHER Hello, Johnny.

JOHNNY What's the matter?

ESTHER My father read me the poems.

JOHNNY What?

ESTHER (*Holding out her hand.*) Here. This is all I've got. (JOHNNY *takes a handful of coins.*) I've been saving up for Christmas. (*She begins to cry, turns, and runs out of the house.*)

JOHNNY (*Deeply touched and furious, sensing something profound and beautiful and terrible.*) Holy Moses. (*His face takes on boyhood's tragic expression of grief, and he begins to cry. He throws the coins against the wall and falls down, sobbing.*) Who the hell wants that stuff? (JOHNNY'S FATHER *comes back.*)

JOHNNY'S FATHER Johnny. (*Going closer.*) Johnny?

JOHNNY (*Sobbing and angry.*) She brought me money.

JOHNNY'S FATHER It's no use crying, Johnny.

JOHNNY (*Jumping up.*) Who's crying? (*He cries harder than ever.*)

JOHNNY'S FATHER Go wash your face. It's nothing.

JOHNNY (*Going.*) Something's wrong somewhere.

[MACGREGOR *finishes the solo, the people are silent with awe and the knowledge that something is wrong.* MACGREGOR'S VOICE *is heard for a moment in a speech.*]

MACGREGOR (*Wearily.*) The years, my friends. I have walked to the end of them. I'm sorry I can no longer play for you. Thank you. Thank you.

[JOHNNY'S FATHER *walks back and forth in the room. He sits down at the table and looks at the food.* MACGREGOR *and* JOHNNY'S GRANDMOTHER *return and sit at the table. The dog lies down in a corner.*]

MACGREGOR (*He lifts the water pitcher, drinks a little.*) They wouldn't let me play. (*He drinks a little more.*) They stole my bugle. (*He drinks a little more.*) They said I was sick. (*He drinks a little more.*) I'm strong as a bull. If they come to take me back, I shall pretend that I am dying. I shall play the death scene from "King Lear." I shall play *all* the death scenes.

[JOHNNY *returns solemnly. They are all at the table. Nobody can eat but the* OLD LADY. *There is a long silence. The* OLD LADY *stops eating.*]

JOHNNY'S GRANDMOTHER What's the matter? Why this terrible gloom? (MACGREGOR *rises.*)

MACGREGOR (*Reciting, remembering lines from Shakespeare, and inventing a few of his own.*)[20] Blow, winds, and crack your cheeks! Rage! blow! You cataracts and hurricanes, spout till you have drenched our steeples, drowned the cocks! You sulphurous and thought-executing fires, singe my white head! Humble thy belly-full, spit fire, spout rain! I never gave you kingdom, call'd you children. Here I stand, your slave, a poor infirm, weak and despised old man. To be or not to be . . . (*Tragically.*) To be—to be—What? A fool? A man mocked by destiny? Turned away from home and fire and love? I am a man more sinned against than sinning. Arms! Arms! Sword! Fire! Corruption in the place! The little dogs and all, Tray, Blanche, Sweetheart. See? They bark at me.

[20] The speech that follows, as the stage directions say, consists of lines from Shakespeare—*King Lear* and *Hamlet*—and lines of MacGregor's own. Most of them are from *King Lear*. MacGregor senses that he (like Lear) is a very old man about to die.

O, that way madness lies—no more of that—let me shun that. My wits begin to turn. (JOHNNY *goes to him and kneels.*) Come on, my boy, how dost my boy? Art cold? Let me alone! Wilt break my heart? And my poor fool is hang'd. No, no, no life! Why should a dog, a horse, a rat have life and thou no life at all? Thou'llt come no more, never, never, never, never! Pray you undo this button—thank you, sir— (*Holds the bugle before him.*) Do you see this? Look on her. Look. Look, there, look there!!

[*While* MACGREGOR *is acting* JOHNNY *returns to the coins on the floor and picks them up one by one and looks at them. The room is in absolute silence. A horse and wagon in the street is heard; then steps on the front porch; then a knock at the door.* JOHNNY'S FATHER *goes to the door. It is* PHILIP CARMICHAEL *and two guards from the Old People's Home. The guards stand at attention at the door.*]

CARMICHAEL We heard him playing. He's very sick. We've come to take him back.

JOHNNY'S FATHER Please come in. (*He enters. To* MACGREGOR.) Mr. MacGregor. (*There is no answer.*)

JOHNNY'S FATHER (*Louder.*) Mr. MacGregor. (*Goes closer.*) Mr. MacGregor, Mr. Mac—

[CARMICHAEL *hurries over to* MACGREGOR *and examines him.*]

CARMICHAEL He's dead.

JOHNNY No, he isn't. He was acting.

JOHNNY'S FATHER By God, he *was* the greatest Shakespearean actor of our day.

CARMICHAEL I'm sorry this had to happen here.

JOHNNY'S FATHER Why not? Why not here? This is where he wanted it to be.

JOHNNY He was only acting, Pa. He isn't dead. (*He goes to* MACGREGOR.) Are you, Mr. MacGregor? (*There is no answer, of course.*)

CARMICHAEL We'll take him back.

JOHNNY'S FATHER Here's his bugle. Keep it with him. (JOHNNY'S FATHER *lifts* MACGREGOR *and carries him out. The guards carry him up the street. The light of the afternoon sun increases to the same intensity as at the beginning of the play. The horse and wagon goes off. There is a moment of strange silence, and the faint far-away sound of the bugle solo. A knock at the door.* JOHNNY'S FATHER *opens the door. It's the young* HUSBAND *and* WIFE. *The* BABY *is crying. They come in.*)

THE WIFE The kid is tired and sleepy.

JOHNNY'S FATHER The house is ready. (*To* JOHNNY.) Get your stuff. (*To the* OLD LADY, *in Armenian.*) We're going. (*He gets a straw suitcase from under the couch and throws his poems, books, envelopes, one loaf of bread, and a few of the other items of food into it. The* OLD LADY *puts a shawl around her head and shoulders.* JOHNNY *leaves all his junk; takes only a handful of coins. The* BABY *stops crying. The dog follows* JOHNNY *around. The music increases in intensity.*)

THE HUSBAND Thank you very much.

THE WIFE Have you some place to go?

JOHNNY'S FATHER Yes we have. Good-by.

THE HUSBAND AND WIFE Good-by. (*They go out of the house to the street.*)

JOHNNY Where the hell do we think we're going, Pa?

JOHNNY'S FATHER Never mind, Johnny. You just follow me.

JOHNNY I'm not mentioning any names, Pa, but something's wrong somewhere.

[*The music grows louder. They walk up the street.*]

Comprehension

1. What does Johnny do when he sees the paperboy? When he sees Mr. MacGregor? What do the actions tell the audience about his character?
2. What favor does Mr. MacGregor ask of Johnny? Why does Johnny delay so long in granting that favor? What incident finally moves him to action?
3. What kind of person is Johnny's father? In his own eyes? In the eyes of Mr. Kosak, the grocer? In the eyes of Mr. MacGregor?
4. Why does Johnny object at first to going to the grocery store for food? What finally persuades him to go?
5. What tactics does Johnny use on Mr. Kosak? With what success?
6. Why is Mr. MacGregor's attention drawn to the jars and cans on the cupboard shelves? What do they contain? What kind of bargain does Mr. MacGregor try to make with Johnny in exchange for their contents?
7. Who finally persuades Mr. MacGregor to play "Drink to Me Only with Thine Eyes" on his bugle for Johnny? What unexpected tribute does Mr. MacGregor receive for his playing?
8. How does Johnny's father introduce Mr. MacGregor to the neighbors? What glimpse into his past does Mr. MacGregor give them?
9. What bargain does Mr. MacGregor make with the neighbors who have gathered in front of the house to hear him play the bugle? How do they react to his song?
10. Where is Mr. MacGregor really from? Under what circumstances does it become known? How does Mr. Carmichael persuade Mr. MacGregor to return with him? In what mood does he part from his new friends—Johnny, Johnny's father, and the grandmother?
11. What do Johnny and the newsboy talk about? What does the

newsboy say he will be when he grows up? What does Johnny say he will be?

12. What language does Johnny's grandmother speak to him? What does she say when she finds out that Mr. MacGregor has returned to the Old People's Home?
13. How does Johnny's father react when he learns that *The Atlantic Monthly* has rejected his poems? How does Johnny react? What does this incident show about the relationship between father and son?
14. Why does Johnny's father leave the furniture in the house?
15. What does Johnny's father give to Mr. Kosak? How does Mr. Kosak react to this gift?
16. Where does Johnny get the grapes? What does Johnny's father think about taking the grapes—does he regard it as stealing? What do they do when they think the farmer is coming?
17. What reasons does Mr. MacGregor give for running away from the Old People's Home? What is his real purpose in returning to the house on San Benito Avenue?
18. What does Esther Kosak give Johnny as a parting gift? What does he do with the gift first? Finally?
19. What is Mr. MacGregor's final speech about?
20. What does Carmichael say when he learns that Mr. MacGregor is dead? What is the reply of Johnny's father? What does the reply mean?

Toward Interpretation

1. Mr. MacGregor comes on stage playing "My Heart's in the Highlands." The words to this song were written by the famous Scottish poet Robert Burns. Here are the four lines of the chorus:

   My heart's in the Highlands, my heart is not here,
   My heart's in the Highlands, a-chasing[1] the deer,
   A-chasing the wild deer and following the roe[2]—
   My heart's in the Highlands, wherever I go!

   How would you describe the theme of this song? What could "the Highlands" be a symbol of? How does Saroyan make use of this theme in the play?
2. Some playwrights are very specific about the details of the set, including the lighting. Discuss Saroyan's use of the sun. How does Johnny feel about the sun? How does his father feel about it? When does the sun come out again?

[1] *a-chasing:* an archaic and dialectal present participle form. Standard English would of course use "chasing."
[2] *roe:* a kind of deer.

3. Saroyan is a master at characterization through gesture and movement. What insights into the characters do the following actions provide:

   "Mr. Kosak swings at a fly, misses, swings again, misses and, objecting to the world in this manner, he chases the fly all round the store, swinging with all his might."

   Johhny and the newsboy bounce an old tennis ball back and forth as they talk about their dead parents.

   While Johnny and his father talk about Mr. MacGregor, Johnny "has been going through various kinds of acrobatics, walking on the porch railing, leaping down, turning somersaults, standing on his head, and so forth. Some of his questions have been asked while he has been standing on his head."

   Johnny's father kicks the rejected poems off the steps of the porch to the ground, takes up the newspaper, and comments furiously on the war and destruction.

4. As the introduction points out, Saroyan's dialogue may seem "wayward and even a little silly, for the characters communicate more through feelings than ideas. They respond not to what is said but to what is intended." The conversation between Johnny and Mr. MacGregor at the beginning of the play is an excellent example of this kind of "wayward" dialogue. What do Johnny and Mr. MacGregor talk about? What is the real purpose of the conversation?

WHITMAN

Section Four
Poetry

Children respond naturally to the delights of poetry in its simpler forms, to the music of its rhythm and rhyme. But the mature and sensitive reader goes far beyond mere pleasure in the music of the words, for poetry increases our awareness of the world about us and gives us new insights. As Robert Frost has said, "Poetry begins in delight and ends in wisdom."

Because poems communicate emotional experiences in patterned language, the meaning of a poem is much more than the meaning to be derived from a simple prose summary. In a poem, the arrangement of words, the sound and the movement, the imagery and the figurative language all combine to convey an intensity of feeling that cannot ordinarily be achieved in prose. The reading of a poem is essentially an emotional experience: the experience of sharing another's feelings, as in the poems of Emily Dickinson or A. E. Housman; the experience of looking with a kind of awe upon the strange ironies of life, as in the poems of Hardy; the experience of recognizing in commonplace facts a hidden significance, as in the poems of Frost.

Our chief delight in reading poetry comes from our response to its music. In the poems that follow you will find many metrical patterns represented, from the conventional iambic feet in Housman to the free verse of Walt Whitman. The iambic foot, which consists of a syllable with weak stress followed by a syllable with heavy stress, is the most common rhythm in English poetry. A line from Frost will illustrate iambic feet:

> Whŏse wóods / thĕse áre / Ĭ thínk / Ĭ knów

The music of poetry comes not only from its meter, but also from the regular recurrence of identical or similar sounds. In many of the poems that follow you will find rhyming words which occur most often at the ends of lines and give a pattern to the poem. Recognizing rhyme can be an important aid in reading aloud effectively.

Rhyme schemes are described with letters of the alphabet. The word at the end of the first line and all words that rhyme with it are *a*. The subsequent rhymes are labeled *b*, *c*, *d*, etc. Notice, for example, the rhyme scheme in the first stanza of Frost's "Stopping by Woods on a Snowy Evening":

Whose woods these are I think I know.	*a*
His house is in the village though;	*a*
He will not see me stopping here	*b*
To watch his woods fill up with snow.	*a*

The iambic foot and the simple rhyme scheme mentioned above represent only two of the great number of musical effects to be found in poetry. Some poets, like Walt Whitman, have found conventional poetic meter and conventional rhyme schemes too restricting. In Whitman's free verse you will find such devices as repetition and parallel phrasing replacing meter and rhyme. The effects are none the less musical, as you can see in this stanza from "A Noiseless Patient Spider":

> A noiseless patient spider,
> I mark'd where on a little promontory it stood isolated,
> Mark'd how to explore the vacant vast surrounding,
> It launched forth filament, filament, filament, out of itself,
> Ever unreeling them, ever tirelessly speeding them.

Words, of course, are the poet's tools. With words he fashions the poem's imagery—the re-creation of sense experience, the rich evocation of things seen and heard, of tastes and smells and sensations of touch. But the poet must use words with great care, for they are subtle and slippery. For one thing, their meaning is never stable. As T. S. Eliot said, words

Slip, slide, perish
Decay with imprecision, will not stay in place,
Will not stay still.

For another thing, words have many meanings. They have literal meanings that can be found in a dictionary, and they have connotative or suggestive meanings as well. *Home* means more than "a house where a person lives." *Mother* means more than "female parent." *Country* means more than "a geographical area or a political organization."

Much of the suggestive power of words comes from figures of speech, of which there are many kinds. The most important of these are *comparisons*—either direct or implied. Frost, for example, in "Mending Wall" says this of the neighbor who insists that the stone wall must be built:

I see him there
Bringing a stone grasped firmly by the top
In each hand, like an old-stone savage armed.
He moves in darkness as it seems to me,
Not of woods only and the shade of trees.
He will not go behind his father's saying. . . .

The neighbor, like a savage in the Stone Age who is incapable of abstract reasoning, moves in darkness—a darkness that is physical ("woods only and the shade of trees") and a darkness that is figurative (mental darkness, without the light of reason). Another important figure of speech—the *symbol*—is also well illustrated in this poem. A symbol is a word or expression that represents something else, that stands for more than what in actuality it is. The wall in Frost's poem comes to be more than a wall—it becomes a symbol of the distrust and misunderstanding between friends and neighbors and even between nations. The poet's use of comparisons, symbols, and other figures of speech is an essential part of his craft.

The poems that follow will provide a good introduction to seven distinguished poets in contemporary English—four American, two English, and one Irish. They will not always be easy to interpret. Poems seldom are, even in one's own language; but they are especially difficult in another language. Their power over the imagination depends in large measure on the reader's familiarity with the words, which allows him to appreciate their sounds and rhythms, their suggestive power, their aptness, and their freshness. You will have to read carefully if you are to grasp the patterns of sound, the figurative language, and the full and precise meanings. Only then will you find the experience of reading poetry in English a valuable one.

Poems
by Robert Frost

Robert Frost (1875–1963) lived in the northeastern part of the United States, known as New England. It is a land of pleasant towns and lovely landscape, rich in history and legend. It is the original land of the Yankees—a name associated with the sturdy traits that the sparse, stony acres are supposed to have fostered. Robert Frost was a spokesman for that land, having spent most of his life on two farms in the state of New Hampshire.

He lived the life he wrote about. "After Apple-picking" and "Mending Wall" are poetic records of actual experiences, as is "Stopping by Woods on a Snowy Evening." The stubborn neighbor in "Mending Wall" and the lonely hired man who came home to die in "The Death of the Hired Man" are people he knew. In his own life he stood at a crossroads like that described in "The Road Not Taken," wondering whether to give himself completely to the writing of poetry or to farming. And the road he took "made all the difference" (as the poem says) in a long and full life.

Oddly enough, Frost was recognized first in England, not America. In the early 1900s, interest in poetry ran high in London and the poetry bookshops gave substantial encouragement to struggling young writers. After selling his farm, which his grandfather had bought him in the hope that he would settle down, he set sail with his family for England. Within a short time he published his first book of poems. He won almost immediate recognition for the simple beauty of his verse; his sensitive, observing spirit; his quick sympathies and gentle understanding—all revealed in simple language that has the tang and twist of Yankee speech. Frost was one of the first American poets of international stature to bring the rhythms of colloquial speech into poetry. Later his books were also published in America, and he returned to another farm in his beloved New Hampshire, where he lived many years.

As you read the poems that follow, look for the universal thoughts and feelings which underlie the picture so vividly sketched. Frost's language is deceptively simple. His poems say more than they seem to.

Stopping by Woods on a Snowy Evening

Whose woods these are I think I know.
His house is in the village though;
He will not see me stopping here
To watch his woods fill up with snow.

My little horse must think it queer 5
To stop without a farmhouse near
Between the woods and frozen lake
The darkest evening of the year.

He gives his harness bells a shake
To ask if there is some mistake. 10
The only other sound's the sweep
Of easy wind and downy flake.

The woods are lovely, dark and deep.
But I have promises to keep,
And miles to go before I sleep, 15
And miles to go before I sleep.

The Road Not Taken

Two roads diverged in a yellow wood,
And sorry I could not travel both
And be one traveler, long I stood
And looked down one as far as I could
To where it bent in the undergrowth; 5

Then took the other, as just as fair,
And having perhaps the better claim,
Because it was grassy and wanted wear;
Though as for that the passing there
Had worn them really about the same, 10

And both that morning equally lay
In leaves no step had trodden black.
Oh, I kept the first for another day!
Yet knowing how way leads on to way,
I doubted if I should ever come back. 15

I shall be telling this with a sigh
Somewhere ages and ages hence:
Two roads diverged in a wood, and I—
I took the one less traveled by,
And that has made all the difference. 20

After Apple-picking

My long two-pointed ladder's sticking through a tree
Toward heaven still,
And there's a barrel that I didn't fill
Besides it, and there may be two or three
Apples I didn't pick upon some bough. 5
But I am done with apple-picking now.
Essence of winter sleep is on the night,
The scent of apples: I am drowsing off.
I cannot rub the strangeness from my sight
I got from looking through a pane of glass[1] 10
I skimmed this morning from the drinking trough
And held against the world of hoary grass.
It melted, and I let it fall and break.
But I was well
Upon my way to sleep before it fell, 15
And I could tell
What form my dreaming was about to take.
Magnified apples appear and disappear
Stem end and blossom end,
And every fleck of russet showing clear. 20
My instep arch not only keeps the ache,
It keeps the pressure of a ladder-round.
I feel the ladder sway as the boughs bend.
And I keep hearing from the cellar bin

[1] The thin sheet of ice over the drinking trough looked like a pane of glass.

The rumbling sound 25
Of load on load of apples coming in.
For I have had too much
Of apple-picking: I am overtired
Of the great harvest I myself desired.
There were ten thousand thousand fruit to touch, 30
Cherish in hand, lift down, and not let fall.
For all
That struck the earth,
No matter if not bruised or spiked with stubble,[2]
Went surely to the cider-apple heap[3] 35
As of no worth.
One can see what will trouble
This sleep of mine, whatever sleep it is.
Were he not gone,
The woodchuck could say whether it's like his 40
Long sleep,[4] as I describe its coming on,
Or just some human sleep.

Mending Wall

Something there is that doesn't love a wall,
That sends the frozen-ground-swell[1] under it,
And spills the upper boulders in the sun;
And makes gaps even two can pass abreast.
The work of hunters is another thing: 5
I have come after them and made repair
Where they have left not one stone on a stone,
But they would have the rabbit out of hiding,
To please the yelping dogs. The gaps I mean,
No one has seen them made or heard them made, 10
But at spring mending-time we find them there.
I let my neighbour know beyond the hill;
And on a day we meet to walk the line
And set the wall between us once again.
We keep the wall between us as we go. 15
To each the boulders that have fallen to each.
And some are loaves and some so nearly balls
We have to use a spell to make them balance:

[2] *spiked with stubble:* pierced or cut (spiked) by the short stems standing after grain has been cut (stubble).
[3] *cider-apple heap:* a pile of apples set aside for making cider, a drink made of apple juice.
[4] The woodchuck is a hibernating animal; that is, it sleeps through the winter.

[1] *frozen-ground-swell:* Freezing expands the damp earth. It shoves the earth up in a "ground-swell," which causes the stone wall to crumble.

'Stay where you are until our backs are turned!'
We wear our fingers rough with handling them. 20
Oh, just another kind of out-door game,
One on a side. It comes to little more:
There where it is we do not need the wall:
He is all pine and I am apple orchard.[2]
My apple trees will never get across 25
And eat the cones under his pines, I tell him.
He only says, 'Good fences make good neighbours.'
Spring is the mischief in me, and I wonder
If I could put a notion in his head:
'*Why* do they make *good* neighbours? Isn't it 30
Where there are cows? But here there are no cows.
Before I built a wall I'd ask to know
What I was walling in or walling out,
And to whom I was like to give offence.
Something there is that doesn't love a wall, 35
That wants it down.' I could say 'Elves' to him,[3]
But it's not elves exactly, and I'd rather
He said it for himself. I see him there
Bringing a stone grasped firmly by the top
In each hand, like an old-stone savage armed. 40
He moves in darkness as it seems to me,
Not of woods only and the shade of trees.
He will not go behind his father's saying,
And he likes having thought of it so well
He says again, 'Good fences make good neighbours.' 45

The Death of the Hired Man

Mary sat musing on the lamp-flame at the table
Waiting for Warren. When she heard his step,
She ran on tip-toe down the darkened passage
To meet him in the doorway with the news
And put him on his guard. "Silas is back." 5
She pushed him outward with her through the door
And shut it after her. "Be kind," she said.
She took the market things from Warren's arms
And set them on the porch, then drew him down
To sit beside her on the wooden steps. 10

"When was I ever anything but kind to him?
But I'll not have the fellow back," he said.

[2] The neighbor has pine trees on his land; the poet raises apple trees.
[3] *I could say 'Elves' to him:* The speaker could tell his neighbor the fairies knocked down the wall.

"I told him so last haying, didn't I?
'If he left then,' I said, 'that ended it.'
What good is he? Who else will harbour him 15
At his age for the little he can do?
What help he is there's no depending on.
Off he goes always when I need him most.
'He thinks he ought to earn a little pay,
Enough at least to buy tobacco with, 20
So he won't have to beg and be beholden.'[1]
'All right,' I say, 'I can't afford to pay
Any fixed wages, though I wish I could.'
'Someone else can.' 'Then someone else will have to.'
I shouldn't mind his bettering himself 25
If that was what it was. You can be certain,
When he begins like that, there's someone at him
Trying to coax him off with pocket-money,—
In haying time, when any help is scarce.
In winter he comes back to us. I'm done." 30

"Sh! not so loud: he'll hear you," Mary said.

"I want him to: he'll have to soon or late."

"He's worn out. He's asleep beside the stove.
When I came up from Rowe's I found him here,
Huddled against the barn-door fast asleep, 35
A miserable sight, and frightening, too—
You needn't smile—I didn't recognize him—
I wasn't looking for him—and he's changed.
Wait till you see."

"Where did you say he'd been?"

"He didn't say. I dragged him to the house, 40
And gave him tea and tried to make him smoke.
I tried to make him talk about his travels.
Nothing would do: he just kept nodding off."

"What did he say? Did he say anything?"

"But little."

"Anything? Mary, confess 45
He said he'd come to ditch the meadow[2] for me."

[1] *be beholden:* be in debt to someone. That is, Silas doesn't want to ask for favors; he wants to earn whatever he gets.
[2] *to ditch the meadow:* to drain the water from the meadow by digging a ditch (or channel) around it into which the water would flow.

"Warren!"

"But did he? I just want to know."

"Of course he did. What would you have him say?
Surely you wouldn't grudge the poor old man
Some humble way to save his self-respect. 50
He added, if you really care to know,
He meant to clear the upper pasture, too.
That sounds like something you have heard before?
Warren, I wish you could have heard the way
He jumbled everything. I stopped to look 55
Two or three times—he made me feel so queer—
To see if he was talking in his sleep.
He ran on[3] Harold Wilson—you remember—
The boy you had in haying four years since.
He's finished school, and teaching in his college. 60
Silas declares you'll have to get him back.
He says they two will make a team for work:
Between them they will lay this farm as smooth!
The way he mixed that in with other things.
He thinks young Wilson a likely lad, though daft 65
On education—you know how they fought
All through July under the blazing sun,
Silas up on the cart to build the load,
Harold along beside to pitch it on."

"Yes, I took care to keep well out of earshot." 70

"Well, those days trouble Silas like a dream.
You wouldn't think they would. How some things linger!
Harold's young college boy's assurance piqued him.
After so many years he still keeps finding
Good arguments he sees he might have used. 75
I sympathize. I know just how it feels
To think of the right thing to say too late.
Harold's associated in his mind with Latin.
He asked me what I thought of Harold's saying
He studied Latin like the violin 80
Because he liked it—that an argument!
He said he couldn't make the boy believe
He could find water with a hazel prong—[4]
Which showed how much good school had ever done him.
He wanted to go over that. But most of all 85

[3] *ran on:* talked continuously about.

[4] *hazel prong:* a forked branch of hazel wood. Some people think it has the power, if used properly, to locate underground water.

He thinks if he could have another chance
To teach him how to build a load of hay—"

"I know, that's Silas' one accomplishment.
He bundles every forkful in its place,
And tags and numbers it for future reference,[5] 90
So he can find and easily dislodge it
In the unloading. Silas does that well.
He takes it out in bunches like big birds' nests.
You never see him standing on the hay
He's trying to lift, straining to lift himself." 95

"He thinks if he could teach him that, he'd be
Some good perhaps to someone in the world.
He hates to see a boy the fool of books.
Poor Silas, so concerned for other folk,
And nothing to look backward to with pride, 100
And nothing to look forward to with hope,
So now and never any different."

Part of a moon was falling down the west,
Dragging the whole sky with it to the hills.
Its light poured softly in her lap. She saw it 105
And spread her apron to it. She put out her hand
Among the harp-like morning-glory strings,[6]
Taut with the dew from garden bed to eaves,
As if she played unheard some tenderness
That wrought on him beside her in the night. 110
"Warren," she said, "he has come home to die:
You needn't be afraid he'll leave you this time."

"Home," he mocked gently.

"Yes, what else but home?
It all depends on what you mean by home.
Of course he's nothing to us, any more 115
Than was the hound that came a stranger to us
Out of the woods, worn out upon the trail."

"Home is the place where, when you have to go there,
They have to take you in."

"I should have called it
Something you somehow haven't to deserve."[7] 120

[5] *tags and numbers it for future reference:* Silas remembers each forkful of hay he places on the wagon, which enables him to unload the hay efficiently.

[6] *harp-like morning-glory strings:* The morning-glory is a flowering vine which may climb on strings stretched like those of a harp.

Warren leaned out and took a step or two,
Picked up a little stick, and brought it back
And broke it in his hand and tossed it by.
"Silas has better claim on us you think
Than on his brother? Thirteen little miles 125
As the road winds would bring him to his door.
Silas has walked that far no doubt to-day.
Why didn't he go there? His brother's rich.
A somebody—director in the bank."

"He never told us that."

"We know it though." 130

"I think his brother ought to help, of course.
I'll see to that if there is need. He ought of right
To take him in, and might be willing to—
He may be better than appearances.
But have some pity on Silas. Do you think 135
If he had any pride in claiming kin
Or anything he looked for from his brother,
He'd keep so still about him all this time?

"I wonder what's between them."

"I can tell you.
Silas is what he is—we wouldn't mind him— 140
But just the kind that kinsfolk can't abide.
He never did a thing so very bad.
He don't know why he isn't quite as good
As anybody. Worthless though he is,
He won't be made ashamed to please his brother." 145

"*I* can't think Si ever hurt anyone."

"No, but he hurt my heart the way he lay.
And rolled his old head on that sharp-edged chair-back.
He wouldn't let me put him on the lounge.
You must go in and see what you can do. 150
I made the bed up for him there to-night.
You'll be surprised at him—how much he's broken.
His working days are done; I'm sure of it."

"I'd not be in a hurry to say that."

"I haven't been. Go, look, see for yourself. 155
But, Warren, please remember how it is:

[7] *Something you somehow haven't to deserve:* something you do not have to deserve but should have without question.

He's come to help you ditch the meadow.
He has a plan. You mustn't laugh at him.
He may not speak of it, and then he may.
I'll sit and see if that small sailing cloud 160
Will hit or miss the moon."

It hit the moon.
Then there were three there, making a dim row,
The moon, the little silver cloud, and she.
Warren returned—too soon, it seemed to her,
Slipped to her side, caught up her hand and waited. 165

"Warren?" she questioned.

"Dead," was all he answered.

Tree at My Window

Tree at my window, window tree,
My sash is lowered when night comes on;
But let there never be curtain drawn
Between you and me.

Vague dream-head lifted out of the ground, 5
And thing next most diffuse to cloud,
Not all your light tongues talking aloud
Could be profound.

But tree, I have seen you taken and tossed,
And if you have seen me when I slept, 10
You have seen me when I was taken and swept
And all but lost.

That day she put our heads together,
Fate had her imagination about her,
Your head so much concerned with outer, 15
Mine with inner, weather.

Fire and Ice

Some say the world will end in fire,
Some say in ice.
From what I've tasted of desire
I hold with those who favor fire
But if it had to perish twice, 5
I think I know enough of hate
To say that for destruction ice
Is also great
And would suffice.

Bravado

Have I not walked without an upward look
Of caution under stars that very well
Might not have missed me when they shot and fell?
It was a risk I had to take—and took.

Stopping by Woods on a Snowy Evening

Comprehension

1. Why does the speaker stop by the woods?
2. Why must the little horse think it strange for him to stop?
3. Why does the horse shake his harness bells?
4. What other sound is there besides the shaking of the bells?
5. Why does the speaker leave?

Toward Interpretation

1. Can you think of any reason why the last line is repeated? What might "miles to go" stand for? What larger meaning might be given to "before I sleep"?

The Road Not Taken

Comprehension

1. What was the speaker sorry about?
2. Why did he choose the "other" road?
3. Did the speaker doubt that he could ever come back to take the other road?
4. Which road did the speaker take? Did his choice make a difference?

Toward Interpretation

1. What makes the speaker doubt that he will come back and take the other road?
2. What do you think the speaker means by "road"?
3. From what you know of the poet himself (see the introduction on page 180), what difference do you think his choice of roads led to? If he had chosen the other road, what might that have led to?

After Apple-picking

Comprehension

1. Did the speaker pick all the apples?
2. Has the weather gotten colder? How do you know?
3. The speaker anticipates the dreams he will have. What does he expect to see in his dreams? Feel? Hear?
4. Is the speaker tired of apple-picking?
5. What happened to the apples that fell to the ground?
6. The speaker wonders if his "sleep" might be like that of a hibernating animal. Which animal is it?

Toward Interpretation

1. By what signs in the orchard are you aware that the apple-picking has been going on?
2. What sensation does the speaker feel just before dozing off after a day of apple-picking?
3. What details does he remember about the scene at the drinking trough that morning?
4. What larger meaning about life do you read into the poem? Consider especially lines 27–29 and 40–41.

Mending Wall

Comprehension

1. What causes the ground to swell and the boulders to fall over?
2. What have hunters done to the wall?
3. Who helps the speaker put the boulders in place every spring?
4. How do they share the labor?
5. Do all the boulders stay easily in place?
6. Why isn't the wall really needed?
7. What does the neighbor say when the speaker tells him that the wall is unnecessary?
8. What does the speaker say he would like to know before building a wall?
9. Does the speaker approve of walls?

Toward Interpretation

1. What does the speaker mean when he says that the neighbor "will not go behind his father's saying"?

2. What do you think is meant by "good neighbors"? "Good" in what respect?
3. What universal trait in human beings is the speaker referring to when he says, "Something there is that doesn't love a wall"? What is that something?

The Death of the Hired Man

Comprehension

1. What did Mary tell Warren when she met him at the doorway?
2. Does Warren want Silas back?
3. Why does Warren object to Silas?
4. Has Silas been reliable?
5. Where did Mary find Silas?
6. How did he look?
7. What did she do for Silas?
8. What did Silas tell Mary he was going to do?
9. Does Mary believe he will do it?
10. Who did Silas talk about? Did he speak coherently—that is, did he make sense when he spoke? What line gives you the answer?
11. Why did Harold study Latin?
12. What would Silas like to teach Harold?
13. What does Warren say is "Silas' one accomplishment"?
14. Why does Mary say Silas has come "home"?
15. What two definitions are given of "home"?
16. Where does Warren say Silas should have gone for help? Why does Mary say he didn't go there?
17. What does Mary tell Warren he mustn't do when he goes to talk with Silas?
18. Why did Warren return so soon?

Toward Interpretation

1. From the conversation on the doorstep between Mary and Warren, what do you learn about Silas?
2. What was Warren's attitude toward Silas in the beginning? Is Mary's attitude the same?
3. What was there about Harold Wilson that bothered Silas?
4. What aspect of human nature is brought out through the character of Silas?
5. In many ways, the story in this poem is similar to the one told in Steinbeck's "The Great Mountain." Discuss some of the similarities.

Tree at My Window

Comprehension

1. Does the speaker draw the curtain on the window between himself and the tree?
2. What do you think the "tongues" of the tree are? Is the talk profound—that is, is it full of deep meaning?
3. What has the tree seen?
4. The tree is concerned with "outer weather." What kind of weather is the speaker concerned with?

Toward Interpretation

1. Why does the speaker feel close to the tree?
2. What words does the speaker use to give the tree human qualities?
3. To which one—the speaker or the tree—does "taken and swept and all but lost" refer? What corresponding words refer to the tree?
4. What does "inner" weather refer to?

Fire and Ice

Comprehension

1. "Some say the world will end in fire." What do others say?
2. What is fire compared to?
3. What is ice compared to?

Toward Interpretation

1. Why does the speaker agree with those who say the world will end in fire?
2. What is the thought that the poem expresses indirectly?
3. Find a verb that is an example of understatement.

Bravado

Comprehension

1. What risk did the speaker have to take?

Toward Interpretation

1. What attitude toward life is implied by the title of the poem?

Poems
by A. E. Housman

A. E. Housman (1859–1936) was a professor and a classical scholar at Cambridge University for many years. Involved as he was in scholarship and teaching, Housman yet found time to write some of the most quietly moving poems in the English language and at his death was universally acknowledged as the greatest English poet of the day. This distinction rests largely on the exquisite perfection of form to be found in the little volume of verse called A Shropshire Lad.

Many legends grew up to account for the pessimism of his poetry. There is a hint in his verses of a personal tragedy that may account for it, though no one really knows the cause. Housman could be delightfully light and ironical ("Oh, When I Was in Love with You"), but his light moments are few. Among his most frequent themes were fading beauty ("Loveliest of Trees"), brief youth ("To an Athlete Dying Young"), and unfaithful love ("Along the Fields As We Came By"). Housman saw himself as a stranger in a world he did not make, an irrational and often brutal world, which, he felt, must nevertheless be endured patiently. His attitude toward life was very similar to that of the ancient Greek stoics who believed that man should keep himself free of passion, unsubdued by either joy or grief, willingly submissive to the laws of nature and man that he cannot change ("The Laws of God, the Laws of Man").

In a book entitled Name and Nature of Poetry, *A. E. Housman compares the writing of verse to the secretions of an injured oyster, which result in a pearl. When he himself was ill or discouraged, he tells us, he found a kind of relief in the writing of verse. Words and phrases, sometimes whole stanzas, would come unaccountably to mind, most often accompanied by a vague idea of the total pattern into which they could later be put. Fitting these fragments together was a hard task at which he worked long and faithfully. As you will see for yourself in the reading of the poems that follow, the final result appears effortless.*

Oh, When I Was in Love with You

Oh, when I was in love with you,
Then I was clean and brave,[1]
And miles around the wonder grew
How well did I behave.

And now the fancy passes by, 5
And nothing will remain,
And miles around they'll say that I
Am quite myself again.

When I Was One-and-Twenty

When I was one-and-twenty
I heard a wise man say,
"Give crowns and pounds and guineas[1]
But not your heart away;
Give pearls away and rubies 5
But keep your fancy free."
But I was one-and-twenty,
No use to talk to me.

When I was one-and-twenty
I heard him say again, 10

[1] *brave:* Here Housman uses an old meaning—fine and splendid in dress.

[1] *crowns and pounds and guineas:* These are fairly large denominations of English money. Here Housman means "give any amount of money."

"The heart out of the bosom
Was never given in vain;
'Tis[2] paid with sighs a-plenty
And sold for endless rue."[3]
And I am two-and-twenty, 15
And oh, 'tis true, 'tis true.

Look Not in My Eyes

Look not in my eyes, for fear
They mirror true the sight I see,
And there you find your face too clear
And love it and be lost like me.
One the long nights through must lie 5
Spent in star-defeated sighs,[1]
But why should you as well as I
Perish? gaze not in my eyes.

A Grecian lad, as I hear tell,
One that many loved in vain, 10
Looked into a forest well[2]
And never looked away again,
There, when the turf in springtime flowers,
With downward eye and gazes sad,
Stands amid the glancing showers 15
A jonquil, not a Grecian lad.

Oh, See How Thick the Goldcup Flowers

Oh, see how thick the goldcup flowers
Are lying in field and lane,
With dandelions[1] to tell the hours[2]
That never are told again.
Oh, may I squire you round the meads[3] 5

[2] *'Tis:* an old way of contracting "it" and "is." The common contraction today is "it's."
[3] *endless rue:* long and bitter disappointment.

[1] *in star-defeated sighs:* defeated by fate.
[2] *A Grecian lad . . . forest well:* Narcissus (the Grecian lad) was a beautiful youth punished by one of the Greek goddesses for his indifference to a lovely maiden. He was made to fall in love with his own reflection in a pool (forest well), pined away in desire for his own reflection, and finally turned into a flower, which was named for him. The jonquil is a species of narcissus.

[1] *goldcup flowers; dandelions:* yellow flowers that bloom in spring. Compare line 10: "the blood runs gold."
[2] *tell the hours:* count the hours.
[3] *squire you round the meads:* walk around the meadow with you.

And pick you posies gay?
—'Twill do no harm to take my arm.
"You may, young man, you may."

Ah, spring was sent for lass and lad,
'Tis now the blood runs gold, 10
And man and maid had best be glad
Before the world is old.
What flowers to-day may flower to-morrow
But never as good as new.
—Suppose I wound my arm right round— 15
"'Tis true, young man, 'tis true."

Some lads there are, 'tis shame to say,
That only court to thieve,
And once they bear the bloom away
'Tis little enough they leave. 20
Then keep your heart for men like me
And safe from trustless chaps.
My love is true and all for you.
"Perhaps, young man, perhaps."

Oh, look in my eyes then, can you doubt? 25
—Why, 'tis a mile from town.
How green the grass is all about!
We might as well sit down.
—Ah, life, what is it but a flower?
Why must true lovers sigh? 30
Be kind, have pity, my own, my pretty,—
"Good-bye, young man, good-bye."

With Rue My Heart Is Laden

With rue[1] my heart is laden[2]
For golden friends I had,
For many a rose-lipt maiden
And many a lightfoot lad.

By brooks too broad for leaping 5
The lightfoot boys are laid;
The rose-lipt girls are sleeping
In fields where roses fade.

[1] *rue:* The meaning is perhaps best given in contemporary English as "sorrow."
[2] *laden:* The past participle of laden (related to load). Here the meaning is "filled" or "burdened with."

Loveliest of Trees

Loveliest of trees, the cherry now
Is hung with bloom along the bough,
And stands about the woodland ride
Wearing white for Eastertide.[1]

Now, of my threescore years and ten,[2] 5
Twenty will not come again,
And take from seventy springs a score,
It only leaves me fifty more.

And since to look at things in bloom
Fifty springs are little room,[3] 10
About the woodlands I will go
To see the cherry hung with snow.

To an Athlete Dying Young

The time you won your town the race
We chaired[1] you through the market-place;
Man and boy stood cheering by,
And home we brought you shoulder-high.

To-day, the road all runners come, 5
Shoulder-high we bring you home,
And set you at your threshold down,
Townsman of a stiller town.[2]

Smart lad, to slip betimes[3] away
From fields where glory does not stay 10
And early though the laurel[4] grows
It withers quicker than the rose.

Eyes the shady night has shut
Cannot see the record cut,[5]
And silence sounds no worse than cheers 15
After earth has stopped the ears:

[1] *Wearing white for Eastertide:* Easter, the festival that celebrates the resurrection of Jesus Christ, is observed in the spring. The cherry tree is blossoming during the Easter season.
[2] *threescore years and ten:* The Bible says that a man can expect a life of threescore years and ten. A score is twenty. Three score plus ten equals seventy years.
[3] *little room:* Here Housman means little time in which "to look at things in bloom."

[1] *chaired:* To get the picture of this scene, you will need to note the verb "chaired." The athlete was carried in a chair on the shoulders of the townspeople.
[2] *stiller town:* Here Housman is referring to the stillness and quietness of the cemetery.
[3] *betimes:* Here the word has its archaic meaning of quickly or promptly.
[4] The laurel, like the palm leaf, is a symbol of victory.
[5] *Cannot see the record cut:* The athlete, dead, will never see anyone make a record better than his.

Now you will not swell the rout[6]
Of lads that wore their honours out,
Runners whom renown outran
And the name died before the man. 20

So set, before its echoes fade,
The fleet foot on the sill of shade,[7]
And hold to the low lintel[8] up
The still-defended challenge-cup.[9]

And round that early-laurelled head 25
Will flock to gaze the strengthless dead,
And find unwithered on its curls
The garland briefer than a girl's.

Along the Field As We Came By

Along the field as we came by
A year ago, my love and I,
The aspen over stile and stone
Was talking to itself alone.[1]
"Oh who are these that kiss and pass? 5
A country lover and his lass;
Two lovers looking to be wed;
And time shall put them both to bed,
But she shall lie with earth above,
And he beside another love." 10

And sure enough beneath the tree
There walks another love with me,
And overhead the aspen heaves
Its rainy-sounding silver leaves;
And I spell[2] nothing in their stir, 15
But now perhaps they speak to her,
And plain for her to understand
They talk about a time at hand
When I shall sleep with clover clad,[3]
And she beside another lad. 20

[6] *swell the rout:* become one of a large crowd.
[7] *sill of shade:* the threshold of death.
[8] *lintel:* archway, or entrance.
[9] *still-defended challenge-cup:* The challenge cup will still be defended—that is, athletes will still go on competing for the prize.

[1] The leaves of the aspen tree make a whispering sound in the wind.
[2] *spell:* understand. That is, he could not understand what the leaves were saying.
[3] *clover clad:* He will be clothed with clover, a low-growing plant. In other words, he will be dead and buried.

The Laws of God, the Laws of Man

The laws of God, the laws of man,
He may keep that will and can;
Not I: let God and man decree
Laws for themselves and not for me;
And if my ways are not as theirs 5
Let them mind their own affairs.
Their deed I judge and much condemn,
Yet when did I make laws for them?
Please yourselves, say I, and they
Need only look the other way. 10
But no, they will not; they must still
Wrest their neighbour to their will,

And make me dance as they desire
With jail and gallows and hell-fire.[1]
And how am I to face the odds[2] 15
Of man's bedevilment and God's?
I, a stranger and afraid
In a world I never made.
They will be master, right or wrong;
Though both are foolish, both are strong. 20
And since, my soul, we cannot fly
To Saturn nor to Mercury,[3]
Keep we must, if keep we can,
These foreign[4] laws of God and man.

Oh, When I Was in Love with You

Comprehension

1. How did the speaker behave when he was in love?
2. Now that he is no longer in love, what will people say about him?

Toward Interpretation

1. What is the mood of the poem—light or sad? Does the speaker seem to take the affair seriously?

[1] *jail and gallows and hell-fire:* Prison (jail) and hanging (on a gallows) are ways in which society's laws are enforced. Hell-fire refers to punishment after death if God's laws are not kept.
[2] *face the odds:* take my chances.
[3] *To Saturn nor to Mercury:* Saturn and Mercury are planets. The poet says we cannot fly away to escape the laws.
[4] *foreign:* As used here, foreign means out of harmony with one's nature. The laws of God and man are often not in harmony with the nature or character of the poet.

When I Was One-and-Twenty

Comprehension

1. What did the wise man tell the speaker that he should not give away?
2. What did the wise man say would happen if the speaker "gave his heart away"?
3. Was the wise man right?

Toward Interpretation

1. Why couldn't the speaker take the advice of the wise man?
2. What happened to make the speaker realize that the wise man's words were true?
3. Does the age of the speaker affect our feeling about the poem—that is, make it humorous instead of pathetic?

Look Not in My Eyes

Comprehension

1. What is the speaker afraid the loved one will see when she looks into his eyes?
2. Does the speaker want his loved one to suffer as he does?
3. What happened when a Grecian lad (Narcissus) looked into a forest well?

Toward Interpretation

1. What is the lesson to be learned from the story about the Grecian lad who looked into a forest well?

Oh, See How Thick the Goldcup Flowers

Comprehension

1. What request does the speaker make of his loved one in the first stanza?
2. What suggestion does he make in the second stanza?
3. Does the speaker say he can be trusted? Can all young men be trusted?
4. Does the young lady have pity on her lover?

Toward Interpretation

1. What is the attitude of the young man toward life and love? Why does he feel that love should not be put off?
2. How does the girl's attitude toward the young man change as the poem progresses? Why does it change?

With Rue My Heart Is Laden

Comprehension

1. What has saddened the speaker? What has happened to the "light-foot boys" and "rose-lipt girls"?

Toward Interpretation

1. What universal truth about life does the poem express?

Loveliest of Trees

Comprehension

1. What is the "loveliest of trees"?
2. Why does the speaker say the tree has white blossoms?
3. How old is the speaker?
4. What does the speaker decide to do?

Toward Interpretation

1. What does the speaker compare the blossoms to in the last stanza?
2. What is the theme of the poem? How does the image of boughs covered with snow reinforce that theme?

To an Athlete Dying Young

Comprehension

1. What did the people do when the athlete won the race?
2. Why are they bringing the athlete home today?
3. How long does the glory last?
4. What "rout," or crowd, will the athlete not become part of?
5. What will the "strengthless dead" find on the athlete's head?

Toward Interpretation

1. Why does the speaker call the athlete a "smart lad"?

Along the Fields As We Came By

Comprehension

1. What prediction did the aspen tree make about the first pair of lovers who passed by?
2. Was the aspen tree right in its prediction?
3. What is the lover worried about? What does he fear the aspen might be saying to "her"?

Toward Interpretation

1. What does the poem seem to be saying about love?

The Laws of God, the Laws of Man

Comprehension

1. Does the speaker want to obey the laws of God and man?
2. Does the speaker want to make others behave as he does?
3. Can the speaker escape these laws?

Toward Interpretation

1. Why does the speaker feel justified in protesting against the laws of God and man? What lines tell you?
2. What reason does he give for accepting these laws?

Poems
by Emily Dickinson

Emily Dickinson (1830–1886), like Robert Frost, is associated with New England. Unlike Frost, however, who wrote of its scenes and its people, Emily Dickinson wrote primarily of herself. Her poetry reveals the impact which her very restricted life had upon her.

For many years she lived as a recluse, seldom venturing outside the hedge that surrounded her father's house except to visit her brother's house next door. Here, along the path between the two houses, she might have been seen, a fleeting vision in white—she dressed almost always in white—tending her flowers or exploring the beauties of nature even within this narrow compass. Indoors, she explored the world of books. She was a deeply religious person, although her form of worship might seem unconventional (see "Some Keep the Sabbath Going to Church"), and her thoughts dwelt often on death and immortality.

Only seven of Dickinson's poems had been published at the time of her death, all anonymously. Gradually, the brief poems she had written and saved for years on mere scraps of paper were brought together. A selection first appeared in 1890. In 1955, a definitive edition was published by the Harvard University Press.

Today Emily Dickinson ranks as one of America's truly great poets. Her poems are fresh and original: she takes liberties with grammar, punctuation, and capitalization; and her innovations in meter are daring. But more particular-

ly it is her whimsical cast of thought with its swift darts at truth that has charmed a nation and extended her reputation abroad.

As you read the sampling of her verse here, you will be fascinated by the suppleness of her rhythm and rhyme, by the vigor of her images, and by the terseness of her thought. In these little gemlike poems you will sense the intensity of feeling that is characteristic of Emily Dickinson.

A Bird Came Down the Walk

A Bird came down the Walk—
He did not know I saw—
He bit an Angleworm in halves
And ate the fellow, raw,

And then he drank a Dew 5
From a convenient Grass[1]—
And then hopped sidewise to the Wall
To let a Beetle pass—

He glanced with rapid eyes
That hurried all around— 10
They looked like frightened Beads, I thought—
He stirred his Velvet Head

Like one in danger, Cautious,
I offered him a Crumb
And he unrolled his feathers 15
And rowed him[2] softer home—

Than[3] Oars divide the Ocean,
Too silver for a seam—
Or Butterflies, off Banks of Noon[4]
Leap, plashless[5] as they swim. 20

Apparently with No Surprise

Apparently with no surprise
To any happy Flower

[1] *a Dew; a Grass:* Here, uncountable nouns (dew and grass) are treated as countable and are preceded by "a." One would expect "a drop of dew and a blade of grass," or "the dew from some convenient grass."
[2] *rowed him:* rowed himself. In lines 15–18, the poet compares a bird's flight to travel in a boat rowed with oars.
[3] *softer home—Than:* The dash after home is misleading. This syntax demands "softer home than. . ."
[4] *Banks of Noon:* The air at noon is compared to a sea in which butterflies swim.
[5] *plashless:* splashless. Butterflies are being compared to swimmers who are so smooth that they do not disturb the water.

The Frost beheads it at its play—
In accidental power—
The blonde Assassin[1] passes on— 5
The Sun proceeds unmoved
To measure off another Day
For an Approving God.

A Narrow Fellow in the Grass

A narrow Fellow in the Grass
Occasionally rides—
You may have met Him—did you not
His notice sudden is—

The Grass divides as with a Comb—[1] 5
A spotted shaft[2] is seen—
And then it closes at your feet
And opens further on—

He likes a Boggy Acre
A Floor too cool for Corn[3]— 10
Yet, when a Boy, and Barefoot—
I more than once at Noon
Have passed, I thought, a Whip lash
Unbraiding[4] in the Sun
When stopping to secure it 15
It wrinkled, and was gone—

Several of Nature's People
I know, and they know me—
I feel for them a transport
Of cordiality—[5] 20

But never met this Fellow
Attended, or alone
Without a tighter breathing
And Zero at the Bone—[6]

[1] *blonde assassin:* a personification of the frost as a killer.

[1] *as with a Comb:* The grass looks like hair parted with a comb.
[2] *spotted shaft:* The snake looks like a long spear handle (shaft).
[3] *a Boggy Acre . . . too cool for Corn:* A boggy (wet, spongy) field is not good for growing corn.
[4] *a Whip lash/Unbraiding:* Whip lashes were often woven with differently colored strips of leather. The design on a snake's skin looks like these braided strips. Here unbraiding means uncoiling.
[5] *transport/Of cordiality:* a feeling of great friendliness or love.
[6] *Zero at the Bone:* here, frightened or suddenly shocked.

I Never Saw a Moor

I never saw a Moor—
I never saw the Sea—
Yet know I how the Heather looks
And what a Billow be.[1]

I never spoke with God 5
Nor visited in Heaven—
Yet certain am I of the spot
As if the Checks[2] were given—

To Make a Prairie[1] It Takes a Clover and One Bee

To make a prairie it takes a clover and one bee,
One clover, and a bee,
And revery.
The revery alone will do,
If bees are few. 5

A Thought Went up My Mind Today

A Thought went up my mind today—
That I have had before—
But did not finish—some way back—
I could not fix the Year—

Nor where it went—nor why it came 5
The second time to me—
Nor definitely, what it was—
Have I the Art to say—

But somewhere—in my Soul—I know—
I've met the Thing before— 10
It just reminded me—'twas all—
And came my way no more—

The Sky Is Low—The Clouds Are Mean

The Sky is low—the Clouds are mean.
A Travelling Flake of Snow
Across a Barn or through a Rut
Debates if it will go—

[1] *be:* Dickinson uses a subjunctive form peculiar to her. The usual form would be "is."
[2] *the Checks:* The conductor on a train puts a ticket (check) on the seat, showing the place to which the passenger is going.

[1] *Prairie:* a rather extensive area of grassy land that is relatively level and without trees.

A Narrow Wind complains all Day 5
How some one treated him.
Nature, like Us is sometimes caught
Without her Diadem.[1]

"Hope" Is the Thing with Feathers

"Hope" is the thing with feathers—
That perches in the soul—
And sings the tune without the words—
And never stops—at all—

And sweetest—in the Gale—is heard— 5
And sore must be the storm—
That could abash the little Bird
That kept so many warm—

I've heard it in the chillest land—
And on the strangest Sea— 10
Yet, never, in Extremity,
It asked a crumb—of Me.

I Died for Beauty

I died for Beauty—but was scarce
Adjusted in the Tomb
When One who died for Truth, was lain
In an adjoining Room—

He questioned softly "Why I failed"?[1] 5
"For Beauty", I replied—
"And I—for Truth—Themself are One[2]—
We Brethren, are",[3] He said—

And so, as Kinsmen, met a Night—
We talked between the Rooms— 10
Until the Moss had reached our lips—
And covered up—our names—[4]

[1] *Without her Diadem:* A diadem is a royal crown. The poet says that nature, like people, does not always appear at her best.

[1] Here Dickinson's use of quotation marks is misleading. We would expect either "Why did you fail?" or "He questioned softly why I failed."
[2] *Themself are One:* example of Dickinson's grammar. We would expect "They are one."
[3] *We Brethren, are:* Again, Emily Dickinson's grammar and diction. We would expect "We are brothers."
[4] In other words, they talked until the moss had sealed their lips and covered the names on their tombstones and they were forgotten.

Because I Could Not Stop for Death

Because I could not stop for Death—
He kindly stopped for me—
The Carriage held but just Ourselves—
And Immortality.

We slowly drove—He knew no haste 5
And I had put away
My labor and my leisure too,
For His Civility—

We passed the School, where Children strove
At Recess—in the Ring— 10
We passed the Fields of Gazing Grain—
We passed the Setting Sun—

Or rather—He passed Us—
The Dews drew quivering and chill—
For only Gossamer, my Gown— 15
My Tippet—only Tulle—[1]

We paused before a House that seemed
A Swelling of the Ground—
The Roof was scarcely visible—
The Cornice—in the Ground— 20

Since then—'tis Centuries—and yet
Feels shorter than the Day
I first surmised the Horses' Heads
Were toward Eternity—

My Life Closed Twice Before Its Close

My life closed twice before its close;
It yet remains to see
If Immortality unveil
A third event to me,

So huge, so hopeless to conceive 5
As these that twice befel.[1]
Parting is all we know of heaven,
And all we need of hell.

[1] Here Dickinson's sentence structure is particularly hard to follow: words are omitted and word order is changed. This is a possible rearrangement: For my gown (was) only gossamer (a filmy, fine kind of cloth) and my tippet (scarf) (was) only tulle (a fine, thin kind of cloth).

[1] *befel*: Dickinson's spelling for befell, meaning happened.

Some Keep the Sabbath Going to Church

Some keep the Sabbath going to Church—
I keep it, staying at Home—
With a Bobolink for a Chorister—
And an Orchard, for a Dome—

Some keep the Sabbath in Surplice— 5
I just wear my Wings—
And instead of tolling the Bell, for Church,
Our little Sexton—sings.

God preaches, a noted Clergyman—
And the sermon is never long, 10
So instead of getting to Heaven, at last—
I'm going, all along.

A Bird Came Down the Walk

Comprehension

1. Did the bird see the speaker at the beginning?
2. What did the bird do to the angleworm?
3. What did he drink?
4. What are his eyes compared to? What is his head compared to?
5. What did the speaker offer the bird?
6. What did the bird do?

Toward Interpretation

1. What is the speaker reminded of as the bird takes off in flight? How many images does Dickinson make you see?

Apparently with No Surprise

Comprehension

1. What happens to the flower?
2. Does the frost intend to destroy the flower?
3. When does the "blonde Assassin"—that is, the frost—pass on?

Toward Interpretation

1. Emily Dickinson often attributes human qualities to the world of nature. What words does she apply to the following that are normally applied to human beings? To the flower? To the frost? To the sun?
2. What implication do you see in the phrase "an Approving God"?

A Narrow Fellow in the Grass

Comprehension

1. How can you notice a snake that is in the grass?
2. Does the snake prefer a wet or a dry field?
3. Was the speaker able to catch a snake?
4. How does the speaker feel about some of "Nature's People"?

Toward Interpretation

1. What feeling is aroused in the speaker when she sees a snake?

I Never Saw a Moor

Comprehension

1. What does the speaker know about a moor and about the sea, even though she has never seen either one?
2. Is the speaker certain that heaven exists?

Toward Interpretation

1. How does the speaker know what a moor looks like or what the sea looks like?

To Make a Prairie It Takes a Clover and One Bee

Comprehension

1. If you do not have a clover and a bee, can you still "make a prairie"?

Toward Interpretation

1. What does the poem say about the importance of imagination? In what way is this poem like the preceding one?

A Thought Went up My Mind Today

Comprehension

1. Was the thought a new one?
2. Was it "finished"?
3. Does the speaker know why the thought came to her a second time?
4. What is the one thing the speaker was sure of?

Toward Interpretation

1. This poem deals with an experience that almost everyone has had

at one time or another. Try to describe this experience in your own words.

The Sky Is Low—The Clouds Are Mean

Comprehension

1. What does the snowflake debate about?
2. What does the wind complain about?
3. In what way is Nature "like Us"?

Toward Interpretation

1. What words are used that generally apply to humans rather than to nature?

"Hope" Is the Thing with Feathers

Comprehension

1. Do people ever give up hope completely?
2. When is hope the "sweetest"?
3. Has hope ever demanded anything of the speaker?

Toward Interpretation

1. What is hope compared to? What words help carry out the comparison?

I Died for Beauty

Comprehension

1. There are two people in the tomb. Who are they?
2. Are beauty and truth related?

Toward Interpretation

1. Why do you think the speaker considers the two dead people as "Brethren" and "Kinsmen"?

Because I Could Not Stop for Death

Comprehension

1. Who were the three passengers in the carriage?
2. Were the passengers in a hurry?
3. Where was the carriage going?
4. What scenes were passed along the way? What was the "House"?

Toward Interpretation

1. What is the speaker's attitude toward death? What lines tell you this?

My Life Closed Twice Before Its Close

Comprehension

1. Does the speaker know for certain that a "third event" will occur?
2. What does the speaker say about "parting"?

Toward Interpretation

1. What caused the speaker's life to close twice? How, other than death, could life be said to "close"?
2. How can "parting" be compared to both heaven and hell?

Some Keep the Sabbath Going to Church

Comprehension

1. Does the speaker go to church on the Sabbath?
2. When is the speaker going to heaven?

Toward Interpretation

1. List the words in the poem that refer to a scene in church. What substitute in nature does the speaker find for each of those words referring to church?
2. What special advantage does the speaker find in keeping the Sabbath in the orchard instead of in church? Does the speaker feel closer to God in church or when she is in an orchard?

Poems
by William Butler Yeats

William Butler Yeats (1865–1939) is regarded as Ireland's foremost poet. During the early part of this century he was a major literary figure in the Western world, widely known not only as a poet but also as a dramatist and a collector of Irish folklore. He was one of the founders of the Irish National Theater, later known as the Abbey Theater, and for many years an ardent patriot in Ireland's struggle for independence. In 1924 he was awarded the Nobel Prize in literature.

When he was a boy of nine his artist-father took him to England to be educated, and often during his youth he was homesick for his beloved Ireland. In the poem "The Lake Isle of Innisfree," it was the "pavements grey" of London that he longed to escape and it was his native land to which he longed to return.

Much of what he did up to middle life was colored by his love for Maud Gonne, a public figure who was devoted to the cause of the Irish Revolution. While he had other loves, it is this one that gives special poignancy to the three love poems included here: "Never Give All the Heart," "The Sorrow of Love," and "When You Are Old." He never forgot her, and in later years he tried again unsuccessfully to marry her when she was once more free. Through her he met, when he was fifty-two, the young woman whom he was soon to marry.

The poem "The Wild Swans of Coole" recalls another woman in his life, Lady Gregory, a long-time friend and disciple who shared in his dream of an Irish theater and participated in its founding. Her estate at Coole, where he saw the wild swans, was often a refuge when he was ill and depressed, and for her he wrote the poem "To a Friend Whose Work Has Come to Nothing."

Though an ardent nationalist, he deplored the unscrupulous methods used by some of the leaders in the turbulent times when Ireland was rebelling against England, and it is this concern that is reflected in the poem "The Leaders of the Crowd."

"The Ballad of Father Gilligan" represents still another feature of his poetry—his interest in the miraculous as part of the folklore of his native land. He loved the peasants of the Irish countryside, and he eagerly collected and later published legends and fairy stories and tales of miracles and wonders. For many years he joined in various movements that dealt with the occult, even seeking the advice of mediums and attending séances.

It was part of Yeats's poetic theory that the writing of verse should be firmly rooted in experience. He also attached great importance to form and style and perfected his own manner slowly over the years. His early poems made use of conventional images, such as flowers and stars, and were written in conventional poetic meters. In general, the rhythms of his later poems were more experimental and, though subtly lyrical, were often closer to the patterns of daily speech. Many of Yeats's later poems are more difficult than those included here. But the poems that follow will amply illustrate his graceful lyricism.

Never Give All the Heart

Never give all the heart, for love
Will hardly seem worth thinking of
To passionate women if it seem
Certain, and they never dream
That it fades out from kiss to kiss; 5
For everything that's lovely is
But a brief, dreamy, kind delight.
O never give the heart outright,
For they, for all smooth lips can say,[1]
Have given their hearts up to the play. 10
And who could play it well enough

[1] *for all smooth lips can say:* here "for" means "in spite of what."

If deaf and dumb and blind with love?
He that made this[2] knows all the cost,
For he gave all his heart and lost.

For Anne Gregory

"Never shall a young man,
Thrown into despair
By those great honey-coloured
Ramparts at your ear,[1]
Love you for yourself alone 5
And not your yellow hair."

"But I can get a hair-dye
And set such colour there,
Brown, or black, or carrot,
That young men in despair 10
May love me for myself alone
And not my yellow hair."

"I heard an old religious man
But yesternight declare
That he had found a text to prove 15
That only God, my dear,
Could love you for yourself alone
And not your yellow hair."

The Sorrow of Love

The quarrel of the sparrows in the eaves,
The full round moon and the star-laden sky,
And the loud song of the ever-singing leaves,
Has hid away earth's old and weary cry.[1]

And then you came with those red mournful lips, 5
And with you came the whole of the world's tears,
And all the trouble of her[2] laboring ships,
And all the trouble of her myriad years.

And how the sparrows warring in the eaves,
The curd-pale moon, the white stars in the sky, 10

[2] *He that made this:* the author of the poem.

[1] *Ramparts at your ear:* This phrase suggests that Anne Gregory wore her hair like protecting walls or fortifications (ramparts) over her ears.

[1] *earth's old and weary cry:* In other words, the sorrow of love is an old grief, common to the whole world.
[2] *her:* the world's.

And the loud chaunting[3] of the unquiet leaves,
Are shaken with earth's old and weary cry.

When You Are Old

When you are old and grey and full of sleep,
And nodding by the fire, take down this book,
And slowly read, and dream of the soft look
Your eyes had once, and of their shadows deep;

How many loved your moments of glad grace, 5
And loved your beauty with love false or true,
But one man loved the pilgrim soul[1] in you,
And loved the sorrows of your changing face;

And bending down beside the glowing bars,[2]
Murmur, a little sadly, how Love fled 10
And paced upon the mountains overhead
And hid his face[3] amid a crowd of stars.

The Song of the Old Mother

I rise in the dawn, and I kneel and blow
Till the seed of the fire flicker and glow;
And then I must scrub and bake and sweep
Till stars are beginning to blink and peep;
And the young lie long and dream in their bed 5
Of the matching of ribbons for bosom and head,
And their day goes over in idleness,
And they sigh if the wind but lift a tress:
While I must work because I am old,
And the seed of the fire gets feeble and cold. 10

The Lake Isle of Innisfree

I will arise and go now, and go to Innisfree,[1]
And a small cabin build there, of clay and wattles[2] made:

[3] *chaunting:* an old way of spelling chanting, which means singing.

[1] *pilgrim soul:* "Pilgrim" has serious religious associations and added to the word "soul," suggests those fine inner qualities which matched the outer beauty of the woman being praised.
[2] *glowing bars:* refers to the hearth, or fireplace.
[3] *his face:* Love's face.

[1] *Innisfree:* a lake in Ireland.
[2] *wattles:* A wattle is a structure made by the weaving together of twigs and branches with larger sticks. This structure can be used to support a thatched roof.

Nine bean-rows[3] will I have there, a hive for the honeybee,
And live alone in the bee-loud glade.

And I shall have some peace there, for peace comes dropping slow, 5
Dropping from the veils of the morning to where the cricket sings;
There midnight's all a glimmer, and noon a purple glow,
And evening full of the linnet's wings.

I will arise and go now, for always night and day
I hear lake water lapping with low sounds by the shore; 10
While I stand on the roadway, or on the pavements grey,
I hear it in the deep heart's core.

The Wild Swans at Coole

The trees are in their autumn beauty,
The woodland paths are dry,
Under the October twilight the water
Mirrors a still sky;
Upon the brimming water among the stones 5
Are nine-and-fifty swans.

The nineteenth autumn has come upon me
Since I first made my count;
I saw, before I had well finished,[1]
All[2] suddenly mount 10
And scatter wheeling in great broken rings
Upon their clamorous wings.

I have looked upon those brilliant creatures,
And now my heart is sore.
All's changed since I, hearing at twilight, 15
The first time on this shore,
The bell-beat of their wings above my head,
Trod with a lighter tread.[3]

Unwearied still, lover by lover,
They paddle[4] in the cold 20
Companionable streams or climb the air;
Their hearts have not grown old;

[3] *Nine bean-rows:* The number nine may have had a mystical significance for Yeats: whether it did or not, the meaning here is probably just "several."

[1] *before I had well finished:* Supply the words "my count" and the meaning becomes clear.
[2] *All:* all the swans.
[3] *Trod with a lighter tread:* This line completes the sentence begun in line 15: "All's changed since I . . . Trod with a lighter tread."
[4] *lover by lover,/They paddle:* The swans swim and fly in mated pairs.

Passion or conquest, wander where they will,
Attend upon them still.

But now they drift on the still water, 25
Mysterious, beautiful;
Among what rushes will they build,
By what lake's edge or pool
Delight men's eyes when I awake some day
To find they have flown away? 30

To a Friend Whose Work Has Come to Nothing

Now[1] all the truth is out,
Be secret and take defeat
From any brazen throat,
For how can you compete,
Being honour bred,[2] with one 5
Who, were it proved he lies,
Were neither shamed in his own
Nor in his neighbours' eyes?
Bred to a harder thing
Than Triumph,[3] turn away 10
And like a laughing string
Whereon mad fingers play
Amid a place of stone,
Be secret and exult,
Because of all things known 15
That is most difficult.

The Leaders of the Crowd

They must to keep their certainty[1] accuse
All that are different of a base intent;
Pull down established honour; hawk for news[2]
Whatever their loose fantasy invent
And murmur it with bated breath, as though 5
The abounding gutter had been Helicon[3]
Or calumny a song. How can they know

[1] *Now:* now that.
[2] *Being honour bred:* being brought up in honor.
[3] *Bred to a harder thing/Than triumph:* That is, honor is harder than triumph.

[1] *They must to keep their certainty:* Leaders, to feel sure of themselves, must. . . .
[2] *hawk for news:* spread about as news.
[3] *Helicon:* a mountain in Greece, supposed by the ancients to be the home of Apollo and the Muses. Here the meaning is that leaders consider any stories they make up ("Whatever their loose fantasy invent") as important as if they had come from Helicon.

Truth flourishes where the student's lamp has shone,
And there alone, that have no solitude?[4]
So[5] the crowd come they care not what may come. 10
They have loud music, hope every day renewed
And heartier loves; that lamp[6] is from the tomb.

The Ballad of Father Gilligan

The old priest Peter Gilligan
Was weary night and day;
For half his flock were in their beds,
Or under green sods lay.[1]

Once, while he nodded on a chair, 5
At the moth-hour of eve,[2]
Another poor man sent for him,
And he began to grieve.

"I have no rest, nor joy, nor peace,
For people die and die"; 10
And after cried he, "God forgive!
My body spake, not I!"

He knelt, and leaning on the chair
He prayed and fell asleep;
And the moth-hour went from the fields, 15
And stars began to peep.

They slowly into millions grew,
And leaves shook in the wind;
And God covered the world with shade,
And whispered to mankind. 20

Upon the time of sparrow-chirp
When the months came once more,
The old priest Peter Gilligan
Stood upright on the floor.

"Mavrone, mavrone![3] the man has died 25
While I slept on the chair";

[4] *that have no solitude:* "That" means "those people." It refers to "they" in line 7.
[5] *So:* Here, "so" means "just as long as."
[6] *that lamp:* the student's lamp in line 8.

[1] *under green sods lay:* were dead and buried.
[2] *the moth-hour of eve:* Moths are insects that fly chiefly at dusk or dawn. Here "eve" is a poetic word for evening.
[3] *mavrone:* an Irish expression of sorrow.

He roused his horse out of its sleep,
And rode with little care.

He rode now as he never rode,
By rocky lane and fen; 30
The sick man's wife opened the door:
"Father! you come again!"

"And is the poor man dead?" he cried.
"He died an hour ago."
The old priest Peter Gilligan 35
In grief swayed to and fro.

"When you were gone, he turned and died
As merry as a bird."
The old priest Peter Gilligan
He knelt him at that word. 40

"He Who hath made the night of stars
For souls who tire and bleed,
Sent one of His great angles down
To help me in my need.

"He Who is wrapped in purple robes, 45
With planets in His care,
Had pity on the least of things
Asleep upon a chair."

Never Give All the Heart

Comprehension

1. When do women consider love hardly worth thinking of? Refer to the *if* clause in line 3.
2. Does love fade away rapidly?
3. Has the speaker been unsuccessful in love?

Toward Interpretation

1. What view of love is expressed in the poem?

For Anne Gregory

Comprehension

1. The poet tells Anne that young men will never love her for herself alone. What will they love her for?
2. What does Anne say she can do with her hair?
3. Does the poet believe that Anne will ever be loved for herself alone?

Toward Interpretation

1. What truth about life does the poet remind Anne of?
2. What does Anne Gregory's yellow hair stand for?

The Sorrow of Love

Comprehension

1. In the first stanza, what three things have hidden away "earth's old and weary cry"?
2. What did the new love bring with her?
3. In the first stanza, the speaker says the sparrows are quarreling. What are they doing in the third stanza?

Toward Interpretation

1. In the first and third stanzas the speaker looks out upon the same scene but with a different attitude. How does he feel in the first stanza? In the third?

When You Are Old

Comprehension

1. What does the speaker tell the woman to dream of when she is old?
2. Many men loved her for her beauty, but one man—the speaker—loved her for another reason. What is it?
3. Did love go away?

Toward Interpretation

1. Describe the two kinds of love that are contrasted in this poem. Which kind do you think the poet feels is more important?

The Song of the Old Mother

Comprehension

1. What must the old mother do?
2. What do the young do while the mother works?

Toward Interpretation

1. What do you think the last line means? What does the fire refer to?

The Lake Isle of Innisfree

Comprehension

1. Where is the speaker going to go?
2. What will the speaker do on the island in the lake? What will he find there?
3. What does the speaker hear "in the deep heart's core"?

Toward Interpretation

1. In what manner will the speaker live at Innisfree?
2. In what lines does he indicate his constant longing for the lake isle?

The Wild Swans at Coole

Comprehension

1. What season of the year is it?
2. How many swans are there on the lake?
3. For how many years has the speaker been counting the swans?
4. Have the swans grown older?
5. What question does the speaker ask in the last stanza?

Toward Interpretation

1. Contrast the speaker's mood the first time he saw the wild swans with his mood when he looked upon them nineteen autumns later.
2. What qualities seem to impress the speaker most about the swans?

To a Friend Whose Work Has Come to Nothing

Comprehension

1. Does the speaker advise his friend to accept defeat?
2. Would it make any difference to the speaker if it could be proved that the other man had lied?
3. "Of all things known," what is the most difficult thing to do?

Toward Interpretation

1. How should a person of honor accept defeat?

The Leaders of the Crowd

Comprehension

1. What must the leaders do to "keep their certainty"?
2. Where does truth really flourish?
3. Do the leaders have solitude?

Toward Interpretation

1. What are some of the implications of the final phrase in the poem, "that lamp is from the tomb"?

The Ballad of Father Gilligan

Comprehension

1. Why was Father Gilligan weary?
2. What happens in stanzas 2, 3, and 4?
3. What was the priest afraid of when he woke up?
4. How did he ride to the sick man's house?
5. What had happened to the sick man during the night?

Toward Interpretation

1. How did Father Gilligan explain what happened during the night?

Poems
by Thomas Hardy

Thomas Hardy (1840–1928) won fame as a poet after he had first established himself as a successful English novelist. As a literary figure he is called "the last of the great Victorians." The Victorian age roughly corresponded to the reign of Britain's Queen Victoria (1837–1901).

As a young man, Hardy wanted most of all to be a poet—not a novelist—and his talents justified his choice. But literary London did not accept him at first, and he was forced to write prose in order to make a living. For twenty-five years he postponed the serious writing of verse. Then in 1896, at the height of his career, he published his last major novel (Jude the Obscure) and turned to poetry for the rest of his long life.

In both prose and poetry his name is associated with that section of midwestern England where he grew up and to which in his novels he gave the name Wessex. Here, roaming the woods and the fields and the pastures, listening to the ballads and tales of the countryside—about lonely crossroads or graveyards—he gradually developed that disillusioned and tragic view of life for which both his novels and his poems are noted. Here he began that long career of "noble indignation" at the cruelties and perplexities of life which he observed and wrote about—disappointment in love, disillusionment, and thwarted hopes. He saw man as struggling helplessly against a God who created the universe without purpose or reason. (See "New Year's Eve.")

Yet Hardy had an unfailing sympathy for the suffering of others and justified his dark outlook on life by saying, "If a way to the Better there be, it exacts a full look at the Worst." That "look" might be a brief narrative account of a chance happening that points up some larger significance ("By Her Aunt's Grave" and "At the Draper's"). The "look" was often ironic ("The Man He Killed") or purely satiric ("In Church").

But there are other moods to be noted in the poems included here. Thomas Hardy could deal affectionately and tenderly with a legend remembered from childhood ("The Oxen") and yield himself completely to the wonder and beauty of nature ("Snow in the Suburbs"). It was a "darkling thrush," on a frozen winter evening, when life seemed at its lowest, that sang a song of blessed hope.

Hardy is not only a skilled craftsman and conscious artist, but also an intense observer of life. In an age of doubt when advances in science raised many disturbing questions about traditional beliefs, Hardy was among the most fearless seekers after truth.

The Oxen[1]

Christmas Eve, and twelve of the clock,[2]
"Now they are all on their knees,"
An elder said as we sat in a flock
By the embers in hearthside ease.

We pictured the meek mild creatures where — 5
They dwelt in their strawy pen,
Nor did it occur to one of us there
To doubt they were kneeling then.

So fair a fancy few would weave
In these years! Yet, I feel, — 10
If someone said on Christmas Eve,
"Come; see the oxen kneel

[1] *The Oxen:* There is an old English legend about the oxen on Christmas Eve. It says that they kneel at midnight to show honor to the Christ child.

[2] *of the clock:* o'clock.

"In the lonely barton by yonder coomb[3]
Our childhood used to know,"
I should go with him in the gloom, 15
Hoping it might be so.

The Shadow on the Stone[1]

I went by the Druid stone[2]
That broods in the garden white and lone,
And I stopped and looked at the shifting shadows
That at some moments fall thereon
From the tree hard by with a rhythmic swing, 5
And they shaped in my imagining
To the shade that a well-known head and shoulders
Threw there when she was gardening.

I thought her behind my back,
Yea,[3] her I long had learned to lack, 10
And I said: "I am sure you are standing behind me,
Though how do you get into this old track?"[4]
And there was no sound but the fall of a leaf
As a sad response; and to keep down my grief
I would not turn my head to discover 15
That there was nothing in my belief.

Yet I wanted to look and see
That nobody stood at the back of me;
But I thought once more: "Nay,[5] I'll not unvision
A shape which, somehow, there may be." 20
So I went on softly from the glade,
And left her behind me throwing her shade,
As[6] she were indeed an apparition—
My head unturned lest my dream should fade.

[3] *the lonely barton by yonder coomb:* the lonely farmyard in the narrow valley which you see from here.

[1] *The Shadow on the Stone:* This is one of the poems written by Hardy after his first wife's death.
[2] *the Druid stone:* In Hardy's garden was a stone which was supposed to have been a part of a stone circle sacred to the Druids, early inhabitants of Great Britain.
[3] *Yea:* yes, used here for emphasis. See note 5 on nay.
[4] *this old track:* Perhaps, this old path—the garden path on which his wife used to walk.
[5] *Nay:* no. Both yea and nay are older forms, no longer in common use.
[6] *As:* as if.

In Church

"And now to God the Father," he ends,
And his voice thrills up to the topmost tiles:[1]
Each listener chokes as he bows and bends,
And emotion pervades the crowded aisles.
Then the preacher glides to the vestry-door, 5
And shuts it, and thinks he is seen no more.

The door swings softly ajar meanwhile,
And a pupil of his in the Bible class,
Who adores him as one without gloss or guile,[2]
Sees her idol stand with a satisfied smile 10
And reënact at the vestry-glass
Each pulpit gesture in deft dumb-show[3]
That had moved the congregation so.

By Her Aunt's Grave

"Sixpence a week," says the girl to her lover,
"Aunt used to bring me, for she could confide
In me alone, she vowed. It was to cover
The cost of her headstone when she died.
And that was a year ago last June: 5
I've not yet fixed it. But I must soon."

"And where is the money now, my dear?"
"O, snug in my purse. . . . Aunt was *so* slow
In saving it—eighty weeks, or near." . . .
"Let's spend it," he hints. "For she won't know. 10
There's a dance tonight at the *Load of Hay*."[1]
She passively nods. And they go that way.

At the Draper's[1]

"I stood at the back of the shop, my dear,
But you did not perceive me.
Well, when they deliver what you were shown
I shall know nothing of it, believe me!"

[1] *to the topmost tiles:* to the highest part of the church.
[2] *without gloss or guile:* without deceit or hypocrisy; innocent.
[3] *dumb-show:* signs or gestures, without words. He is acting out for his own satisfaction the scene described in the first stanza.

[1] *Load of Hay:* the name of a dance hall.

[1] *Draper's:* in British usage, one who sells cloth and clothing.

And he coughed and coughed as she paled and said, 5
"O, I didn't see you come in there—
Why couldn't you speak?"—"Well, I didn't. I left
That you should not notice I'd been there.

"You were viewing some lovely things. *'Soon required*
For a widow, of latest fashion'; 10
And I knew 'twould upset you to meet the man
Who had to be cold and ashen

"And screwed in a box before they could dress you
'In the last new note in mourning,'
As they defined it. So, not to distress you, 15
I left you to your adorning."

Snow in the Suburbs

Every branch big with it,
Bent every twig with it;
Every fork like a white web-foot;[1]
Every street and pavement mute:

Some flakes have lost their way, and grope back upward, when 5
Meeting those meandering down they turn and descend again.
The palings[2] are glued together like a wall,
And there is no waft of wind with the fleecy fall.

A sparrow enters the tree
Whereon immediately 10
A snow-lump thrice his own slight size
Descends on him and showers his head and eyes.
And overturns him
And near inurns[3] him,
And lights on a nether[4] twig, when its brush 15
Starts off a volley of other lodging lumps with a rush.

The steps are a blanched slope,
Up which, with feeble hope,
A black cat comes, wide-eyed and thin;
And we take him in. 20

[1] *Every fork like a white web-foot:* The snow has filled in the spaces so that each dividing branch (fork) looks like the foot of a duck (web-foot).
[2] *palings:* In fences made with pales (narrow pointed stakes), there is usually a space between each pale. The snow has now filled in the spaces, glueing them together like a wall.
[3] *inurns:* puts him in an urn; buries him.
[4] *nether:* an older word meaning "lower."

The Man He Killed

"Had he and I but met
By some old ancient inn,
We should have sat us down to wet
Right many a nipperkin![1]

"But ranged as infantry, 5
And staring face to face,
I shot at him as he at me,
And killed him in his place.

"I shot him dead because—
Because he was my foe, 10
Just so: my foe of course he was;
That's clear enough; although
"He thought he'd 'list,[2] perhaps,
Off-hand-like[3]—just as I—
Was out of work—had sold his traps[4]— 15
No other reason why.

"Yes, quaint and curious war is!
You shoot a fellow down
You'd treat, if met where any bar is,
Or help to half-a-crown."[5] 20

New Year's Eve

"I have finished another year," said God,
"In gray, green, white and brown;
I have strewn the leaf upon the sod,
Sealed up the worm within the clod,
And let the last sun down." 5

"And what's the good of it?" I said,
"What reasons made you call
From formless void this earth we tread,
When nine-and-ninety can be read[1]
Why nought should be at all? 10

[1] *Right many a nipperkin:* A nip or nipper is a drink. The *-kin* on the end means small. In other words, the soldier would have had several drinks with the man.
[2] *'list:* short for enlist. The apostrophe stands for an omitted syllable—omitted in order to maintain rhythm.
[3] *Off-hand like:* without thinking much about it.
[4] *his traps:* the tools of his trade.
[5] *help to half-a-crown:* lend him money.

[1] *nine-and-ninety can be read:* In other words, nine-and-ninety reasons can be given why the earth should not have been created at all.

"Yea, Sire;[2] why shaped you us, 'who in
This tabernacle[3] groan'—
If ever a joy be found herein,
Such joy no man had wished to win
If he had never known!" 15

Then he: "My labors—logicless—
You may explain; not I:
Sense-sealed[4] I have wrought, without a guess
That I evolved a Consciousness
To ask for reasons why. 20

"Strange that ephemeral creatures who
By my own ordering are,
Should see the shortness of my view,
Use ethic tests I never knew,
Or made provision for!" 25

He[5] sank to raptness as of yore,
And opening New Year's Day
Wove it by rote as theretofore,
And went on working evermore
In his unweeting[6] way. 30

The Darkling[1] Thrush

I leaned upon a coppice gate[2]
When Frost was specter-gray,
And Winter's dregs made desolate
The weakening eye of day
The tangled bine-stems scored the sky 5
Like strings from broken lyres,[3]
And all mankind that haunted nigh[4]
Had sought their household fires.

[2] *Yea, Sire:* Sire means lord. Yea means truly or indeed. Both words, as used here, are obsolete.
[3] *This tabernacle:* literally, a place of worship. Here the meaning is figurative: tabernacle could refer to the world or, more narrowly, the body, the "earthly tabernacle."
[4] *Sense-sealed:* without sense or thought.
[5] *He:* God.
[6] *unweeting:* unknowing—that is, without knowledge of what he was doing.

[1] *Darkling:* a poetic word meaning existing in darkness. Note how "darkling" helps to set the scene and the mood of a poem written at the end of the day, the end of the year, and the end of the century.
[2] *coppice gate:* a gate in a hedge.
[3] *bine-stems . . . lyres:* Bine-stems are stems of climbing vines. They made lines (scored) against the sky, like the strings from broken musical instruments (lyres).
[4] *haunted nigh:* lived nearby.

The land's sharp features seemed to be
The Century's corpse outleant;[5] 10
His crypt the cloudy canopy,[6]
The wind his death-lament.
The ancient pulse of germ and birth
Was shrunken hard and dry,
And every spirit upon earth 15
Seemed fervorless as I.

At once a voice burst forth among
The bleak twigs overhead
In a full-hearted evensong
Of joy illimited; 20
An aged thrush, frail, gaunt and small,
In blast-beruffled plume,[7]
Had chosen thus to fling his soul
Upon the growing gloom.

So little cause for carolings 25
Of such ecstatic sound
Was written on terrestrial things
Afar or nigh around,
That I could think there trembled through
His happy good-night air 30
Some blessed hope, whereof he knew
And I was unaware.

31 December 1900

The Oxen

Comprehension

1. What did the elder say the oxen were doing on Christmas Eve?
2. Did the young speaker believe that the oxen were kneeling?
3. What would the speaker do if someone asked him now to go and see the oxen kneeling?

Toward Interpretation

1. Contrast the point of view expressed in the first two stanzas with that expressed in the last two.

[5] *Century's corpse outleant:* The dead century leaned or stretched out. See the date at the end of the poem.
[6] *His crypt the cloudy canopy:* His burial place (crypt) was the sky (cloudy canopy).
[7] *blast-beruffled plume:* The bird's feathers have been ruffled by the wind.

The Shadow on the Stone

Comprehension

1. What did the speaker imagine he saw as he looked at the "shifting shadows" made by the tree on the Druid stone?
2. Why wouldn't the speaker turn his head to see if someone was really standing behind him?
3. What did the speaker finally do?

Toward Interpretation

1. In a way, the theme of this poem is very similar to that of "The Oxen." How would you describe this similarity?

In Church

Comprehension

1. Is the congregation moved by the preacher's sermon? What words describe the response of the listeners?
2. What does the preacher do after he closes the vestry door?
3. Who sees him?

Toward Interpretation

1. What must have been the effect on the pupil as she watched the preacher act out his sermon before a glass?

By Her Aunt's Grave

Comprehension

1. Why did the aunt bring money to her niece?
2. How long has the girl waited to fix her aunt's headstone?
3. What does her lover suggest that they do with the money?

Toward Interpretation

1. Will the girl buy a headstone for her aunt's grave?
2. What is ironic about the phrase "for she could confide in me alone, she vowed"?

At the Draper's

Comprehension

1. Why did the wife go to the shop?
2. Who else was there? Did the wife see him?

3. Why did the husband say he left?
4. What was his wife doing when he left?

Toward Interpretation

1. Pick out some of the ironic lines and explain the irony.

Snow in the Suburbs

Comprehension

1. Is the scene quiet? Is there any wind?
2. What happens to the sparrow that enters the tree?
3. What happens after the lump of snow falls off the sparrow?
4. What does the black cat look like? What do they do with the cat?

Toward Interpretation

1. What does the cat add to the poem?

The Man He Killed

Comprehension

1. What would have happened if the two men had met at an inn?
2. What happened when they faced each other as soldiers?
3. What reason does the speaker give for killing the other man?
4. Did he dislike the man he killed?

Toward Interpretation

1. What words might be substituted for "quaint" and "curious"?
2. What is the ironic fact about war that the speaker in the poem calls "quaint and curious"?

New Year's Eve

Comprehension

1. What does God say as the poem opens?
2. What questions does the speaker ask God at the beginning of the second stanza?
3. What is the speaker's attitude toward life? Does he think it is worth living?
4. Does God say he has created man for a reason?
5. What does God say is strange about the human beings he has created?

6. Did man's questions cause God to change his ways or work any differently?

Toward Interpretation

1. What conception of the universe does the poem suggest?

The Darkling Thrush

Comprehension

1. What time of day is it? What line gives you the answer?
2. Were there any other persons around, or was the speaker alone?
3. What date was the poem written? How does this fact explain the poet's reference to "the Century's corpse"?
4. What word does the speaker use to describe his feelings at the end of the first stanza?
5. What happened that changed the mood of the scene from one of complete desolation?

Toward Interpretation

1. What is the speaker's mood in the first stanza? What change of mood comes over him as he listens to the bird's song?

Poems
by Walt Whitman

Walt Whitman (1819–1892) once desribed his poems in Leaves of Grass *as a language experiment. He believed that a new world, a new time, and a new people needed a new poetry that would embrace all experience. In his revolt against the artificial literary language of his day he created his own poetic diction marked both by lofty rhetoric and by the familiar usages of everyday speech. Slang, coined words, and foreign borrowings added freshness and vigor. Only a bold and unfettered language would serve to celebrate the body as well as the soul, the factory as well as the farm, the butcher boy as well as the poet.*

Whitman's poetry was not only far-ranging in subject matter and bold in language but also daring in its rejection of rhyme and traditional stanzaic forms. "The sunshine of the light of letters is simplicity," he wrote. The "elegance" of traditional metrical forms he described as "curtains" hanging between the poet and the reader. Believing, as Emerson did, that "the poetic quality is not marshalled in rhyme or uniformity," he pleaded for "the free growth of metrical laws." In place of narrow restrictions of meter and form, such as the traditional iambic pentameter, Whitman substituted larger cadences which he used with great subtlety. In place of regular rhyme, he substituted the verbal effects of oratory. To give form to this "free verse," he turned to rhetorical devices such as repetition and parallelism. To unify his longer poems, he employed stanzas of widely varying length, in which an idea could be developed, images could be clustered, or a symbolic pattern could be woven.

All of Whitman's poetry was collected in a single volume called Leaves of Grass, *which was first published in 1855 and constantly revised and expanded until the final edition of 1892. This final edition constitutes a kind of spiritual autobiography in which the poems are arranged to correspond roughly to the poet's own growth and development from youth to old age. The hundreds of poems in* Leaves of Grass *concentrate on a small number of favorite themes. Most of the important themes can be found in the poems that follow: the material and the spiritual, the ideal and the practical, are one; truth can be most clearly perceived by direct obervation of nature; God is everywhere and in everything; life does not stop with death; all men and women, regardless of wealth or condition, are equally important in the universe; and every experience, no matter how slight, contributes to a man's growth.*

Whitman was the new poet that a new nation was looking for. Few American poets have been as quickly and enduringly internationalized. His reputation has risen steadily, and today most critics would agree with Emerson that Leaves of Grass *contains "incomparable things said incomparably well."*

When I Heard the Learn'd Astronomer

When I heard the learn'd astronomer,
When the proofs, the figures, were ranged in columns before me,
When I was shown the charts and diagrams, to add, divide, and
  measure them,
When I sitting heard the astronomer where he lectured with much
  applause in the lecture-room,
How soon unaccountable[1] I became tired and sick, 5
Till rising and gliding out I wander'd off by myself,
In the mystical moist night-air, and from time to time,
Look'd up in perfect silence at the stars.

I Saw in Louisiana a Live-Oak Growing

I saw in Louisiana a live-oak growing,
All alone stood it and the moss hung down from the branches,

[1] *unaccountable:* for a reason or reasons that cannot be explained. The usage is peculiar to Whitman. One would expect unaccountably in this context.

Without any companion it grew there uttering joyous leaves of dark green,
And its look, rude, unbending, lusty, made me think of myself,
But I wonder'd how it could utter joyous leaves standing alone there without its friend near, for I knew I could not, 5
And I broke off a twig with a certain number of leaves upon it, and twined around it a little moss,
And brought it away, and I have placed it in sight in my room,
It is not needed to remind me as of my own dear friends,
(For I believe lately I think of little else than of them,)
Yet it remains to me a curious token, it makes me think of manly love; 10
For all that, and though the live-oak glistens there in Louisiana solitary in a wide flat space,
Uttering joyous leaves all its life without a friend a lover near,
I know very well I could not.

Give Me the Splendid Silent Sun

1

Give me the splendid silent sun with his beams full-dazzling,
Give me juicy autumnal fruit ripe and red from the orchard,
Give me a field where the unmow'd grass grows,
Give me an arbor, give me the trellis'd grape,
Give me fresh corn and wheat, give me serene-moving animals teaching content, 5
Give me nights perfectly quiet as on high plateaus west of the Mississippi, and I looking up at the stars,
Give me odorous at sunrise a garden of beautiful flowers where I can walk undisturb'd,
Give me for marriage a sweet-breath'd woman of whom I should never tire,
Give me a perfect child, give me away aside from the noise of the world a rural domestic life,
Give me to warble spontaneous songs recluse by myself, for my own ears only, 10
Give me solitude, give me Nature, give me again O Nature your primal sanities!
These demanding to have them,[1] (tired with ceaseless excitement, and rack'd by the war-strife,)
These to procure incessantly asking, rising in cries from my heart,

[1] The syntax of this and the following line is somewhat obscure. The general sense, however, is clear enough. Here is one possible paraphrase: "I, demanding to have these things, (the joys of Nature), I, incessantly asking to have these things, these things that are rising in cries from my heart. . . ."

While yet incessantly asking still I adhere to my city,
Day upon day and year upon year O city, walking your streets, 15
Where you hold me enchain'd a certain time refusing to give me up,
Yet giving to make me glutted, enrich'd of soul, you give me forever
faces;
(O I see what I sought to escape, confronting, reversing my cries,
I see my own soul trampling down what it ask'd for.)

2

Keep your splendid silent sun, 20
Keep your woods O Nature, and the quiet places by the woods,
Keep your fields of clover and timothy, and your corn-fields and
orchards,
Keep the blossoming buckwheat fields where the Ninth-month bees
hum;
Give me faces and streets—give me these phantoms incessant and
endless along the trottoirs![2]
Give me interminable eyes—give me women—give me comrades and
lovers by the thousand! 25
Let me see new ones every day—let me hold new ones by the hand
every day!
Give me such shows—give me the streets of Manhattan![3]
Give me Broadway,[3] with the soldiers marching[4]—give me the sound
of the trumpets and drums!
(The soldiers in companies or regiments—some starting away, flush'd
and reckless,
Some, their time up, returning with thinn'd ranks, young, yet very
old, worn, marching, noticing nothing;) 30
Give me the shores and wharves heavy-fringed with black ships!
O such for me! O an intense life, full to repletion and varied!
The life of the theatre, bar-room, huge hotel, for me!
The saloon of the steamer! the crowded excursion for me! the
torchlight procession!
The dense brigade bound for the war, with high piled military
wagons following; 35
People, endless, streaming, with strong voices, passions, pageants,
Manhattan streets with their powerful throbs, with beating drums
as now,

[2] *trottoirs:* sidewalks, a French word. This is an example of Whitman's fondness for foreign borrowings.
[3] *Manhattan; Broadway:* The main part of New York City is on the island of Manhattan, and Broadway is probably its most famous street. But Whitman here (as elsewhere) is using Manhattan as a symbol for any large, crowded city, teeming with life.
[4] *soldiers marching:* This line and the two lines that follow describe soldiers going to and returning from the battles of the American Civil War (1861–1865).

The endless and noisy chorus, the rustle and clank of muskets, (even the sight of the wounded,)
Manhattan crowds, with their turbulent musical chorus!
Manhattan faces and eyes forever for me. 40

There Was a Child Went Forth

There was a child went forth every day,
And the first object he looked upon and received with wonder or pity or love or dread, that object he became,
And that object became part of him for the day or a certain part of the day . . . . or for many years or stretching cycles of years.

The early lilacs became part of this child,
And grass, and white and red morningglories, and white and red clover, and the song of the phœbe-bird, 5
And the March-born lambs, and the sow's pink-faint litter, and the mare's foal, and the cow's calf, and the noisy brood of the barnyard or by the mire of the pondside . . and the fish suspending themselves so curiously below there . . and the beautiful curious liquid . . and the water-plants with their graceful flat heads . . all became part of him.

And the field-sprouts of April and May became part of him . . . . wintergrain sprouts, and those of the light-yellow corn, and of the esculent roots of the garden,
And the appletrees covered with blossoms, and the fruit afterward . . . . and woodberries . . and the commonest weeds by the road;
And the old drunkard staggering home from the outhouse of the tavern whence he had lately risen,
And the schoolmistress that passed on her way to the school . . and the friendly boys that passed . . and the quarrelsome boys . . and the tidy and freshcheeked girls . . and the barefoot negro boy and girl, 10
And all the changes of city and country wherever he went.
His own parents . . he that had propelled the fatherstuff at night, and fathered him . . and she that conceived him in her womb and birthed him . . . . they gave this child more of themselves than that,
They gave him afterward every day . . . . they and of them became part of him.

The mother at home quietly placing the dishes on the suppertable,
The mother with mild words . . . . clean her cap and gown . . . . a wholesome odor falling off her person and clothes as she walks by: 15
The father, strong, selfsufficient, manly, mean, angered, unjust,

The blow, the quick loud word, the tight bargain, the crafty lure,
The family usages, the language, the company, the furniture . . . . the yearning and swelling heart,
Affection that will not be gainsayed[1] . . . . The sense of what is real . . . . the thought if after all it should prove unreal,
The doubts of daytime and the doubts of nighttime . . . the curious whether and how, 20
Whether that which appears so is so . . . . Or is it all flashes and specks?
Men and women crowding fast in the streets . . if they are not flashes and specks what are they?
The streets themselves and the facades of houses . . . . the goods in the windows,
Vehicles . . teams . . the tiered wharves, and the huge crossing at the ferries;
The village on the highland seen from afar at sunset . . . . the river between, 25
Shadows . . aureola and mist . . light falling on roofs and gables of white or brown, three miles off,
The schooner near by sleepily dropping down the tide . . the little boat slacktowed astern,[2]
The hurrying tumbling waves and quickbroken crests and slapping;
The strata of colored clouds . . . . the long bar of maroontint[3] away solitary by itself . . . . the spread of purity it lies motionless in,
The horizon's edge, the flying seacrow, the fragrance of saltmarsh and shoremud; 30
These became part of that child who went forth every day, and who now goes and will always go forth every day,
And these become of him or her that peruses them now.[4]

From "Song of Myself"

Chant 6

A child said, What is the grass? fetching it to me with full hands;
How could I answer the child? . . . . I do not know what it is any more than he.
I guess it must be the flag of my disposition,[1] out of hopeful green stuff woven.

[1] *will not be gainsayed:* will not be denied.
[2] *slacktowed astern:* pulled slowly behind.
[3] *maroontint:* the color of maroon, a dark red.
[4] *And these become of him or her that peruses them now:* And all the things mentioned in the poem (these) become part of the reader (him or her) who reads about them (persues them) now.

[1] *flag of my disposition:* symbol of the way I feel about things.

Or I guess it is the handkerchief of the Lord,
A scented gift and remembrancer designedly dropped, 5
Bearing the owner's name someway in the corners, that we may see
and remark, and say Whose?
Or I guess the grass is itself a child. . . . the produced babe of the
vegetation. . . .

Tenderly will I use you curling grass,
It may be you transpire[2] from the breasts of young men,
It may be if I had known them I would have loved them; 10
It may be you are from old people and from women, and from off-
spring taken soon out of their mothers' laps,
And here you are the mothers' laps.

This grass is very dark to be from the white heads of old mothers,
Darker than the colorless beards of old men,
Dark to come from under the faint red roofs of mouths.[3] 15

O I perceive after all so many uttering tongues!
And I perceive they do not come from the roofs of mouths for nothing.
I wish I could translate the hints about the dead young men and women,
And the hints about old men and mothers, and the offspring taken
soon out of their laps.
What do you think has become of the young and old men? 20
And what do you think has become of the women and children?

They are alive and well somewhere;
The smallest sprout shows there is really no death,
And if ever there was it led forward life, and does not wait at the end
to arrest it,
And ceased the moment life appeared. 25

All goes onward and outward . . . . and nothing collapses,
And to die is different from what any one supposed, and luckier.

Chant 21

I am the poet of the Body and I am the poet of the Soul,
The pleasures of heaven are with me and the pains of hell are with me,
The first I graft and increase upon myself, the latter I translate into a
new tongue.

I am the poet of the woman the same as the man,
And I say it is as great to be a woman as to be a man, 5
And I say there is nothing greater than the mother of men.

[2] *transpire:* Just as moisture can be given off by the skin of humans or by leaves, the grass may come from the breasts of young men who are buried below.

[3] Lines 14 and 15 will become clear if you begin them with "This grass is . . . ."

I chant the chant of dilation or pride,
We have had ducking and deprecating about enough,
I show that size is only development.

Have you outstripped the rest? are you the President? 10
It is a trifle, they will more than arrive there every one, and still pass on.

I am he that walks with the tender and growing night,
I call to the earth and sea half-held by the night.

Press close bare-bosomed night—press close magnetic nourishing night!
Night of south winds—night of the large few stars! 15
Still nodding night—mad naked summer night.

Smile O voluptuous cool-breathed earth!
Earth of the slumbering and liquid trees!
Earth of departed sunset—earth of the mountains misty-topped!
Earth of the vitreous pour of the full moon just tinged with blue! 20
Earth of shine and dark mottling the tide of the river!
Earth of the limpid gray of clouds brighter and clearer for my sake!
Far-swooping elbowed earth—rich apple-blossomed earth!
Smile, for your lover comes.

Prodigal, you have given me love—therefore I to you give love! 25
O unspeakable passionate love.

Chant 22

You sea! I resign myself to you also—I guess what you mean,
I behold from the beach your crooked inviting fingers,
I believe you refuse to go back without feeling of me,
We must have a turn together, I undress, hurry me out of sight of the
land,
Cushion me soft, rock me in billowy drowse, 5
Dash me with amorous wet, I can repay you.

Sea of stretched ground-swells,
Sea breathing broad and convulsive breaths,
Sea of the brine of life and of unshoveled yet always-ready graves,
Howler and scooper of storms, capricious and dainty sea, 10
I am integral with you, I too am of one phase and of all phases.[1]

[1] *of one phase and of all phases:* The poet may be referring here to the phases of the moon, which influence the ocean tides.

Chant 31

I believe a leaf of grass is no less than the journey-work[1] of the stars,
And the pismire[2] is equally perfect, and a grain of sand, and the egg of
the wren
And the tree-toad is a chef-d'oeuvre[3] for the highest,
And the running blackberry would adorn the parlors of heaven,
And the narrowest hinge in my hand puts to scorn all machinery, 5
And the cow crunching with depressed head surpasses any statue,
And a mouse is miracle enough to stagger sextillions[4] of infidels.

A Noiseless Patient Spider

A noiseless patient spider,
I mark'd where on a little promontory[1] it stood isolated,
Mark'd how to explore the vacant vast[2] surrounding,
It launched forth filament, filament, filament, out of itself,
Ever unreeling them, ever tirelessly speeding them. 5

And you O my soul where you stand,
Surrounded, detached, in measureless oceans of space,

Ceaselessly musing, venturing, throwing, seeking the spheres to connect
them,
Till the bridge you will need be form'd, till the ductile anchor hold,
Till the gossamer thread you fling catch somewhere, O my soul. 10

Passage to India

I

Singing my days,
Singing the great achievements of the present,
Singing the strong light works of engineers,
Our modern wonders, (the antique ponderous Seven outvied,)[1]

[1] *journey-work:* A journey-man is a workman who is skilled and experienced.
[2] *pismire:* ant.
[3] *chef-d'oeuvre:* a great work of art, a masterpiece.
[4] *sextillions:* In the United States, sextillion is written as the number 1 followed by 21 zeros. In Great Britain, sextillion is written as the number 1 followed by 36 zeros. The meaning here is "a vast number, beyond our power to count."

[1] *promontory:* a high piece of land jutting out into the ocean and almost surrounded by water. The word is important to the poem.
[2] *vacant vast:* Here "vast" is used as a noun. The expression "vacant vast" means empty, boundless space.

[1] *the antique ponderous Seven outvied*: The seven wonders of the world in ancient times are surpassed by the modern wonders that are being celebrated in this poem: the Suez Canal, the railroad spanning the North American continent, and the trans-Atlantic cable—(the "eloquent gentle wires").

In the Old World the east the Suez canal, 5
The New by its mighty railroad spann'd,
The seas inlaid with eloquent gentle wires;
Yet first to sound, and ever sound, the cry with thee O soul,
The Past! the Past! the Past!

The Past—the dark unfathom'd retrospect! 10
The teeming gulf—the sleepers and the shadows!
The past—the infinite greatness of the past!
For what is the present after all but a growth out of the past?
(As a projectile form'd, impell'd, passing a certain line, still keeps on,
So the present, utterly form'd, impell'd by the past.) 15

2

Passage O soul to India!
Eclaircise[2] the myths Asiatic, the primitive fables.

Not you alone proud truths of the world,
Nor you alone ye[3] facts of modern science,
But myths and fables of eld,[3] Asia's, Africa's fables, 20
The far-darting beams of the spirit, the unloos'd dreams,
The deep diving bibles and legends,
The daring plots of the poets, the elder[3] religions;
O you temples fairer than lilies pour'd over by the rising sun!
O you fables spurning the known, eluding the hold of the known,
  mounting to heaven! 25
You lofty and dazzling towers, pinnacled, red as roses, burnish'd with
  gold!
Towers of fables immortal fashion'd from mortal dreams!
You too I welcome and fully the same as the rest!
You too with joy I sing.

Passage to India! 30
Lo, soul, seest thou not[3] God's purpose from the first?
The earth to be spann'd, connected by network,
The races, neighbors, to marry and be given in marriage,
The oceans to be cross'd, the distant brought near,
The lands to be welded together. . . . 35

[2] *Eclaircise*: The French verb *eclairer* means "to enlighten, illuminate." "Eclaircise," Walt Whitman's own coinage, is another example of his fondness for foreign words.
[3] *ye*: you, archaic. There are other examples of archaic vocabulary and grammar in the lines that follow. *of eld*: of old; *elder*: older; *seest thou not*: don't you see.

When I Heard the Learn'd Astronomer

Comprehension

1. Where is the poet at the beginning of the poem?
2. Where does the poet go?

Toward Interpretation

1. What difference do you see in the two experiences—the one inside, the other outside the lecture hall?

I Saw in Louisiana a Live-Oak Growing

Comprehension

1. Did the oak stand alone or were there other trees around it?
2. What is there about the look of the tree that makes the poet think of himself? What three adjectives does he use?
3. What did the poet wonder about?
4. Could the poet be "joyous" if he was alone?
5. What did the poet do with the leafy twig he broke off the tree?
6. What does the poet think of lately?
7. What does the leafy twig make him think of?
8. What does the tree do that the poet cannot do?

Toward Interpretation

1. The poet refers twice to "uttering joyous leaves." What is unusual about the choice of the verb *utter*? What do you think he means by it?
2. What do you think the tree might symbolize for Whitman? How does he use this symbol to reveal his feelings about friendship?

Give Me the Splendid Silent Sun

Comprehension

1. In line 11, the poet asks "Nature" to give him its "primal sanities." What does this phrase mean to you?
2. In line 17, the poet says that the city gives him "forever faces." What does this phrase mean to you?

Toward Interpretation

1. Discuss the organization of the poem. What lines refer to the joys of life in the country? How does the emphasis shift after "still" in line 14? In what lines is nature rejected? What lines deal with the joys of life in the city?
2. Both this poem and "I Saw in Louisiana" share a common theme. What is it?

There Was a Child Went Forth

Comprehension

1. What happened to the first object the child looked upon as he went out every day?
2. All the details listed in the poem became part not only of the child who "went forth." At the end of the poem, Whitman says these experiences will also become part of other people. Who are they?

Toward Interpretation

1. Comment on the progression of the details in the poem by answering the following questions:
   a. In lines 4–7, what do all the details have in common?
   b. In lines 9 and 10, what do the details have in common?
   c. What is the general subject of lines 12–19?
   d. What kind of detail is used at the close of the poem, from line 26 on?

Song of Myself: Chant 6

Comprehension

1. What question does the child ask at the beginning? Does the poet know the answer?
2. How many times does the poet use the phrase "I guess"?
3. Line 7 introduces an idea that the poet develops throughout the rest of the poem. What does he say the grass "seems" to him now?
4. What are the blades of grass compared to in line 16?
5. What does the "smallest sprout" show?

Toward Interpretation

1. To what five different things does the poet compare a handful of grass?
2. What three hints of truth do the "uttering tongues" speak?

Song of Myself: Chant 21

Comprehension

1. At the beginning of "Chant 21," the poet describes what he will write about in his verse. What will he be "poet of"?
2. Does the poet think that pride is to be condemned?
3. What does the poet identify with in the lines following line 17?

Toward Interpretation

1. What do you think the speaker means when he says "I am the poet of the Body and I am the poet of the Soul"?
2. In lines 12–16 the speaker addresses the night as if it were a living being. What phrases suggest the animate, almost human quality of the night?
3. In lines 17–26 the speaker addresses the earth. What phrases does he apply to the earth that suggest its animate, almost human nature?

Song of Myself: Chant 22

Comprehension

1. In what way do the poet and the sea "have a turn together"?

Toward Interpretation

1. In this chant, the poet addresses the sea as one would a lover. What phrases suggest the human qualities of the sea?

Song of Myself: Chant 31

Comprehension

1. What objects does the poet select for his praise?

Toward Interpretation

1. The six lines given here illustrate one of Whitman's favorite themes. What is it?

A Noiseless Patient Spider

Comprehension

1. In the first stanza what is the spider doing?
2. In the second stanza what does the poet compare the spider to?

Toward Interpretation

1. What similarities does the poet see between the spider and himself?

Passage to India

Comprehension

1. What change of subject occurs in line 8? What word marks the transition?
2. What does the poet say about the relation of the present to the past (lines 13–15)?
3. Does the poet reject the accomplishments of the present in favor of those of the past?

Toward Interpretation

1. In this poem "India" does not refer to a specific country. It is instead a symbol for something much larger and more inclusive. What does this symbol suggest to you?
2. How does the poet relate the present to the past in the lines beginning with "The earth to be spann'd"?
3. What is the similarity between the theme of this poem and that of "A Noiseless Patient Spider"?

Poems

by Gwendolyn Brooks

Gwendolyn Brooks is a widely read and respected Afro-American writer. Born in 1917 in Topeka, Kansas, she started a poetry notebook at the age of eleven; at thirteen she published her first poem. Of writing poetry she says, "I like the concentration, the crush; I like working with language, as others like working with paints and clay, or notes."

Gwendolyn Brooks celebrated black life in America long before it was fashionable to do so and, even more unusual, when it was simply not expected that a black person, especially a woman, should aspire to be a writer. At first she was not appreciated by those members of her own race who were ashamed of their color; today she is recognized as an elder "sister" asserting the new black awareness.

Her work is frankly racial but in the context of a broad humanity: "It is my privilege to present Negroes not as curios but as people." White readers have always responded to the universal elements in her compassionate portrayals of life in southside Chicago, the black section of the city, as in her first book of poetry, A Street in Bronzeville *(1945), in* Annie Allen *(1949), which she calls her "Anniad" and which won the Pulitzer Prize for poetry in 1950, and in her autobiographical novel* Maud Martha *(1953), a tender story about a young girl's growing up. It takes a "bitter birth and intrinsic sorrow," she says, to truly understand what it means to be black in a society in which the black has had to rise from slavery to a new pride in self against great odds. "We Real Cool," from* The Bean Eaters *(1960), suggests how precarious that existence can be. She calls* In the Mecca *(1968) her "epic of black humanity": "Hope occurred, and charity, sainthood, glory, shame, despair, fear, altruism. Theft, material and moral."*

Many of her poems in the 1960s and '70s take account of political events (the integration of the schools, the death of Malcolm X, the riots in Chicago after the assassination of Martin Luther King), but her voice is never shrill nor militant. Though she is aroused about the contradictions in American life ("The time/cracks into furious flower"), she speaks with the same dignity and depth of feeling, the same strength in seeming simplicity that have always marked her work. In the poetry before 1967 she constrains her power in traditional forms (iambic pentameter, the sonnet, the ballad). Since then, as in In the Mecca, Riot, *and* Family Pictures, *in keeping with the new consciousness ("Blackness/is a going to essences and to unifyings"), she has experimented with free forms.*

Gwendolyn Brooks is helping young black writers in workshops and is participating in neighborhood cultural events, and she has moved from a "white establishment" publisher to an exclusively black press, the Broadside Press of Detroit. She visited East Africa in 1971, confirming her sense of identification with her African heritage. Her autobiography, Report from Part One *(1972), reveals her integrity and strong sense of affirmation of life and of self and, like her poetry, radiates strength and beauty. In the words of one of her admirers, "She is the continuing storm that walks with the English language as lions walk with Africa."*

kitchenette building[1]

We are things of dry hours and the involuntary plan,[2]
Grayed in, and gray. "Dream" makes a giddy sound, not strong
Like "rent," "feeding a wife," "satisfying a man."

But could a dream send up through onion fumes
Its white and violet, fight with fried potatoes 5

[1] *kitchenette building:* an apartment building with very small rooms and tiny kitchens called kitchenettes.
[2] *involuntary plan:* The occupants are not there by their own choice, by their own free will; they are there because they have to be, because they have no other place to go.

And yesterday's garbage ripening in the hall,
Flutter, or sing an aria down these rooms

Even if we were willing to let it in,
Had time to warm it, keep it very clean,
Anticipate a message, let it begin? 10

We wonder. But not well! not for a minute!
Since Number Five[3] is out of the bathroom now,
We think of lukewarm water, hope to get in it.

the preacher: ruminates behind the sermon[1]

I think it must be lonely to be God.
Nobody loves a master. No. Despite
The bright hosannas, bright dear-Lords,[2] and bright
Determined reverence of Sunday eyes.

Picture Jehovah[3] striding through the hall 5
Of His importance, creatures running out
From servant-corners[4] to acclaim, to shout
Appreciation of His merit's glare.

But who walks with Him?—dares to take His arm,
To slap Him on the shoulder, tweak His ear, 10
Buy Him a Coca-Cola or a beer,
Pooh-pooh His politics, call Him a fool?

Perhaps—who knows?—He tires of looking down.
Those eyes are never lifted. Never straight.
Perhaps sometimes He tires of being great 15
In solitude. Without a hand to hold.

piano after war[1]

On a snug evening I shall watch her fingers,
Cleverly ringed, declining to clever pink,
Beg glory from the willing keys. Old hungers

[3] *Number Five:* the occupant of apartment number five. There is only one bathroom per floor, instead of bathrooms in each apartment.

[1] *ruminates behind the sermon:* thinks to himself about the deity he addresses.
[2] *The bright hosannas, bright dear-Lords:* refers to the congregation's vocal responses. As the preacher talks, the congregation calls out "hosanna" and "dear-Lord," which are exclamations of praise.
[3] *Picture Jehovah:* Imagine Jehovah (another name for God).
[4] *creatures running out/From servant-corners:* Perhaps this suggests the members of the congregation, lowly as servants, catching a glimpse of God in his greatness.

[1] *piano after war:* A black veteran of World War II is listening to the piano. ("Piano after war" and "mentors" must be read together as a double sonnet.)

Will break their coffins,[2] rise to eat and thank.
And music, warily, like the golden rose 5
That sometimes after sunset warms the west,
Will warm that room, persuasively suffuse
That room and me, rejuvenate a past.
But suddenly, across my climbing fever
Of proud delight—a multiplying cry. 10
A cry of bitter dead men[3] who will never
Attend a gentle maker of musical joy.
Then my thawed eye[4] will go again to ice.
And stone will shove the softness from my face.[5]

mentors

For I am rightful fellow of their band.[1]
My best allegiances are to the dead.
I swear to keep the dead upon my mind,
Disdain for all time to be overglad.
Among spring flowers, under summer trees, 5
By chilling autumn waters, in the frosts
Of supercilious winter—all my days
I'll have as mentors those reproving ghosts.[2]
And at that cry, at that remotest whisper,
I'll stop my casual business. Leave the banquet. 10
Or leave the ball—reluctant to unclasp her
Who may be fragrant as the flower she wears,
Make gallant bows and dim excuses, then quit
Light for the midnight that is mine and theirs.

the sonnet-ballad[1]

Oh mother, mother, where is happiness?
They took my lover's tallness off to war.
Left me lamenting. Now I cannot guess
What I can use an empty heart-cup[2] for.
He won't be coming back here any more. 5

[2] *Old hungers/Will break their coffins:* Desires once thought dead will be revived, will come to life.
[3] *bitter dead men:* men killed in the war.
[4] *thawed eye:* eye wet from weeping.
[5] *stone will shove the softness from my face:* His face will become lifeless again, like stone.

[1] *of their band*: of the soldiers that have been killed in the war.
[2] *those reproving ghosts*: the ghosts of the soldiers who "cry" or "whisper" their disapproval and rebuke.

[1] *sonnet-ballad:* a form Miss Brooks says she "invented." Like the ballad, it tells a story, a story of grief and loss; but it is in the form of a sonnet.
[2] *an empty heart-cup:* Her heart, like a cup, has been emptied.

Some day the war will end, but, oh, I knew
When he went walking grandly out that door
That my sweet love would have to be untrue.
Would have to be untrue. Would have to court
Coquettish death,[3] whose impudent and strange 10
Possessive arms and beauty (of a sort)
Can make a hard man hesitate—and change.
And he will be the one to stammer, "Yes."
Oh mother, mother, where is happiness?

First fight. Then fiddle.

First fight. Then fiddle.[1] Ply the slipping string
With feathery sorcery;[2] muzzle the note
With hurting love; the music that they wrote
Bewitch, bewilder. Qualify to sing
Threadwise.[3] Devise no salt, no hempen thing[4] 5
For the dear instrument to bear. Devote
The bow to silks and honey. Be remote
A while from malice and from murdering.
But first to arms, to armor. Carry hate
In front of you and harmony behind. 10
Be deaf to music and to beauty blind.
Win war. Rise bloody, maybe not too late
For having first to civilize a space
Wherein to play your violin with grace.

Life for my child is simple, and is good

Life for my child is simple, and is good.
He knows his wish. Yes, but that is not all.
Because I know mine too.
And we both want joy of undeep and unabiding things,
Like kicking over a chair or throwing blocks[1] out of a window 5
Or tipping over an icebox pan[2]

[3] *Coquettish death:* a personification of death as a coquette, a vamp, a seductress.

[1] *Then fiddle:* Then play the violin. The word "fiddle," whether a noun or a verb, is now largely confined to dialectal or jocular use.
[2] *With feathery sorcery:* lightly and skillfully, as if with magical power.
[3] *Qualify to sing/Threadwise:* prepare the strings properly.
[4] *Devise no salt, no hempen thing:* Do not make rough strings, strings of salt or rope. See the next sentence: "Devote/The bow to silks and honey."

[1] *blocks:* children's toy blocks.
[2] *icebox pan:* Before electric refrigerators, iceboxes were cooled by large blocks of ice. There were pans under the icebox to catch the water from the melting ice.

Or snatching down curtains or fingering an electric outlet
Or a journey or a friend or an illegal kiss.[3]
No. There is more to it than that.
It is that he has never been afraid. 10
Rather, he reaches out and lo[4] the chair falls with a beautiful crash,
And the blocks fall, down on the people's heads,
And the water comes slooshing[5] sloppily out across the floor.
And so forth.
Not that success, for him, is sure, infallible. 15
But never has he been afraid to reach.
His lesions are legion.[6]
But reaching is his rule.

WE REAL COOL[1]

The Pool Players.
Seven at the Golden Shovel.[2]

We real cool. We
Left school. We

Lurk late. We
Strike straight. We

Sing sin. We
Thin gin. We 5

Jazz June.[3] We
Die Soon.

[3] *an illegal kiss:* a child's sly and expected kiss.
[4] *lo:* a poetic interjection expressing wonder.
[5] *slooshing:* a word based on "sloshing" that Brooks uses to describe the sound of water falling and spreading across the floor.
[6] *His lesions are legion:* Like all children, he has many bumps and bruises.

[1] *We Real Cool:* an expression difficult to render in standard English. It means something like "We think we are the greatest, the best." The poem is in black dialect. One mark of this dialect is the omission of a form of *be*: "We *are* real cool." The term *cool*, however, is not restricted to black dialect. It is used in slang as a general term of approval: things, people, situations can all be "cool," meaning roughly "all right." The use of *real*, instead of *really* or *very*, is characteristic of informal English.
[2] *The Pool Players./Seven at the Golden Shovel:* Seven boys are playing pool, or billiards, at a pool hall called the Golden Shovel.
[3] The following paraphrase, admittedly inadequate, will probably clarify the general meaning of the poem: "We dropped out of school. We stay out late at night ('lurk late'), and when we fight with knives we 'strike straight.' Our speech is earthy and racy ('We/Sing sin'.) We dilute gin with water." One possible interpretation of "We jazz June" is "We boast and brag to a girlfriend." (June is a girl's name.)

old people working (garden, car)

Old people working. Making a gift of garden.
Or washing a car, so some one else may ride.
A note of alliance, an eloquence of pride.
A way of greeting or sally to the world.[1]

The time cracks into furious flower

The time[1]
cracks into furious flower. Lifts its face
all unashamed. And sways in wicked grace.
Whose[2] half-black hands assemble oranges
is tom-tom hearted[3] 5
(goes in bearing oranges and boom).
And there are bells for orphans[4]—
and red and shriek and sheen.
A garbageman is dignified
as any diplomat. 10
Big Bessie's[5] feet hurt like nobody's business,
but she stands—bigly—under the unruly scrutiny, stands in the wild weed.

In the wild weed[6]
she is a citizen,
and is a moment of highest quality; admirable. 15

It is lonesome, yes. For we are the last of the loud.
Nevertheless, live.

Conduct your blooming in the noise and whip of the whirlwind.

kitchenette building

Comprehension

1. Who are the speakers, the "we" of the poem, and where are they?
2. How does "dream" contrast with "rent, feeding a wife, satisfying a man"?
3. What is the antecedent of "it" throughout the third stanza?

[1] The last two lines will be clearer if you preface them with a phrase such as "These acts constitute . . . ."

[1] *The time:* refers to the 1960s, when the black protest movement in the United States was at its peak.
[2] *Whose:* the time whose.
[3] *is tom-tom hearted:* has the urgency of the tom-tom, the African war drum.
[4] *bells for orphans:* perhaps funeral bells, tolling for the parents who have perished in the struggle for recognition.
[5] *Big Bessie's:* Big Bessie, one of the apartment dwellers, is perhaps a symbol for the lowly black women. Big Bessie, as well as the garbageman, has as much dignity as a diplomat.
[6] *In the wild weed:* perhaps "In this chaotic and uncertain time."

Toward Interpretation

1. What do you think is meant by "things of dry hours" and "Grayed in, and gray"?
2. What might the dreams of these poor tenement dwellers be? What is the compromise they must settle for? (stanza 4)

the preacher: ruminates behind the sermon

Comprehension

1. Who is speaking and what does he imagine?
2. What picture of Jehovah does the preacher give in the second stanza?
3. In the third stanza, the preacher tries to imagine God in more familiar terms. How is this familiarity suggested through actions and phrases?
4. What does the preacher conclude in the last stanza?

Toward Interpretation

1. What special meaning do you think "Nobody loves a master" would have for a black reader of the poem?
2. The first line states the theme of the poem. How does the view of God given here differ from the conventional one?

piano after war

Comprehension

1. How does the piano music affect the speaker?
2. How does his mood suddenly change?

Toward Interpretation

1. What is universal about the general theme of the poem?
2. What images suggest the revival of the joys and warmth of the past? What images describe the collapse of these feelings?

mentors

Comprehension

1. What does the speaker say he will "Disdain for all time"?
2. What are some of the pleasures the speaker will reject?

Toward Interpretation

1. This poem, like "piano after war," has a universal theme. What is it?

Comprehension

1. What is the situation in the poem?
2. The girl says that her lover "would have to be untrue." Who is the rival for her affections?

Toward Interpretation

1. In a traditional ballad, the loved one would be "untrue" because he had found another woman. In what fresh, new terms is this time-honored situation expressed?

First fight. Then fiddle.

Comprehension

1. What must be done before the violin can be played "with grace"?
2. Does the poem end on a hopeful note?

Toward Interpretation

1. The poem is developed around a central image, that of playing the violin. What broader meaning might this image have for the black readers to whom the poem is addressed?

Life for my child is simple, and is good

Comprehension

1. What kinds of things does the child customarily take joy in?
2. What does the child continue to do, despite his bumps and bruises?

Toward Interpretation

1. The first part of the poem is a description of the pleasure the child takes in play. The turning point is announced in the line: "No. There is more to it than that." What significance does this simple play have in the life of the child?

WE REAL COOL

Comprehension

1. All the statements except the last seem of the same order. How is the last sentence different?

Toward Interpretation

1. This is a collective biography, a group portrait of young boys in the black ghetto. For all their bravado, is there anything in the form and tone of the poem that suggests their basic insecurity?

old people working (garden, car)

Comprehension

1. The old people are engaged in two unselfish acts. What are they?

Toward Interpretation

1. What is the purpose of making a garden and washing a car? What do these unselfish acts accomplish?

The time cracks into furious flower

Comprehension

1. The poem describes a mood, not an action. What is the spirit of the moment?
2. Which details point up the sense of crisis, and which point up the sense of confidence?

Toward Interpretation

1. Discuss the meaning of the flower image in the first and last sentences of the poem.

1 2 3 4 5 6 7 8 9 10 VHVH 84 83 82 81 80 79 78 77 76 75